Cities in the 1990s

local choice for a balanced strategy

By

Gerry Stoker
and
Stephen Young

Series editors: John Benington and Mike Geddes

Published by Longman Information and Reference,
Longman Group UK Ltd, 6th Floor, Westgate House, The High,
Harlow, Essex CM20 1YR
Telephone: Harlow (0279) 442601; Fax: Harlow (0279) 444501:
Telex: 81491 Padlog

A catalogue record for this book is available from the British Library

ISBN 0-582-10224-3

Printed in Great Britain by BPCC Wheatons Ltd, Exeter

*To those who believe
in making planning work*

Longman Local Government Library

The Warwick Series on Local Economic and Social Strategies

This series is designed to contribute to the ability of policy makers and managers in local government to meet the challenges of the 1990s. The focus is on strategic questions of local economic and social change. The series deals with issues which confront local government (and local public services more widely) at the level of corporate or inter agency strategy (for example, industrial restructuring, Europeanisation, ageing, poverty, transport, the environment). These issues are challenging local government to move beyond its traditional and primary role as a distributor and deliverer of services and to explore the potential for influence in new economic roles (as a major employer, investor and purchaser within the local economic roles (as a major employer, investor and purchaser within the local economy) and in its political and ideological roles (as a democratically elected body, with a mandate to represent the interests of the whole community).

The series will present the results of applied research and innovative policy initiatives in key areas of local government strategy, policy making, organisation and management. Its primary aim is to contribute to the development of good practice in local government policy making and corporate management, but it will also contribute to a better conceptual understanding of the role and functioning of the local state.

We hope this series will stimulate a lively and critical exchange of ideas and experience about policy making in the public sector. The editors welcome contributions to the debate from local policy makers, managers and academics.

John Benington and Mike Geddes

Contents

Preface   vi

Introduction   1

1   Bringing local government back in   5
2   The challenge for cities   19
3   Entrepreneurial planning   37
4   Sustainable development at the level of the city   64
5   Decentralisation and area approaches   97
6   The contribution of third force, not-for-profit organisations   119
7   Lobbying Whitehall and Brussels   151
8   Networks: the new driving force   179
9   Conclusions   191

Index   205

Preface

The case for this book rests on our feeling that there is a gap in the literature on cities. To be sure, publications of all kinds continue to proliferate, especially on inner city issues. Some of it is descriptive. Some of it is generalised. Some of it is polemical. Some of it is negative. Much of it analyses the impacts on cities and people of policies and wider pressures for change. But too little is focussed on the perspectives of policy-makers. When asked whether they have read a particular article, pamphlet or book their responses usually go something like 'Yes, it was very interesting, but what can I do with it?' or 'Quite fascinating, but it is too generalised'; or 'the trouble is that the writer wanted to change the political system. I'm working to this month's committee cycle; and trying to find time to think about next year's budget.' So we have tried to relate to the needs of senior policy-makers in cities. It is not a 'how to do it' book. It is one that seeks to conceptualise and contextualise the issues confronting policy-makers. It aims to be an analysis of the key issues and problems that need addressing.

Over the last 20 years many have tried to help us understand the complexities of cites, the nature of decision-making processes at all levels of government, and the range of implementation problems that arise. We have also learnt from academic colleagues and students; from interviews all over the country, from the front rooms of those running neighbourhood-based not-for-profit projects, to Marsham Street offices; from the informal chats that are so fascinating at conferences; and from the meetings of a range of academic and professional associations. Stephen would particularly like to mention the study tours organized by the Town and Country Planning Association; and Gerry his years at INLOGOV. We are especially grateful to John Hudson, Chris Wood, Chris Bannister, Paul Wilding, Riki Therivel, John Stewart and Vivien Lowndes who have commented on draft chapters. But these are our views and not those of any of the organisations or people with which we are associated. Whatever the faults we are responsible for them.

Apart from our intellectual debts, we are also indebted to those who have converted our writing into this book. Catherine Smith, Joanne Crolla-Parkhouse and Shahnaz Holder have cheerfully coped with Stephen's illegible scribbling; and Grace Hunter, Margaret Leckie and Alison Bennett with Gerry's more readable scrawl. We are also grateful to our editors Mike Geddes and John Benington; and to James Banfield at Longmans for their patient help and encouragement.

But it is the nearest and dearest who always bear the real costs of living with writers especially when they have too many other things to do anyway. Stephen's debts are to Anne for her love and support, and her distractions. She has also womanfully accompanied him on all sorts of strange expeditions exploring inner city sites, and lost green corridors. In such places he was especially grateful for the realism behind the questions that started 'But...?' Gerry gives his thanks and love to Deborah, Bethany, Robert and Benjamin.

Stephen Young, *Manchester*
Gerry Stoker, *Glasgow*
March 1993

Introduction

This book is about the positive role for local authorities in regenerating urban areas. The argument is made by way of an extensive review of the experience of local government and local communities in tackling the problems they face. Concrete policy options are considered at various stages but this book is not aimed at providing a comprehensive review of substantive, urban policies. Indeed part of the argument of the book is that to think in terms of policies being applied on a uniform basis, to tackle the problems of cities, is mistaken. It belies the variety and complexity of the challenges facing our towns and cities. This book, then, makes the case for an approach to solving urban problems that relies on local leadership to make strategic choices and balance the diverse interests of the communities that live in urban areas. Local authorities, working through and alongside other interests, can, by developing a new style of government, provide that leadership. This book seeks to explore the core characteristics of this new system of urban governance and how its empowering style and approach to city government can be fostered.

Chapter 1 outlines the general case for bringing local government back in. Such a case needs to be made because of the extent to which the role of local authorities has been side-lined by successive central government interventions. Articles in the national press about how to tackle inner city problems often give little credence to the role of local authorities. Those in local government may in some instances have lost heart or lack a clear view of what is the appropriate role for local authorities. In short to develop the argument of our book we need to overcome the doubts and uncertainties surrounding the value and role of local authority intervention in meeting the challenge of urban problems.

We build our case for giving elected local government a key role in urban regeneration around four arguments. First urban problems require local solutions and the local knowledge embedded within local authorities means they can tailor policies to meet the particular conditions of their locality. Second the challenges facing cities demand a response from a range of agencies, and local authorities are in a position to ensure that effective networks between different agencies and interests are developed. Third tackling problems requires leadership. Local authorities can offer that leadership in a way that blances the concerns of different interests. Finally, it is argued that local authorities have a special role in ensuring the legitimacy of urban decision-making.

Chapter 2 is divided into two parts. The first half of the chapter establishes that, despite the efforts of many, substantial problems remain in cities. A range of statistical and other information is reviewed to show how many residents of cities suffer substantial economic and social disadvantages. The deteriorating infrastructure of cities and environmental concerns are also identified as key challenges facing policy-makers. The second half of the chapter argues that, in light of the substantial evidence of continuing disadvantage suffered by many city residents and the other problems of cities, a balanced regeneration strategy is required for the new governance of cities. The physical, growth orientated renewal strategies of the 1980s need to be extended to provide a wider vision. To meet the challenge facing cities we need strategies that give opportunties to 'have-nots' as well as 'haves' and in which the commitment to growth is complimented by a concern with sustainable development.

Chapter 3 begins the process of exploring the different elements of the new style of governance required in cities. The underlying theme of the chapter is the emergence of a new type of entrepreneurial planning to encourage private investment and economic development in cities. This type of planning is market orientated in the sense that it seeks to establish the conditions for private sector economic activity yet it involves a complex range of activities for the public sector. This chapter outlines a step-by-step guide to these activities and the implementation problems that need to be tackled. Entrepreneurial planning is not just about recreating the market, it is also about getting people, vitality and even a sense of festival back into neglected areas. The chapter concludes with some thoughts about how the people dimension to entrepreneurial planning can be developed. The challenge for the 1990s is to apply the techniques of entrepreneurial planning to tackle social as well as economic or physical regeneration.

Chapter 4 introduces the need for sustainable planning. It is argued that sensitivity to the environment is not a bolt-on extra that local authorities can simply adopt, rather it requires a whole new way of thinking. The chapter aims to provide a guide to how a commitment to greening the city can be realised in practice. The aim is to try to work out what sustainable planning means at the level of the city, especially given the conclusion of the 1992 UN Earth Summit that if the environment challenge was to be met action at the local level was the key. This chapter outlines criteria by which new proposals and established conditions can be judged in environmental terms. It considers the resources that need to be mobilised to meet environmental challenges and emphasises how local authorities need to work through and alongside other organisations. The chapter makes it clear that environmental issues cannot be ignored and urges local authorities to lead a concerted effort to move from tokenistic responses to positive, long-term programmes for greening the city.

Chapter 5 restates the case for what has for long been a plan of urban policy: the need for initiatives aimed at particular geographical pockets within the broader boundaries of cities. The experience of area approaches in the 1970s and decentraliation in the 1980s is reviewed. It is concluded that such approaches tend to attract unreasonably high expectations but if they are seen as one part of a wider strategy they can make a valuable contribution. The bulk of the chapter is then devoted to an examination of the potential and pitfalls of area approaches and decentralisation. A concluding section reviews the main lessons from past experience and indicates the way forward for decentralisation in the 1990s.

Chapter 6 is concerned with the growing band of 'third force organisations' and the contribution they can make to a balanced strategy of regeneration. Third force organisations operate on a not-for-profit basis and include various charities, community groups, voluntary sector bodies and other agencies. This new breed of organisation is independent and outside government like a pressure group, but instead of trying to simply persuade government into action they get involved in implementation and in carrying out projects. The chapter reviews the advantages and disadvantages of third force organisations. It outlines what policy-makers need to understand about these organisations in order to enable them to offer appropriate support. It considers various stages in the development of third force organisations. Various strategies for local authorities seeking to encourage third force organisations are explored. It is concluded that such organisations should have a vital part to play in encouraging a politics of empowerment in the 1990s.

Chapter 7 explores the process of lobbying Whitehall and Brussels for funding and other support to underwrite the kind of local initiatives we have been discussing. Behind the more politicised relations of conflict that exist between central and local government there are many opportunities to develop a more positive dialogue. The enhanced role for the European Community means that a capacity to lobby in Brussels is also an essential part of the toolkit of urban governance. This chapter explains the strategies and tactics of lobbying.

Chapter 8 examines the new style of working that has been at the heart of the more substantive chapters. Networking — the pooling of resources in a co-operative manner to achieve shared purposes — underlies much of the new style of governance that we argue for in this book. The chapter identifies the distinctive features of the networking style and explores what makes networks 'tick'. The key dilemmas associated with networking are briefly reviewed. It is concluded that at its best networking can provide a flexible and responsive approach to the challenge of governing our cities. However it is noted that networks are not immune from the strains of operating in the context of a political system that distributes scarce resources and driven by competing ideologies and interests.

The concluding chapter is divided into three parts. First a call is made for local authorities to develop an overall sense of how different regeneration strategies might be applied to different parts of their areas. Second, in order to bolster its claims for civic leadership, we argue that the local government community should give serious attention to reforming its structure of internal decision-making. In particular we argue the case for experimenting with an elected mayor or political executive. Although we note that, if such a measure was adopted, a strengthening of the systems of accountability would also be required. Much of this book has argued the need for local intervention and action. We conclude by examining the sort of national urban policy that is implied by our commitment to local choice.

1 Bringing local government back in: The importance of local choice

Local government has to be seen not as an inhibition to the exercise of choice but as a prime means of providing choice for both individuals and communities. Its legitimacy lies not only in the ballot box but in daily contact of members and officers with the communities we serve, communities in which collective needs and aspirations have to be balanced with each other and with the needs and aspirations of individuals. The atomisation of local government through the hiving off of responsibilities to appointed agencies negates the strategic role which is at the core of local government's rationale, whether in the form of planning or providing services, or acting as spokesmen for an individual area.

(Jeremy Beecham, Chairman of the Association of Metropolitan Authority 1992).

The task of this introductory chapter is to make the general case for 'bringing local government back in'. That such a case needs to be made cannot be doubted. The policies of central government since 1979 have marginalised the role of local authorities. Urban Development Corporations, Training and Enterprise Councils, Local Enterprise Companies in Scotland, City Technology Colleges, Task Forces are among the agencies set up by central government to by-pass elected local authorities. City Challenge launched in 1991 in some respects revised the trend and appeared to give local authorities a clear leadership role. But the proposed

Urban Regeneration Agency launched in July 1992 appears to revert to the formula in which central government vests power in a special purpose agency. The conflict-laden days of the 1980s appear to have passed but at best central government ministers appear to see local authorities as one interest group among many. Local authorities are viewed not as partners in government but as pressure groups to be appeased.

In making our case for local government we are not only challenging the central thrust of the Conservatives' urban policy since 1979 but we also seek to attack two substantial 'schools of thought' within local authorities. One group — the pessimists — argue that the role and financial position of elected local government has been so undermined that no positive ways forward remain. We would not dispute that the constraints can be considerable — the financial thought-jacket which was tight in 1980s appears likely to be even tighter in the 1990s. Yet opportunities remain and building on the experience of local authorities we will show how these may be exploited. This is not to deny, of course, that the availability of more resources would make the solution of urban problems easier.

A second group within local government — the complacent — argue that if resources were available local authorities as they proved in the 1950s, '60s and '70s could do the job of urban regeneration. While many good developments did take place in those years we must also recognise that there were many failures. Moreover the challenges of the 1990s are different in form and scope. They demand a new way of working from local authorities.

We build our case for 'bringing local government back in' around four roles.

1. Urban problems require local solutions and local authorities can provide the local knowledge necessary to tailor policies to meet the particular conditions of their localities.
2. Tackling urban problems often requires an integrated response from a range of agencies and interests. Local authorities can act as a catalyst to ensure effective networking among agencies.
3. Developing appropriate policies requires strategic leadership and vision. Local authorities can provide that leadership in a way that balances the concerns of different interests.
4. Decisions about how to tackle urban problems should be seen as accountable and legitimate. Local authorities can provide a forum for ensuring the legitimacy of urban decision-making.

None of these roles can be uniquely reserved for local authorities. Yet no other organisation is as well-equipped to undertake all four roles. The capacity within local authorities to bring together these four roles in tackling urban problems makes an overwhelming argument for bringing local authorities back in. Local authorities have a role in urban regeneration by virtue of their position within localities as major service providers, employers, purchasers and landowners. Yet our argument for local authorities to take a lead role goes beyond their particular powers and responsibilities. It rests on their potential to offer community government.

The need for local solutions and knowledge

As Chapter 2 makes clear, the scale and range of urban problems is such that national or even European-wide intervention is necessary to tackle the issues of de-industrialisation, social deprivation, physical decay and failing infrastructure. In short many urban issues may be problems in cities but not necessarily problems of cities. The underlying cause of urban problems may lie in broad processes of social and economic restructuring which have national or global dimensions. Tackling urban problems can never, in the light of such factors, simply be left to cities. Yet equally it is a mistake to believe that national or supra-national intervention is the key. What is required is a framework for action in which supra-national, national and local intervention all have a part to play.

Given the focus of this book our prime concern is with the scope for local intervention. The scope is considerable because of the localised character of urban problems. As Solesbury (1990, p.26) comments:

Urban policy in the 1990s must address directly a much more varied agenda. That variety has two dimensions: variety in issues, and with the mix of issues varying between places as they respond individually to the wider processes of economic, social and environmental change. In consequence, individual towns and cities will tend to have their own unique agenda — rather than a common agenda — of issues to address.

Places have a unique mixture of potential and problems.

Diversity is much greater than the dominant image of the North/ South divide allows. Robson (1988) reviewing the plight of those inner cities, rightly notes the particular problems of big cities and the sustained influence of a North/South divide. The British image of the urban is conditioned by a perspective which contrasts the declining, large industrial cities in the North with the booming, newer, smaller cities and towns in the South East and East Anglia. The recession of the early 1990s, which has been more severe in the South East and East Anglia, has only slightly dented this image. Yet behind the broad pattern of uneven development lies a more complex reality. Growth areas and prosperous enclaves are to be found in the North and deprivation and disadvantage exists in parts of the South. Smaller towns and cities have their own problems and difficulties. Moreover within any particular urban area the pattern of decline and growth is more complex than any simple generalisation about boom or bust areas might suggest. As Solesbury (1990, p.26) argues 'on closer examination, and increasingly, the policy issues in Manchester differ from those in Liverpool, Sevenoaks from Maidenhead, Bath from Oxford, Morecombe from Eastbourne and so on. Places are individual and diverse'.

If these arguments are accepted then the case for detailed local knowledge and involvement in the design of urban policies is clear. Local authorities are in a position to provide that local knowledge. Yet we would not claim that they are uniquely able to provide such knowledge.

In theory at least it would be possible for locally-based agents of central government to gain a significant level of local knowledge. Indeed few could dispute that certain regional officials from, for example, the Departments of Environment or Trade and Industry have a detailed local grasp. Of course problems caused by the rapid turnover of officials and the detached way in which many operate limit the development of local understanding. Local business people may also have a certain type of local knowledge. Indeed some business interests in property and building may rely on that local knowledge to provide economic opportunities. Voluntary agencies and community groups — the range of 'third force organisations' we consider in Chapter 6 — have a particular contribution to make in local knowledge and understanding. Their local knowledge may enable them to see opportunities where others see only problems.

Local authorities cannot claim to be the sole source of local knowledge but they can claim to be a key source through the detailed and technical work of their professional officers and the daily presence in their local communities of councillors. At times a local authority may fail to harness or bring together in a manageable form its range of local knowledge. Yet there can be

little doubt of the strong potential for providing such knowledge by
local authorities and that in many instances successful urban policy
interventions have drawn on the deep well of local knowledge
contained within local authorities.

Co-ordination through networking

If the problems of our towns and cities are to be tackled, then what
is required is a sustained effort from a variety of sources. Such
effort has indeed been forthcoming. Many living in urban
communities, despite in some cases a daily struggle to survive, have
banded together in groups and organisations to tackle the problems
of their area. Local politicians and officials have also played a key
part. Private and corporate interests have launched initiatives. The
churches and the voluntary sector have developed programmes.
Finally national-level government has engaged in a diverse range
of policy initiatives. So much so that the Audit Commission in
1989 accused central government programmes of creating 'a
patchwork quilt of complexity and idiosyncrasy' (Audit
Commission 1989). The very proliferation of interests involved in
tackling urban issues raises the issues of co-ordination. Multi-
agency involvement in urban problem-solving is a phenomenon
that is not going to disappear. Further no urban gathering or
conference would be complete without the ritual call for and
endorsement of the need for more co-ordination.

But what do people mean by co-ordination? In a famous study
of the problems of implementation associated with an urban
renewal programme in the United States, Pressman and Wildavsky
(1974, pp. 135-5) pour scorn on those that argue that the solution
to urban problems is more co-ordination. They argue that co-
ordination lacks a clear meaning and focus in circumstances where
participants in a common project disagree over goals and means. It
would be nice to assume that people do not work at cross-purposes
but given the different backgrounds and starting-points of those
involved in multi-agency working such conflict is best taken as a
given.

One response to the problem of co-ordination would then be to
set up an agency to impose order and coerce others to go along
with its policy goals. Co-ordination in this sense becomes a form of
power. People are co-ordinated by being told what to do within a
hierarchical frame of reference or to use the jargon of organisational analysis the solution is vertical integration. A central
government agent such as a local prefect in the French system of

administration, before its reform, might be seen as having such a role. Do those calling for co-ordination want it imposed in a hierarchical way by central government or its agent?

A second response to the case for co-ordination is to ask for machinery which, in effect, grants a veto to all those with a stake in the matter. Co-ordination becomes the search for consent which given a context of conflict and disagreement can become a recipe for inaction. Horizontal integration within a bureaucratic/ hierarchical frame of reference leaves in place the autonomy and rationale of each unit. Each interest is granted a place in the decision-making table and the option of protecting its special interests and 'sacred cows'. Such machinery has at times been associated with inner city partnerships. A House of Commons (1983) report on Liverpool's inner city partnership committee in the early 1980s showed how conflicts were not resolved and effective policy solutions did not emerge.

We suggest that the search for co-ordination does not necessarily imply coercion by a higher authority or an endless search for consensus. Pressman and Wildavsky's work is premised on the assumption of co-ordination through hierarchy, either by way of vertical or horizontal integration. We would offer another approach: co-ordination through networks. Co-operation is obtained, and subsequently sustained, through the establishment of relations premised on solidarity, loyalty, trust and reciprocity rather than through hierarchy. Under the network model, organisations learn to co-operate by recognising their mutual dependency; through discussion, negotiation and open communication; and by the development of shared knowledge and experience. The outcome of successful networking is a long-term commitment to one another and shared goals.

We will return to the issue of networking in Chapter 8. For the present we will simply argue that local authorities are able to make a particularly valuable contribution to the development of effective local networks. First their relative permanence provides a solid base for developing the long-term commitment associated with networking. Local authorities are part of the government scene with a history, a strong position in the present and an assurance that they will be around in some form in the future. Compared to other potential networkers — central government agencies, local community groups and business interests — local authorities have a certain solidity and substance. Of course there is a danger that these characteristics may become so exaggerated that the authority becomes ossified and insular — uninterested in new ideas and the wider environment. Yet a committed authority can turn these potential stumbling blocks into building blocks for local networks.

To undertake a networking role it is necessary for a local authority to become a learning authority (Clarke and Stewart, 1992(a)). There can be no doubt about the difficulty of achieving such learning from both within and outside the authority. Yet local authorities, in so far as they become committed learners, can stimulate the debate, exchange and mutual understanding necessary to effective networking. Forums for the exchange of views, advisory panels drawing on expertise in the community, short-term attachments and secondments, recruitment of officers with wider experience than local government, research in partnership with local communities or universities can all provide the basis for learning and ultimately network building. Many local authorities undertake such activities and all are well-placed to do so.

A final element in networking in which local authorities can make a particular contribution is through the provision of resources. Resources are necessary to oil the wheels of networks. Local authorities can offer subsidies and grants but in many ways more important are the benefits in kind: premises, land, statistical information, technical expertise and so on. Such items can form the basis for the reciprocity which binds together networks.

Tackling urban problems requires co-ordination. Networking provides a valuable tool for achieving co-ordination. Local authorities have a number of qualities that make them potentially very important contributors to local network-building. By definition networks involve organisations other than the local authority yet the building of local networks would seem to be greatly enhanced if local authorities are involved in an active and substantial way. As Clarke and Stewart (1992(b) p. 27) comment:

> City government has become the job of a whole set of agencies with separate tasks whose separation from one another can limit change. To prevent this fragmentation being disruptive a network of co-operation needs to be built from the fragments.

Strategic vision and civic leadership

City government is about co-operation and coalition-building. Yet behind these processes lurk other issues: what is the purpose of co-operation and which interests should be involved? Strategic vision and civic leadership are necessary to make choices for the networks and coalitions that are assembled. Local authorities can play a central role in providing such leadership. They can mold the diverse interests and perspectives present in a locality into a shared vision. They can manage the tension between achieving capacity to obtain goals and ensuring that some interests — in particular those lacking resources with which to bargain — are not excluded from the process. The focus on leadership in the current discussion goes beyond the biographies of leading men and women in local government. It is concerned with the opportunities for leadership understood as a process of strategic vision and collective organisation.

Leadership is about providing and promoting strategic vision. But do local authorities have the capacity to offer such a vision and make it a vision shared within the wider community of local interests? Benington (1986, pp. 16–17) argues in the 1980s that local authorities could 'mobilise the weight of the state':

> A local authority, when it uses its authority as a body elected to represent the interests of the whole community, has a capacity to redefine problems, to move certain issues into the centre of political attention and to begin to shift the balance of power in favour of new interests.

But are the resource-constrained local authorities operating in the fragmented world of local governance in the 1990s capable of providing such leadership? The answer to this question in the abstract depends on your view of the world of politics and the political system (*cf* Jones 1989).

Those with a more mechanical view of the political world see political actors as operating in the context of a complex set of external forces and influences. It is recognised also that political actors have their own energies and their own goals. Indeed political actors are often assumed to have a rather narrow economic rationality and to be driven by self-interest. The political process consists of 'actions and reactions, forcing and adjustments' which govern the resulting interactions.

> The political world envisioned by this analysis is one of high information and systematic predictable interactions among well-behaved variables. It is a world of certainty and clarity. Its actors are driven by single motives that can be achieved in straightforward ways, although the resulting interactions can be enormously complex.
>
> (Jones 1989, p. 8)

Leadership in this world is molded by a complex of social and economic forces and is heavily structured by the institutional environment and the resources at the disposal of different political actors.

From this perspective leaders operating in a fragmented environment with limited resources will be seen as very constrained. Forces of social and economic change may sweep them along without any sense of control or influence on their part. Local authorities as leaders from such a perspective may have little to offer in the 1990s. Lacking in resources and faced with a fragmented environment the local authority is unlikely to produce an effective strategic response to societal changes.

A second perspective on politics, however, provides grounds for greater optimism about the opportunities for local authority leadership. This perspective offers a more biological view of the political world. It is a world of substantial indeterminancy. Actors may lack a clear view of their goals and considerable doubt may exist about how best to achieve their goals. If we assume that there is some fluidity about how people define their preferences and how these relate to their goals and actions, a key role for leadership emerges. Leaders 'can more easily persuade others that a policy relates to their ends in politics... leaders may be able to convince others that their preferences correspond to the leader's policy proposal' (Jones 1989, pp. 9–10). Rhetoric, the endowment of meaning to a situation, definitions of the problem became central to the political process. The task of leadership in the light of unstable and changing events is to define how issues should be understood and what are appropriate policy responses.

The biological view of politics brings into focus a second dimension to understanding leadership. Developing and promoting a shared vision is part of the challenge of leadership. A second element is achieving the capacity to make things happen. In the uncertain and fluid biological world, leadership faces the challenge of how to aggregate efforts for a common purpose or how to assemble a regime which blends capacities and so obtains a sustained impact in key policy areas. The achievement and maintenance of a capacity to govern is not an easy task confronted as city leaders are by social change, economic transformation, a continuing influx of new actors and the potential for collective action breakdowns due to conflict or indifference (cf Stone 1989).

Achieving the capacity to make things happen increases in difficulty as complexity of the task that is to be undertaken grows. Further, in the case of many urban policies, an effective response requires mobilising more than governmental resources; it involves gaining the commitment of non-governmental actors. It is with respect to this undertaking that government actors in market-oriented societies can face a crucial dilemma. Resources essential to achieving many societal benefits lie in the control of a select group of interests, in particular business corporations. Their decisions in relation to investment, the management of production and the reward of their employees have a crucial bearing on the welfare of a locality. Achieving an effective mobilisation of effort involving local businesses alone is challenging in itself. Government and local authorities should also consider the interest of those with less resources with which to bargain, 'That is a particularly difficult task because there is always a tension between representativeness and the capacity to govern' (Stone 1989, p. 156). The management of this tension is an essential challenge of urban government — one which a local authority more than any other organisation can claim as its own. Business leadership is by its nature partisan. The agents of central government can claim an interest in developing broad-based coalitions but it can be difficult for appointed officials to undertake such a task. The elected, representative nature of local authorities should make them the natural protectors and promoters of balanced social and economic agendas and strategies.

The legitimacy of urban decision-making

Tackling urban problems involves creating a 'capacity to get things done' but in a democracy achieving such a capacity is not sufficient. The exercise of power needs to be legitimate. This argument is more than a normative assertion. It rests also on the pragmatic grounds that to be effective in the long run power-holders must be seen to be legitimate. A legitimation deficit undermines public support and commitment to programmes of change and ultimately undermines the ability of power-holders to mobilise resources and promote co-operation and partnership.

The current fragmented system of urban governance offers little comfort to those concerned with legitimacy. Jones and Stewart (1992) suggest that what has been created is 'a new magistracy' — a lay non-elected elite.

> Elected representatives are being replaced by a burgeoning army of the selected. They are found on training and enterprise councils, health authorities, housing action trusts and urban corporations.

Many more such individuals take places on the governing bodies of the new universities, hospital trusts and other local agencies. Indeed there appears to be in some cases a considerable overlapping in the membership of different appointed bodies. These agencies of non-elected local government share a common problem: 'this new pattern of governance has a fault line: 'non-accountability'. The rise of a fragmented and poorly understood system of urban governance threatens the legitimacy of the system of urban policy-making.

How can we bring greater legitimacy back to the structure of urban governance? Beetham (1991, p. 19) suggests that there are three dimensions to the legitimacy of a political system. Beetham's criteria come not from abstract philosophical reflection but from empirical observation of the workings of political systems.

> For power to be fully legitimate...three conditions are required: its conformity to established rules; the justifiability of the rules by reference to shared beliefs; the express consent of the subordinate, or the most significant among them, to the particular relations of power.

Legitimacy according to this approach is not an all-or-nothing affair. Within any political system there will be some ambiguity about rules and some who do not accept their validity and who will not give their consent to the power-holders. The point is that it is possible to make the rules of power more or less legitimate. In short a system can be designed and operated in a way that either decreases or increases its legitimacy. The current confused and fragmented structure of urban governance has helped to create a substantial legitimation deficit. Bringing elected local authorities back into a lead role can help to overcome this deficit.

Following Beetham's criteria, decisions about the future of cities should be made in accordance with the established rules that are widely understood and recognised within the locality. As Lewis (1992, pp. 60–61) comments, the conduct of inner city regeneration through a maze of institutions creates a system that fails 'to be rational, open, clear, committed and accountable'. Decisions in relation to urban regeneration should be conducted in the open not under cover. What we have is 'government by moonlight' not 'government in the sunlight'. He concludes: 'Constitutional principles require that constitutional actors be readily identified and that they should be readily called into account' (p. 69). Local authorities offer the best hope of developing a process of decision making that is more open, understood and accountable. Local authorities have statutory responsibilities in relation to freedom of information. They have a duty to consult over economic development and land-use planning matters. Councillors can be held to account to some degree in their surgeries, public meetings, the media and through elections. This is not to suggest that the mechanisms of local democracy are perfect (see discussion in Chapter 9). It is to suggest that elected local government provides a better starting point in the search for legitimacy than either business leaders or agents of central government.

A second dimension to legitimacy in urban regeneration is that decisions must emanate from what is widely perceived among both dominant and subordinate groups as a rightful source of authority. 'The rules must provide that those who come to hold power have the qualities appropriate to its exercise; and the structure of power must be seen to serve a recognisably general interest, rather than simply the interests of the powerful' (Beetham 1991, p. 17). Local authorities with respect to this second dimension of legitimacy again offer the best option. The calibre of local authority leaders may at times be inadequate and some local authority leaders may on occasion pursue sectional or narrow interests. Yet the potential remains great for local authority leaders to be seen as powerful exponents of community interests.

The calibre of local authority leaders has at times been questioned by central government and by business. Indeed a CBI Report (1988) comments:

> Local politicians cannot normally be expected to provide the visionary leadership required...the local business community must therefore step up to the responsibilities of leadership.

Yet business figures in Britain have been relatively reluctant to take a leadership role. Where they are involved it is not evident that they have provided an overwhelming new dynamic to policy-making. There appears to be a number of major obstacles confronting the rise of a coherent business leadership at the local level. First there is the problem of capacity. Major corporate companies are organised on a national and international basis. Their local managers often lack the time, commitment or authority to become effective local leaders. There is a tendency in some cases for major companies to second those managers who are approaching retirement or whose use to the company is limited further. Local business people that do offer their services may have a very particular interest — in property development for example — which limits their ability to take a wider view of the area's needs. This is not to deny the significance of the contribution of some business leaders but to indicate that the qualities of business leaders as a group cannot give them an automatic legitimacy with the public. Moreover the position of business leaders as legitimate community leaders is fundamentally in doubt because they are prone to being seen as acting in the interests of the powerful and not in the interests of the subordinate.

The third dimension of legitimacy is perhaps the one that most pushes the role of local authorities to the fore. The third level of legitimacy involves the giving of a demonstrable expression of consent on the part of the subordinate. Local authorities through elections, surveys, public meetings, consultation exercises and so on are plainly in a position to obtain public expressions of consent. Some Urban Development Corporations have sought similar public approval for their projects yet their non-elected status always raises questions over their actions. Is legitimacy given to such agencies or do they take it by a combination of propaganda and public relations? Legitimacy requires a giving of demonstrable consent by the public. An election or a referendum provides the most powerful symbolic expression of such consent. As such the elected status of local authorities gives them a special role in ensuring the legitimacy of urban decision-making.

Concluding comment

This chapter has made the case for giving elected local government a central role in urban regeneration. Two points are perhaps worth emphasising in terms of the argument we have assembled. First we have made our argument on pragmatic grounds to a greater extent than philosophical terms. There is a broader normative and philosophical argument to be made for local government but our position as developed here, draws on the experience and practice of urban politics and management. The second point to emphasise is that, despite the grounded nature of our argument, we are not seeking to defend all the current practice of elected local authorities. Rather, our aim is to support those new ways of working and thinking that are present in the local government community. Our argument is for a different type of elected local government bringing an empowering style to meet the challenge of urban governance.

References and bibliography

Audit Commission (1989) *Urban Regeneration and Economic Development* London: HMSO.
Beecham, J. (1992) *Municipal Review and AMA News* **730**, Aug/Sept.
Beetham, D. (1991) *The Legitimation of Power* London: Macmillan.

Benington, J. (1986) 'Local economic strategies: paradigms for a planned economy' Local Economy **1**, 1, 7–33.

CBI Report (1988) *Initiatives Beyond Charity: Report of the CBI Task Force on Business and Urban Regeneration* London: CBI.

Clarke, M. and Stewart, J. (1992(a)) *The Learning Authority* Luton: Local Government Management Board.

Clarke, M. and Stewart, J. (1992(b)) The challenge for the government of the cities' *Local Government Policy Making* **18**, 4, March, 25–28.

House of Commons (1983) *The Problems of Management of Urban Renewal (Appraisal of the Recent Initiatives in Merseyside) Report: Vol. 1.* Third Report from the Environment Committee, London: HMSO.

Jones, B. (1989) 'Causation, constraint and political leadership' in B. Jones (ed.) *Leadership and Politics* Lawrence: University Press of Kansas.

Jones, G. and Stewart, J. (1992) 'Selected not elected' *Local Government Chronicle* 13 November, 15.

Lewis, N. (1992) *Inner City Regeneration* Buckingham: Open University Press.

Pressman, J. and Wildavsky, A. (1984) *Implementation* Berkeley, CA: University of California Press.

Robson, B. (1988) *Those Inner Cities* Oxford: Clarendon Press.

Solesbury, W. (1990) 'Reconstructing national urban policy for the 1990s' unpublished but see by same author 'Reframing urban policy' *Policy and Politics* **21**, 1, 1993, 31–38.

Stone, C. (1989) 'Paradigms, power and urban leadership' in B. Jones (ed.) *Leadership and Politics* Lawrence: University Press of Kansas.

2 The challenge for cities: A question of balance

The picture that emerges of the light and prospects of inner cities cannot be other than bleak.

(Brian Robson 1983, p.39)

The Government wants inner city residents to have more opportunity to share in the new prosperity.

(H.M. Government, 1988, *Action for Cities* London: HMSO)

It is fashionable to talk about potential rather than problems in policy debate. The leader of Trafford, in welcoming guests to the 1992 Association of Metropolitan Authorities Conference, claimed: 'We don't admit to problems in Trafford, only opportunities'. This comment was quickly followed by a qualification: 'although it must be said that the ongoing effects of the current recession have had an impact throughout the borough but, in particular, within inner city areas' (Warbrick 1992, p. 127). Trafford council leader like many before him has the difficult task of being positive about the future and yet being realistic about the problems his area faces.

There is no denying that the problems of cities are considerable. A report produced in 1992 by the Policy Studies Institute (PSI) brings home in dramatic terms the scale of the challenge that remains despite the various efforts made to tackle problems since the mid-1970s. The report uses official statistics to examine progress with respect to factors such as employment, poverty and housing in 36 of the most deprived areas within Britain. It concludes that despite 15 years of policy effort aimed at urban areas deprivation and disadvantage remain strongly entrenched. 'In general the gap between conditions and opportunities in deprived areas and other kinds of place...remains as wide as it was a decade and a half ago. In some respects the gap has widened' (Policy Studies Institute 1992, p. 82).

The first half of this chapter looks briefly at the problems facing cities. A full analysis of these problems is not provided. The main aim is to establish the scale of the challenge facing cities in the 1990s, notwithstanding the achievements of past interventions. The second half of the chapter defines what should be the focus of regeneration strategies in the future. The dominant strategy of the 1980s — growth, orientated physical renewal — needs to be extended to include a wider vision of the purpose of regeneration. The challenge is to achieve a 'balanced city' in which growth is complemented by concern about sustainable development; physical regeneration is pursued alongside social and employment objectives; 'have-nots' as well as 'haves' gain through change; and strategies of empowerment ensure the participation of all in the decision-making process.

The problems of cities

The problems of cities are considered along a number of dimensions in the first half of this chapter:

- economy and employment;
- social polarisation;
- training and education;
- physical decay and environmental concerns;
- crime and social unrest.

Economy and employment

The weakening of the economic base of cities is at the heart of many of the problems they face. The patterns of change vary from city to city. Areas such as the West Midlands suffered the collapse of key sectors of manufacturing; including the machine tool, engineering and car industries. During the 1970s the industrial base of Birmingham shrank by a third (Spencer *et al.* 1986). In Sheffield in 1971 there were 139,000 people employed in the manufacturing industry. Ten years later the number had declined to 90,000, and by 1987 it had collapsed to 58,000 (Sheffield City Council, 1987).

The mid-1980s onwards revealed signs of a national economic recovery, with some deprived urban areas also showing substantial decreases in unemployment. The PSI report, however, shows that while unemployment fell in a third of deprived urban areas between 1983–91, it remained the same or increased in the other two thirds (see Table 2.1).

During the 1980s businesses have continued moving out of towns and cities. Some have closed. Others have sought new or greenfield locations. The last decade or so has seen suburban business parks and urban fringe development increase to a substantial degree. Space in business parks, for example, has grown since the beginning of the 1980s from almost nothing to 72 million square feet — the size of Birmingham and Bristol's city centre office space put together (*The Economist*, 23 May 1992, p. 31). Britain's established cities, then, still suffer from the attractions of greenfield locations elsewhere.

The challenge facing Britain's cities increasingly is recognised as having a European dimension. The creation of the Single European Market, a more competitive and integrated market, may well widen disparities between regions. Locational advantage would appear to lie with more central regions and cities, such as Paris and Frankfurt, with many of Britain's older industrial cities left out in the cold. The impact of industrial restructuring in part stimulated by the Single European Market could be particularly acute in some UK cities partly because of the spatial concentration of vulnerable industries in such areas (such as auto and aerospace factories) and partly because of the very low economic base from which many of Britian's cities start. Over 40 per cent of Europe's declining industrial areas, eligible for European Commission Objective 2 funding, are in the UK (Benington and Taylor 1993).

Social polarisation

Robson (1988, p. 17) points out the flight to the suburbs is a long-standing phenomenon in British cities, with the more middle-class and affluent groups leading the way. Between 1951 and 1981 the largest towns and cities lost on average one-third of their population. This process slowed but continued in many areas during the 1980s. London lost 218,000 people (2.3 per cent of its population) through migration in the mid 1980s. Birmingham lost 113,000 people (4.3 per cent) and Manchester lost 70,000 (2.7 per

Table 2.1: Unemployment in selected deprived urban areas 1983, 1991

| | Unemployment ('000) | |
	1983	1991
Scotland		
Clydebank	4.0	2.8
Glasgow	75.7	49.8
Inverclyde	8.0	5.7
Monklands	9.7	5.4
North West region		
Blackburn	9.5	6.7
Burnley	6.2	3.8
Knowsley	21.1	12.7
Liverpool	56.2	40.0
Manchester	43.6	32.4
Preston	9.0	6.2
Rochdale	14.5	9.4
Salford	19.0	12.3
West Midlands region		
Birmingham	94.3	66.9
Coventry	27.9	17.5
Sandwell	28.3	17.6
Wolverhampton	22.7	15.3
Wales		
Blaenau Gwent	6.4	3.4
Rhondda	5.3	4.0
Northern region		
Middlesborough	16.1	9.7
Yorkshire and Humberside region		
Bradford	30.9	23.1
Kingston-upon-Hull	23.6	17.8
East Midlands region		
Leicester	22.1	16.7
Nottingham	21.6	19.0
Greater London		
Brent	15.3	16.2
Greenwich	13.3	13.3
Hackney	18.6	18.4
Hammersmith and Fulham	10.7	10.1
Haringey	15.5	18.0
Islington	14.7	14.2
Kensington and Chelsea	8.5	6.3
Lambeth	23.0	22.1
Lewisham	15.7	17.3
Newham	15.9	16.9
Southwark	18.2	18.8
Tower Hamlets	15.8	14.3
Wandsworth	15.3	14.7

Source: Adapted from PSI (1992) Tables 2.6, 2.9, 2.10, 2.11 and 2.12.

cent). The figures from the 1991 census confirm the picture of slow continuing population loss in most cities. Although an element of uncertainty has been created because the returns for the census were disproportinately weak in some areas, because of people's unwillingness to respond for fear of being traced by poll tax collectors. In contrast to the general trend some inner London boroughs do show signs of population growth.

Associated with population loss has been an increase in poverty and deprivation within large cities. As Robson (1988, p. 23) comments:

'Migration has always been age and ability selective. Inevitably the resorting of the population has changed its social composition in space. The piling up of the poor and deprived in urban areas in not as consistent as might popularly be thought, but there is no doubt that there has been a considerable relative polarization of the poor in the urban areas'.

The social polarisation evident in many towns and cities has, if anything, increased in the last decade or so. Various dimensions to social polarisation include:

• The proportion of people in poverty — measured in terms of those qualifying for social security benefits — has grown in many inner city areas and remained at high levels in others. In England as a whole 13.9 per cent of the adult population could be counted as poor in 1989–91. The percentage figures for deprived urban areas ranged during the same period from a low of 15.9 in Kensington and Chelsea to a staggering 36.2 in Liverpool (see Table 2.2).

• Premature death among adults in deprived urban areas remains higher than elsewhere. Table 2.3 presents figures for deprived urban areas in terms of standardised mortality ratios (SMR). These figures take account of differences in age and sex of the population in areas and are calculated around a national rate expressed as 100. Most deprived urban areas have an SMR above 100 which means that they have more deaths than would be expected given their population structure.

• Homelessness has increased substantially during the 1980s, with large increases in the number of households accepted as homeless by local authorities in deprived urban areas. The rise in homelessness is specially notable in London but is also observable in urban areas such as Manchester, Clydebank, Blaenau, and Gwent (see Table 2.4).

Table 2.2: Claimants receiving income support/supplementary
          benefit in selected deprived urban areas of England
          1983–5, 1989–91

	Percentage of estimated adult population	
	1983–85	**1989–91**
Greater London		
Brent	15.4	18.5
Greenwich	19.4	18.8
Hackney	29.5	32.4
Hammersmith and Fulham	20.8	20.0
Haringey	23.1	27.2
Islington	28.4	26.5
Kensington and Chelsea	17.5	15.9
Lambeth	27.4	28.9
Lewisham	21.5	22.1
Newham	24.4	27.3
Southwark	29.0	27.6
Tower Hamlets	34.7	32.6
Wandsworth	20.8	18.1
North West region		
Knowsley	32.9	33.8
Liverpool	34.4	36.2
Manchester	22.2	32.0
Rochdale	22.0	16.2
Salford	25.0	22.3
West Midlands region		
Birmingham	22.2	23.9
Coventry	23.1	19.3
Sandwell	25.6	20.2
Wolverhampton	24.7	21.9
England	15.9	13.9

Source: Adapted from PSI (1992) Table 4.1.

Table 2.3: Standardised mortality ratios in selected deprived urban
        areas 1980, 1990

	Great Britain = 100	
	1980	1990
Greater London		
Brent	86	85
Greenwich	104	97
Hackney	92	103
Hammersmith and Fulham	94	99
Haringey	93	97
Islington	93	98
Kensington and Chelsea	83	99
Lambeth	91	103
Lewisham	94	102
Newham	97	104
Southwark	98	98
Tower Hamlets	104	103
Wandsworth	96	104
North West region		
Blackburn	119	120
Burnley	137	128
Knowsley	112	108
Liverpool	112	112
Manchester	113	114
Preston	98	116
Rochdale	111	113
Salford	122	115
West Midlands region		
Birmingham	106	107
Coventry	98	106
Sandwell	109	107
Wolverhampton	104	105
Wales		
Blaenau Gwent	122	113
Rhondda	122	113
Scotland		
Clydebank	112	118
Glasgow	107	113
Inverclyde	107	114
Monklands	111	122

Source: Adapted from PSI (1992) Tables 4.7, 4.8.

Table 2.4: Homelessness in selected deprived urban areas 1980, 1990

	Households accepted as homeless by local authorities in second quarter of year, per 1,000 households	
	1980	1990
Greater London		
Brent	2.8	3.0
Greenwich	1.5	4.1
Hackney	3.1	5.6
Hammersmith and Fulham	4.2	3.7
Haringey	1.6	3.7
Islington	3.2	6.4
Kensington and Chelsea	1.9	1.4
Lambeth	2.4	3.4
Lewisham	2.2	3.5
Newham	2.2	5.2
Southwark	2.1	7.0
Tower Hamlets	1.6	3.5
Wandsworth	3.0	3.3
North West		
Blackburn	0.8	2.4
Burnley	0.7	1.6
Knowsley	1.2	1.3
Liverpool	1.2	1.3
Manchester	1.6	11.1
Preston	1.0	2.2
Rochdale	0.6	2.3
Salford	0.8	1.2
Midlands		
Birmingham	2.7	1.9
Coventry	0.4	1.4
Sandwell	0.3	1.2
Wolverhampton	0.8	1.3
Leicester	3.0	2.5
Nottingham	0.8	2.5
Yorkshire and Humberside		
Bradford	1.1	1.5
Kingston-upon-Hull	0.6	1.5
Scotland		
Clydebank	0.6	4.6
Glasgow	1.8	1.1
Inverclyde	1.6	3.1
Monklands	0.8	1.1
Wales		
Blaenau, Gwent	0.9	2.3
Rhondda	0.9	0.4
	1.1	1.4

Source: Adapted from PSI (1992) Table 5.7.

Training and education

The importance of education and training in providing opportunities for the disadvantaged citizens of urban areas is widely recognised. Policy initiatives from Educational Priority Areas to City Technology Colleges testify to the perceived need to give special attention to this area. The 1992 PSI report reviewing the performance of such initiatives makes rather grim reading. It suggests that despite the success of some projects the general trend in education and training has seen the disadvantaged position of the population of the most deprived urban communities confirmed. Key findings include:

- The worsening of pupil-teacher ratio in primary schools in many deprived local education authorities in England against the national trend (see Table 2.5).
- examination achievements in deprived areas are weak compared with more wealthy areas. Table 2.6 illustrates this point with respect to England. Table 2.7 looks at evidence from Scotland, where the link between poverty (measured by access to clothing grants) and weak examination performance is clear.
- People from deprived areas were less likely to get a training place and more likely to remain unemployed after leaving Employment Training and Youth Training schemes. The PSI report points out that the difference was not great but was persistent.

Physical decay and environmental concerns

Changing economic fortunes for cities has left them with large tracts of despoiled and abandoned land. Such land may be owned by local authorities, quasi-governmental agencies or private interests. The pattern of ownership can be mixed and even confused. Derelict land and physical decay have been recognised as city problems for a long time. The 1970s and 80s have seen local authorities restore large acreages of land but in many cases cities have 'still ended up with even more dereliction than they started with' (Robson 1988, p. 36). The problem of derelict land, that requires some sort of remedial treatment before it can be put to use, is part of a wider problem of vacant urban land. A Government sponsored research report estimates that in England there were some 150,000 acres of vacant urban land in 1990. This grand total constitutes an area the size of Cleveland county and represents 5 per cent of the total urban area of England. The concentration of vacant land ranges from 11 per cent in the Northern region to 3 per cent in the South East and Greater London (Shepherd and Abakuks 1992).

Table 2.5: Pupil:teacher ratios in primary schools in selected deprived urban areas in England, 1981 and 1990

	1981	1990
Brent	18.4	20.8
Haringey	19.7	21.8
Newham	20.7	23.1
Inner London Education Authority	17.5	18.8
Birmingham	23.2	23.5
Coventry	22.1	22.4
Sandwell	23.4	22.2
Wolverhampton	19.4	19.8
Knowsley	22.7	21.4
Liverpool	20.8	21.7
Manchester	22.4	21.8
Rochdale	23.2	21.9
Salford	21.5	22.0
Bradford	20.2	19.7
England	22.6	22.0

Source: Adapted from PSI (1992) Table 3.2.

Table 2.6: Those leaving secondary school with five or more CSE grade 1 and/or 'O' level grades A–C, and/or GCSE grade A–C[1] in selected deprived urban areas in England

	Percentage of all school leavers	
	1979/80, 80/1, 81/2	1987/80, 88/9, 89/90
Brent	17.5	23.3
Haringey	15.0	19.8
Newham	12.8	14.3
Inner London Education Authority	14.0	17.4[2]
Birmingham	18.5	22.7
Coventry	19.8	21.3
Sandwell	12.6	17.4
Wolverhampton	14.9	21.2
Knowsley	11.4	11.6
Liverpool	16.5	20.7
Manchester	15.7	20.2
Rochdale	16.5	24.5
Salford	14.5	24.9
Bradford	18.9	16.9
England	21.9	28.6

1. *Aggregations of school leavers in groups of three academic years.*
2. *Data for inner London boroughs used for 1989/90.*
Source: Adapted from PSI (1992) Table 3.3.

Table 2.7: Link between poverty and performance: an illustration
from Scotland's schools

	Comparisons of 3+ Highers and Clothing grants 1989/90	
	3+ Highers	% pupils clothing grants
Lenzie	57.4	4
Gryffe	53.1	2
Bearsden	52.5	5
Boclair	50.9	5
Williamwood	50.8	2
Douglas	47.8	7
Kyle	47.6	5
Marr	46.8	4
Eastwood	45.2	5
Greenock Academy	45.1	13
Paisley Grammar	43.3	13
Turnbull	42.3	11
Notre Dame, Glasgow	40.9	29
St Pius	*	51
Wellington	*	58
Glenwood	*	50
Cranhill	*	55
Craigbank	*	60
St Leonard	*	56
John Street	*	50
Springburn	*	53
Merksworth	*	48
Garthamlock	*	49
Kingsridge	*	62
St Augustine's	*	53
Possilpark	*	61
Lochend	*	55

* = Below one per cent
Source: The Herald Thursday, 5 March, 1992, p. 22.

Other physical problems are also present in many cities.
Challenges include council tower blocks and housing estates and
vast numbers of private homes in need of repair and renovation.
Again, a picture emerges of considerable progress on improvement
and renovation and yet a considerable backlog of work remaining.
A DoE survey in 1985 estimated that £18.8 billion would be
required to undertake repair and modernisation work to local
authority stock in England alone. Average spending on such work
in the 1980s was only 1.4 billion a year and the initial years of the
1990s have seen spending decline. In short 'the backlog continues
to grow' (PSI Report 1992, p. 62).

In many cities there are severe problems with a collapsing infrastructure which dates from the nineteenth century. Sewers, roads, pavements and utility lines are not adequate to the demands of the 1990s. The challenge of maintaining and improving the machinery of the city is considerable. As Solesbury (1990) comments: 'Beyond the visible buildings, parks, roads and railways, there are invisible network carrying water, power, electronic and optic impulses; and also the intangible qualities of air and water, noise, townscape and landscape. | Property, infrastructure and environment must all perform adequately if the economic and social life of the city is to thrive.'

There is an increasing awareness of issues around the quality of the environment in cities. Concerns include:

- air and water quality;
- solid waste disposal;
- accessibility of 'public realm' street;
- retention of familiar and valued buildings.

Above all, cities are vast consumers of natural resources and potentially prone to energy shortages and other environmental disasters. Equally, the potential contribution of 'cleaner' cities to the global environment is increasingly recognized (Stewart and Hams 1992).

Crime and social unrest

Crime is a problem in many cities and towns. As the Morgan Report (1991) points out, despite the growth of Neighbourhood Watch and other local level initiatives aimed at crime prevention, the number of recorded crimes has been increased substantially over the last four decades. The number of notifiable offences recorded by the police in England and Wales has risen from about 1 per 100 of the population in the 1950s to 5 per 100 in the 1970s and to over 8 per 100 in 1990. Urban residents, especially those living in or close to more deprived areas suffer disproportionately not only from violent crime but also from burglary, theft, vandalism and street crime. Table 2.8 illustrates this point by looking at crime figures in selected urban and non-urban country areas in 1990.

Urban unrest and disturbances appear to have been a constant theme of the 1980s, with outbreaks occurring again in the 1990s. The summer of 1992 alone saw unrest in at least eight towns or cities. All this suggests the enduring potential for social tensions in British cities to erupt into outbreaks of violence on the streets.

Table 2.8: Notifiable offences recorded by the police per 100,000 population in selected urban and non-urban police force areas

England and Wales	Main categories of crime			
	Violent Crime	Burglary, Fraud & Theft	Criminal Damage	Total offences
Urban				
Greater Manchester	494	10,299	2,242	13,112
Merseyside	535	7,466	1,507	9,614
London Metropolitan	820	8,726	2,001	11,642
West Midlands	568	7,985	1,512	10,123
South Yorkshire	468	6,508	1,252	8,286
West Yorkshire	586	9,000	1,766	11,420
Northumbria	475	9,889	2,819	14,236
South Wales	412	8,017	2,171	10,649
Cleveland	553	10,743	2,018	13,363
Non-urban				
Cheshire	312	4,505	889	5,786
Cumbria	459	4,147	1,146	6,782
Devon and Cornwall	310	4,960	866	6,167
Norfolk	326	5,978	952	7,298
Suffolk	355	4,441	1,013	5,888
Sussex	320	5,500	805	6,700
Warwickshire	288	5,498	991	6,811
Dyfed-Powys	464	3,128	791	4,427

Source: Home Office (1992) *Criminal Statistics, England and Wales 1990,* Cmd 2935, London: HMSO.

Defining the challenge: a balanced city

The presentation in the first half of this chapter of the problems of cities inevitably makes bleak reading. Many of the basic indicators of the health of cities provide a rather pitiless account of the vast scale of the problems that remain despite the efforts of many urban citizens and policy-makers to tackle them over recent years. Few would dispute the claim of the PSI report: 'the decay at the heart of Britain's cities is one of the biggest challenges faced by its government' (1992, p. 1).

The recounting of the extent of the problems that remain in our cities is not to encourage a fatalistic resignation. Nor is it our view that all the policies of the past have failed. What is required is careful reflection on the strengths and weaknesses of past approaches. Given the argument of Chapter 1 about the importance of local solutions, we are reluctant to think in terms of universal policy prescriptions. In the discussion below we offer some general thoughts on the nature of an appropriate balanced urban strategy for the 1990s.

Concern for the welfare of all citizens

The first point to be made is that any strategy should provide opportunities for all the citiziens of cities. As a bold statement this guideline for urban strategy is likely to attract widespread political support. The argument underlying our promotion of it, however, involves recognising a criticism of the dominant approach of the 1980s. Growth and market-oriented strategies tend to lead to 'the 75 per cent solution' (Brindley and Stoker 1988). They produce a pattern of urban renewal which is broadly beneficial to the top three-quarters of the income distribution but which can leave many inner city residents on low incomes feeling excluded and ignored. The evidence reviewed in the first half of this chapter provides a considerable challenge to the view that an increase in general prosperity automatically improves prospects for all residents. The disadvantages faced by residents of the more deprived areas of our country remain stubbornly in place. 'Trickle down' theories which suggested that economic prosperity and recovery in the 1980s would bring benefits to all have been discredited on both sides of the Atlantic (cf. Hambleton 1991). To quote one American writer: 'the rising tide may have lifted all yachts, but it did not lift all boats' (Michel 1991).

The creation of 'boom' conditions within one locality does not guarantee that the benefits in terms of employment and other opportunities are made available to the citizens of that locality. A classic and well-known illustration of this phenomenon is provided by the regeneration stimulated by the London Docklands Development Corporation (LDDC). Redevelopment in the area led to creation of 'new' jobs in the office and service sector but a skills mismatch prevented many local residents from getting the jobs with the result that the number of unemployed residents in the LDDC area was greater in April 1988 than in July 1981 at the launch of the development corporation (House of Commons 1988). The new housing provided within the LDDC area has also tended to have a socially exclusive character. As Brindley *et al.* (1989, p. 120) comment 'the private sector regeneration of Docklands is producing a collage of private realms, each barricaded behind its own security system'. The London Docklands experience provides in many respects an extreme case but there are similar stories, if less spectacular, to be told in other localities. The issue of how to design solutions which create opportunities for all citizens emerges as a critical concern of the 1990s.

The need for a broad-based approach

Given a concern with all citizens then what is required is 'a many sided and comprehensive urban policy' (Hambleton 1991, p. 25). In designing strategies for a city, all programmes — not just those specifically deemed as urban — should be a focus of attention. A balanced approach requires moving beyond piecemeal strategies towards a capacity to link the efforts of those concerned with the future of cities in economic, social and cultural fields.

Developing a comprehensive approach presents a considerable challenge to many local authorities. Birmingham, for example, has had to answer criticism that its focus on the physical renewal of the city centre has led to the neglect of outlying areas of the city or a down-playing of person-based provision in education or social services. Many local authorities have been confronted with the irony of gaining additional resources from central government under the Urban Programme or City Challenge only to lose central grant allocation under general funding arrangements. In general, central government has tended to offer a piecemeal package of initiatives and has failed to recognise the cross-cutting impact of many of its policies. Support and help available at the European levels of government has a similar character. The EC has a range of programmes which are central to tackling urban problems yet it would be difficult to see these policies as anything other than piecemeal and potentially cross-cutting.

To achieve the capacity to make links between programmes is a task which should be driven by local knowledge and priorities. The argument of Chapter 1 about the importance of local choice leads us to the view that if balanced, broad-based strategies to tackle the problems of cities are to emerge then it is within localities that the attempts 'to impose order on chaos' should start. This is not to deny the need for national and international action. It is to argue that effective, balanced strategies are most likely to emerge when informed by local knowledge and commitment.

A commitment to sustainable development

A balanced strategy requires respect for environmental concerns. The goal of sustainable developments has not only a concern with economic vitality but also has been defined as 'improving the quality of human life while living within the carrying capacity of supporting eco-systems' (see Stewart and Hams 1992, p. 7). It is imperative that such a goal becomes incorporated into the policy approaches of the future because of the pressures placed on eco-systems by human economic activity in the 'developed' world. Global warming, declining natural resources and the problem of waste production are signs of a process of development challenging the limits of the earth's carrying capacity. A commitment to sustainable development requires that we alter 'our activities whenever possible to use less resources, to use them more efficiently and recycle waste into new resources' (Stewart and Hams 1992, p. 7).

Cities are inevitably involved in meeting the environmental challenge because they are significant users of resources and a location for much economic and social activity. Local government can have a key part to play in promoting sustainable development because of its qualities outlined in Chapter 1: closeness to the issues; an ability to provide a focus for co-ordinated action; a leadership capacity; and the ability to respond to and gather public support. To realise this potential, a commitment to sustainable development should form part of a balanced approach to urban regeneration.

A strategy of empowerment

The final element in a balanced approach to the problems of cities is a commitment to a strategy of empowerment. There has been a tendency to think in terms of regeneration as requiring better co-ordination among political, social and business elites. The 1980s has seen a number of forums in which the 'movers and shapers' or the 'great and the good' have been brought together in an umbrella organisation to develop strategies and new solutions for the prob-lems of cities. Glasgow's civil leadership formed 'Glasgow Action', Aberdeen has 'Aberdeen beyond 2000' and Sheffield has its Eco-nomic Regeneration Committee. These bodies may well provide a valuable focus for city renewal but a balanced approach demands that attention and opportunity be given to the 'have-nots'.

Power is not equally spread in society so a strategy of empowerment is necessary to ensure the strengthening of the position of those who are on the sidelines of the decision-making process. As Clarke and Stewart (1992, p. 2) argue, 'Empowerment is about increasing the power of the public in relation to the institutions and organisations whose activities affect their way of life'. Empowering can involve giving opportunities for choice to individuals. It can mean making concrete the citizen's right to information and consultation. It can also involve providing opportunities for groups and communities to influence, through collective action, the environment in which they live.

Conclusions

This chapter has established that despite the efforts of many over the last two decades the problems of cities are considerable. We have not provided a detailed analysis of those problems but rather indicated the scale of the challenge that remains. If the relative disadvantage suffered by many inter-city residents is to be confronted a recognition of the limited impact of past policies is an important starting point. A recognition of the failings of the past has not however encouraged us to unveil a series of new utopias or panaceas. Our proposals are in many cases modest and yet they do require a fundamental shift in thinking. It means moving away from a narrow concentration on 'big' initiatives and towards a long-term concerted strategy. The essence of that balanced strategy is examined in various dimensions in the remainder of the book.

Concern for the welfare of all citizens is addressed in Chapter 3 in a discussion of how economic regeneration can be developed to add a social dimension. The commitment to sustainable development is directly considered in Chapter 4. Chapter 5 argues that an area or decentralised focus can help to ensure a broad-based approach to urban policy. Chapter 6 looks at the way that 'third force organisations' can contribute to a strategy of empowerment. Throughout the book the need for a balanced, long-term approach is emphasised.

References and bibliography

Benington, J. and Taylor, M. (1993) 'Changes and challenges facing the UK welfare state in the Europe of the 1990s' *Policy and Politics,* **21**, 2, 121–34.

Brindley, T. and Stoker, G. (1988) 'Partnership in inner city urban renewal — a critical analysis' *Local Government Policy Making* **15**, 2, September, 3–12.

Brindley, T., Rydin, Y. and Stoker, G. (1989) *Remaking Planning* London: Unwin Hyman.

Clarke, M. and Stewart, J. (1992) *Citizens and Local Democracy. Empowerment: A Theme for the 1990s* Luton: Local Government Management Board.

Hambleton, R. (1991) *Another Chance for Cities? Issue for Urban Policy in the 1990s.*

House of Commons (1988) *Third Report of the Employment Committee — The Employment Effects of Urban Development Corporations* (1991) HC 327, London: HMSO.

Morgan Report (1991) *Safer Communities: the local delivery of crime prevention through the partnership approach*, Independent Working Group Report, chaired by James Morgan, to the Home Office Standing Conference on Crime Prevention.

Robson, B. (1988) *Those Inner Cities* Oxford: Clarendon Press.

Sheffield City Council (1987) *Sheffield Working it Out* Sheffield: Sheffield City Council.

Shepherd, J. and Abakuks, A. (1992) *The National Survey of Vacant Land in Urban Areas of England* London: HMSO.

Solesbury, W. (1990) *Reconstructing National Urban Policy for the 1990s.* Unpublished but see by the same author: (1993) 'Reframing Urban Policy' *Policy and Politics* **21**, 31–38.

Spencer, K. *et al.* (1986) *Crisis in the Industrial Heartland. A Study of the West Midlands* Oxford: Clarendon Press.

Stewart, J. and Hams, T. (1992) *Local Government for Sustainable Development* The UK Local Government Agenda for the Earth Summit. Luton: Local Government Management Board.

Warbrick, C. (1992) 'Aiming to be number one' *Municipal Review and AMA News No. 730*, August/September, 127.

Willmott, P. and Hutchinson, R. (1992) *Urban Trends: A report of Britain's Deprived Urban Areas* London: Policy Studies Institute, Michel (1991).

3 Entrepreneurial planning

...The output from the contemporary planner is action-oriented, rather then process-oriented. It is necessary for the contemporary planner to understand the mechanisms of the private sector, to work at speed, and frequently to use informal means of expression (such as 'development frameworks' with no statutory status, rather than more formal and fossilised statutory plans). The need is for flexibility and invention in the way the planner works.   (Lock 1988, p. 27)

In the declining parts of Britain in the late 1970s and early 1980s there was a severe lack of new private sector investment. For policy-makers, this presented itself not just in terms of lost jobs, but in the form of huge tracts of disused land. Such sites usually had outdated buildings and were in no fit state for immediate redevelopment. During the late 1970s and the 1980s policy-makers working in quasi-governmental agencies (QGAs) and local government and consultancies began to tackle this problem. They used subsidies to intervene in the market to 'lever' private sector investment onto these kinds of sites. Some refer to this as 'leverage planning' (Lock 1988; Brindley *et al.* 1989, Chapter 2). Another widely used term was 'entrepreneurial planning'. This is adopted here.

In the late 1970s and early 1980s the target of the entrepreneurial approach was vacant, disused sites in typical inner-city areas or de-industrialised urban regions where the market was not functioning. New investment proposals were not coming forward. These sites varied in size from huge steel complexes like Shotton, through plots sterilised by such things as earlier munitions or chemicals activity, as on the Mersey and Clyde estuaries, down to smaller pieces of land. An example is the site surrounding a single disused building like the old Central Station in Manchester. Sometimes these areas were linear in shape, as with empty buildings and parcels of vacant land alongside unused canals.

In a nutshell, the problem facing policy-makers on sites like these in areas where there is no demand is the lack of private sector investment. Some of them — like the Central Station one — had been disused for years. In other cases, as in many inner city areas, the long term result of a site being vacant was to infect the surrounding area so that the decay was spreading. The challenge was to convert these sites into areas where there was some degree of demand from the market, so that economic pressures could take over. The argument was that if policy-makers succeeded in levering private sector investment onto sites like these, this would stimulate market forces into operating. If this could be done, private sector investment would become an attractive proposition again.

However, entreprenerial planning is not just about recreating the market. It has the wider goal of getting people and vitality — even a sense of festival — back into neglected areas. It aims to inject them with life and excitement, so that there is a buzz, even on Sunday evenings. One example of this approach was the encouragement given to the Arnolfini and Watershed arts complexes as 'people drawing projects' in the Bristol docks.

The initial target of entrepreneurial planning was projects on big empty sites in prominent positions. As the techniques for levering in private investment were developed, they were applied to areas with lots of buildings that were empty or occupied but in poor condition. Examples here are Bradford's Little Germany and Hull's Old Town areas. There was thus an infinite variety in the types of site which were being tackled. A feature they all had in common was degraded environmental conditions.

In the literature there are articles about individual projects. There are also attempts to get beyond the case studies to identify best practice approaches. For example a DoE study picks out the features that schemes have in common (Department of the Environment 1988). This chapter is an attempt to get beyond that approach to create a model that can be applied to sites of all sizes in rundown areas. It is based on visits, sometimes necessitating sturdy mountain boots to cope with the rubble strewn and muddy terrain to reach such places — with and without development potential — in different parts of the country. These have included not just the London docks (and bits of Barcelona and Paris), but towns and cities around a zig-zag route from Salford to Plymouth, Exeter to Dundee, Glasgow to the Tees estuary, Leeds to the Docks at Pembroke, and across to the East Thames corridor at Gravesend.

The object of the visits, which usually involved detailed interviews with practitioners, has been to collect material from which to distil a general argument. The model is thus based on examples, but these are not mentioned in the text unless it is appropriate to give a detailed explanation.

The main purpose of this chapter is to develop a model that can be used to lever private sector investment onto vacant sites, and into built-up but run-down neighbourhoods in declining areas. It draws on the experience of the 1980s and early 1990s. The first section sets out a step by step approach — a 'five stage' model — that policy-makers can follow as a set of guidelines. They draw together the main issues that need to be confronted. The discussion is mainly in terms of flagship projects and schemes on big vacant sites. The second section analyses five key implementation problems, both on empty sites and in more built up areas. The focus then shifts briefly to the changing role of the planner and the wider significance of these approaches. The final section looks at the prospects for entrepreneurial planning in the 1990s. The underlying theme, highlighted by Lock's quote at the start of this chapter, is the emergence of a new type of planning.

The five stages of entrepreneurial planning

This section sets out the five stages in the entrepreneurial planning approach. It reveals the complexities of levering investment onto a large site.

Stage one: securing access to the site

The initial step with these so-called brown-field sites is to deal with any factors blocking redevelopment. These might be, for example, the landowner's or potential developer's unwillingness to carry out any site preparation or reclamation before building can start. The aim of stage one is for the local authority or leading public sector organisation to secure access to the site to set things in motion. Sometimes there is a single owner, sometimes the site is in multi-ownership. Purchasing the lease(s) or freehold(s), or reaching agreement with the owner(s), can remove the initial block, thus enabling the redevelopment process to begin.

Stage two: land renewal

This involves a variety of tasks. There is the filling in of docks, the demolishing of outdated buildings, the clearing of industrial remains, and perhaps the culverting of rivers and the laying of drains. Next, there is the removal of eyesores; and the landscaping, tree planting and environmental improvement work to carry out. In addition, there are the roads, services, electronic cabling and other infrastructure to go in. If buildings are to be retained for conversion to new uses at stages three or four, work has to be carried out to ensure they are weather-proofed. The aim of stage two is to leave the site ready for redevelopment. The financing of land renewal projects is discussed under the subsidies heading after the five stage model has been outlined.

Stage three: public sector investment projects

On a big site it is possible to inject confidence into an area through capital schemes initiated and carried out by the public sector on its own. The aims here are to demonstrate an area's potential to the private sector; and to signal public sector commitment to staying and turning it round. The local authorities involved in the Swansea Docks for example put in a museum, a leisure centre, and a new County Hall. At Hull the City Council persuaded English Estates to put up a speculative office development. Such schemes are quite separate from land renewal and infrastructure provision. Their aim is to convince potential private sector investors that an apparently run-down area has a positive and prosperous future.

In run-down areas with buildings already there, a different approach is to make grants available to the existing private sector firms. Establishing Conservation Areas, or Industrial Improvement Area type regimes offers financial support. As the grants are not 100 per cent there has to be a private sector input. Such regimes can thus stimulate private sector spending and commitment to the area — as in the Lace Market area of Nottingham. A variation is to improve access for local businesses and to put in some units to let. Such approaches, and refurbishing any buildings the local authority owns, demonstrate commitment to an improved future for the area.

Stage four: initiating private sector investment

There are four options at this stage. First, the Conservation Area type approach described above can create a new, more optimistic climate in an area. In Hull's Old Town for example such designations attracted £25 million of private sector investment in refurbishment between 1978 and 1986.

Next, policy-makers can try to induce a positive reaction towards recent site improvements from the private sector. Design briefs are usually drawn up and circulated to show the kinds of development that the planning authority hopes to see on specific sites. The London Docklands Development Corporation (LDDC) practised a more open-ended approach, preparing sites for redevelopment and waiting to see what proposals came forward from the private sector. The 'we can only do that if...' or 'that's not viable but...' type of responses from the private sector produces dialogue with the lead public sector agency. In practice, this often results in an amended scheme, or introduces some form of subsidy, as via City Grant. If this approach does not lead to firm proposals the problem is what to try next.

A third option is to think up projects for specific sites. This involves developing the concept as a whole — its scope, its design, its financial details and so on. Having put together a package it then has to be marketed to the investing institutions to ensure a private sector input. An example here is turning the old Central Station in Manchester into the G-Mex Centre for conferences and exhibitions. A variation on this option is to identify specific projects that an area needs before looking for a suitable site. An example here is the Scottish Exhibition Centre which was developed as a concept within the Scottish Development Agency (SDA), worked up in the context of a site, and then sold as a package to the investment institutions.

If no private sector development is forthcoming for a reclaimed site, the other option is to identify gaps in the market and take the lead. If projects 'pioneered' by the public sector are successful, they will then get copied by the private sector. In the Clydebank Enterprise Zone for example, the SDA cleared a huge tract of land when it demolished the Singer sewing machine works. On part of this, a developer was persuaded to put up advanced factory units. Basically, the SDA's approach was to agree to pay the developer most of the rental if a unit stayed vacant. The units were successfully let. In the second phase, the SDA found it could reduce the proportion of the rental that it guaranteed, and still persuade developers to build. The rental guarantee had acted as a catalyst in awakening their interest. The public sector had thus shown the private sector there was a gap in the market and an opportunity for profitable investment.

Stage four is the acid test of the whole process. Private sector firms will only sign documents committing them to a site in a run-down area if they have confidence in its future. Stage four is essentially about seeing whether that confidence has been created. Sometimes an area's prospects can suddenly leap forward. Once the office block referred to above on the waterfront at Hull had been let, Trust House Forte very quickly put forward proposals for a hotel on an adjacent site.

Stage five: implementing private sector schemes

This is the final part of the implementation process. It involves the on-site works on the reclaimed land to carry out the schemes prepared at stage four. Individual projects may be just one element, or the dominant part of the regeneration process on the site in question. Development itself needs to be seen as a separate stage in case implementation problems arise. There may have been unexpected complications over access to a site. Funding cuts may have delayed public sector projects causing the green shoots of confidence to wilt and die. Escalating costs may lead to one partner withdrawing. A project may need to be reconsidered and perhaps amended. It may be necessary to repeat stage four before development can be completed. Alternatively a site may grow. The Wigan Pier Project expanded when Trencherfield Mill was closed. That building was incorporated into a more ambitious scheme.

The five stage model as a whole: complexity

Reducing the diverse complications of urban regeneration to five stages inevitably rides roughshod over some of the nuances involved. The aim here is to draw principles out from the collective urban renewal experience of the 1980s. However, two particular over-simplifications merit discussion because they can affect the process of applying the five stages.

The first point is that the five stages are, of course, an over-precise representation of events. In reality, the stages get mixed up with one another. This is particularly the case where a huge area is involved — say of derelict dockland. Big sites need dividing up into smaller land packages, each of which has to be taken through the five stages separately. In practice, the division of a big site into smaller packages often follows on from how quickly access can be secured to specific areas, and funds raised to carry out the process of land renewal. What happens in practice is that stages three and four may be reached on some parts of a huge site before there is much progress with stage two, or even stage one on adjacent bits of land. The stages thus tend to overlap each other on different parts of a big site.

The second over-simplification is that these five stages ignore the surrounding area. In the light of experience some developers argue that there is little point in doing, say, a luxury housing project or high tech office complex, if it will be an island in a sea of decay. If the surrounds are unattractive, people will not want to live or work there, and the value and saleability of the units will fall.

If schemes are to be successful, urban regeneration projects need to be integrated into the surrounding context. The borders to a large site may be made up of such things as a canal and other waterfronts, major and minor roads, existing industrial estates, areas of housing, a supermarket and its car park, open space, and other land uses. Treatment for these border sites needs to be considered in parallel with the project as a whole if effective integration is to be achieved. Environmental improvement schemes from stage two may be appropriate, as may other public sector projects that are not infrastructure — like those considered in stage three. The positive way to tackle this issue is to go for things like high quality street furniture and paving; facilities for local people; flood-lighting of prominent buildings; and good landscaping schemes that integrate the site with its surrounds. In some circumstances it may be possible to get developers to pay for, or contribute to, these integrating works. There have been examples of a more negative approach. One way of trying to safeguard the environmental context of new private housing is simply to build an enormous wall to blot out the view of, for example, a run-down council estate.

Figure 3.1 shows the application of the five stage model to a large disused tract of land with potential for economic regeneration somewhere in a typical inner city area or de-industrialised region in a capitalist western industrial democracy (TICAODRIACWID). It is a hypothetical example which integrates the two 'over-simplification' points discussed above. It illustrates how a large site can be broken down into separate land packages — three in this case. Also it brings the surrounding area in as two separate border sites. In reality it will usually be necessary to break the surrounds up into a series of small land parcels requiring different handling.

Applying the five stages to brown-field sites enables policy-makers to build, step by incremental step, towards successful on-site development. The aim of stage one is to gain access to the disused land in question. The aim of stage two is the creation of the urban equivalent of a greenfield site. Stage three should help to inject confidence into the process of economic regeneration

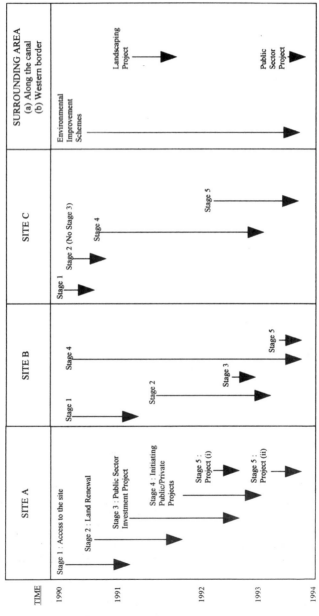

Figure 3.1: Relating the five stages model to a large hypothetical site somewhere in a typical inner city area or de-industrialised region in a capitalist western industrial democracy (TICAODRIACWID)

Sites A, B, and C are three separate sections of a large disused plot of land with potential for economic regeneration in TICAODRIACWID

SITE A

Stage 1 : Access to the site

Stage 2 : Land Renewal

Stage 3 : Public Sector Investment Project

Stage 4 : Initiating Public/Private Projects

Stage 5 : Project (i)

Stage 5 : Project (ii)

SITE B

Stage 1

Stage 2

Stage 3

Stage 4

Stage 5

SITE C

Stage 1

Stage 2 (No Stage 3)

Stage 4

Stage 5

SURROUNDING AREA
(a) Along the canal
(b) Western border

Environmental Improvement Schemes

Landscaping Project

Public Sector Project

TIME

1990

1991

1992

1993

1994

through public sector capital schemes. If private sector investment is to be levered into the area then stage four is the most critical. The aims here are to hold discussions with developers, institutional investors and other potential partners; to reach agreement; to resolve the legal problems; and to put together a tailor-made financial package. If these tasks are not successfully carried out, confidence has not been restored, the market will not have been recreated, and private sector schemes will not be implemented at stage five.

Making things happen: the five Ss

The five stage approach tackles the question of what to do. The discussion now focuses on *how* to do it. There are five specific tasks to carry out if a site is to be taken through the five stages to successful regeneration. These can be summed up as five Ss — choosing the right *site*; developing a *strategy*; exploiting available *subsidies*; *spotlighting* successful schemes; and assembling a team of people with all the relevant *skills*. Obviously no two schemes are the same and these five tasks have to be carried out in a variety of ways. The point of this section is to show the scope of what has to be done.

Sites

The first task is to decide which site to focus on. By the 1990s industrial closures and inner city problems had left many buildings empty and huge tracts of urban land vacant. Given the cuts, and the limited resources for land renewal, it is impossible to redevelop everywhere. Choices have to be made about where to concentrate resources. An important consideration is trying to identify which sites have the greatest potential in terms of what was once called the Covent Garden effect. It refers to what happened in Covent Garden in central London. This was one of the earlier 1970s regeneration schemes. The area was affected by closures and blight. But a successful public/private partnership strategy produced a turn-round. New life was injected into the area as people were attracted back and private sector investment began to emerge. A small amount of public money had produced a large amount of private sector investment.

The aim is to choose sites where some initial public expenditure levers in some private sector investment, with the result that market forces are released, and further private sector investment is generated. The ultimate objective is for the public sector to withdraw. If this is possible it will be because the market has been recreated, and demand for land and buildings has been firmly established.

Strategies

The second task is to develop a strategy for the site. There is a certain paradox here. On the one hand entrepreneurial planning is about renewing disused land and opening it up to market pressures. Yet on the other, some kind of strategy has practical advantages. It helps give the developer confidence in the future of the area. It reassures the banker that the infrastructure will go in, and the neighbouring land uses will not undermine the security of the investment. A strategy also helps the local authority to rein in and channel market pressure once investment starts to take off. Some kind of framework thus helps to maintain momentum once it has been established (Department of the Environment 1988, pp. 18–19, & 23–27; Lock 1988, pp. 26–8).

The strategy needs to define the boundaries of the site on which economic regeneration is to be focused. A number of features come into play. These include picking sites given an identity by distinctive, natural boundaries; sites on the fringe of a more prosperous part of a city; and sites where the surrounding environment can be improved and the island problem, as referred to above, does not arise. Policy-makers also point to the need to pick sites which include plots that can be made attractive to investors quickly; and ones where environmental improvements can be dramatic. A quick impact helps boost confidence. An example here is tackling big gap sites in say, a dockland area where a number of existing uses are to be retained, and much of the infrastructure is already in place. Another feature is to look at the site in terms of its potential for public sector schemes that will help to inject confidence into the area. The overall size of a site needs to be thought of in terms of whether there are adequate public sector resources to tackle it over, say a five year period. Another consideration is including land the authority owns within the overall site. This can subsequently strengthen an authority's bargaining position whilst negotiating with developers.

The strategy needs to analyse land-ownership and possible future land-uses — retail, office, light industry, leisure, heritage, housing, and so on. This needs to be looked at from the perspective of the private sector. Market surveys — or at least discussions with commercial estate agents — will be needed to look at the demand for small firm units, or a hotel, or housing at a particular value. Economic regeneration has to be rooted in private sector perceptions about markets, and about the potential of the site in question. Social housing provides an example. It is often argued for, but the developers' pespective is that it is only possible if it is part of a bigger scheme that will create the profits to carry it.

Land-use options have to be related to the immediate surrounding area — the housing, recreation, employment and other needs of local residents, and any broader local plan or UDP. Entrepreneurial planning projects are frequently focused on dead, neglected areas. They need to be integrated with the vibrant, bustling parts of the city to bring people and energy back in. Putting in new roads can open up large vacant disused sites that have been locked away out of reach. If the roads are carefully placed they can also help to integrate the projects yet to be built with the surrounding area. High quality public spaces are an important part of this. Another approach is to encourage development that retains heritage features. In the Bristol docks planners laid particular emphasis on this as a means of integrating new development into the existing city. The strategy needs to identify such guiding principles.

Many argue that it is a mistake to spend too much time on complex goals because this limits flexibility. More important is the need to identify priority projects at stages two and three to help achieve a quick impact. Where public sector finance is involved it is possible to promote such schemes during a property slump while waiting for the upturn. This happened at the Quarry Hill site in Leeds where the new Playhouse theatre was built. This was followed by an office complex to house the headquarters of the Government's benefits agency.

Apart from developing principles and proposals, the strategy needs to focus strongly on implementation. It is necessary to work out the implications of the five stage approach for a particular site in terms of the organisations involved. The five stage model focuses on processes, not on organisations and their budgets. In different cities there will be different departmental structures within local authorities, and varying combinations of QGA, government, and EC programmes involved. Each of the five stages needs to be broken down into component parts, and allocated to the appropriate organisations. Information about the financial implications, and what needs to be budgeted for in which financial year for each organisation or committee has to be drawn together. Projects can then be effectively phased. As discussed above, a huge site will need dividing up into more maneagable plots, each with its own boundaries. The strategy needs to set out the authority's commitment over the several years it will take to turn a site round. (Sources of funds are dealt with below under the third task — exploiting available subsidies.)

The strategy also needs to establish clear monitoring arrangements. The main purpose of this is to assess progress across the site as a whole, and over integration with the surrounding areas. For example it is essential to keep a close check on how potential developers are responding on different parts of the site. It may be necessary to have a fundamental rethink or merely to change the design guidance. The monitoring arrangements need to trigger the questions. Monitoring is also important from the point of view of good relations with funding bodies. They will always want reassurance that progress is on schedule.

There are different views about having a consultation period on a draft strategy. Some authorities and UDCs have done it on a minimal basis via discussions with landowners and other local economic interests. However this can backfire. For example, Leeds Development Corporation (LDC) was forced to back track in the Kirkstall Valley. Local groups objected to its approach. This led to a 'planning for real' participation exercise, the production of a community plan, and a revised LDC strategy. Where local communities are affected by proposals, trouble can be avoided by involving them in the consultation process. There is an important link here to the earlier discussion of site boundaries. If speed is of the essence it is best, if possible, to exclude not just areas of local housing from a big regeneration project, but also community facilities including allotments, sports fields and other open spaces for informal recreation.

Some would put developing a strategy as the first task before deciding on a site. In practice, there is some overlap because there needs to be some analysis before the boundaries of the target site can be defined. The tasks have been put in this order to emphasise the way entrepreneurial planning focuses so strongly on implementation. Others would put these studies as a plan preparation stage before stage one on land renewal. But these are strategies rather than full-blown plans. They emphasise proposals and the implementation implications, rather than reams of survey and analysis. Some authorities have questioned the need for a plan at all. They have concentrated on short informal documents focused just on areas subject to change. A small site with one or two proposals is more the 'back of an envelope' job than a scheme in need of a detailed plan. On bigger sites, plan or strategy preparation on the one hand, and implementation on the other, can actually proceed *in parallel* with each other. A planning authority can tackle stages one and two while thinking about stages four and five. For example, discussions with a particular developer may breakdown. If the first option at stage four leads nowhere, another can be explored while land renewal proceeds. This is what happened in 1986–87 with the Salford Quays development.

The strategy documents that have been prepared in Britain are commonly described as documents with themes. They have tended to be short, informal and non-statutory. They have a philosophy, broad aims for different parts of the site, and priorities. Planning briefs come later. Flexibility is allowed for. Contemporary urban regeneration emphasises realism, action and implementation, and reduces the time spent on plan preparation (Lock 1988). That is the spirit of the age. It is about going for it — *and making it happen.*

Subsidies

The third task is to work out which grants, loans and other subsidies are available for a particular scheme (Department of the Environment 1988, pp. 29–31). Three main types of subsidy are possible. First there are direct subsidies where one of the three tiers of government — Whitehall, QGA, local authority — makes money available to a firm, as with City Grant. Next, there are indirect subsidies where government money is spent on a project to help a scheme go ahead. Here the finance is not given direct to the firm that benefits from the investment. A typical example is where a local authority uses Derelict Land Grant at the land renewal stage. Thirdly, there are the safety net subsidies where a government agency commits itself to spend money in certain circumstances. The cases of the SDA agreeing to pay developers part of the rent if a unit is not let come into this category.

A bewildering variety of grants, loans and other subsidies are available under each heading from all three tiers of government and from Brussels. One of the most comprehensive summaries to appear was published regularly in the *Architects Journal* through the 1980s see the 1989 one for example (Butler and Moore). It omits the arts moneys that are sometimes relevant. Also as a result of the Chancellor's Autumn Statement in 1992 the Urban Programme is being phased out and a new capital receipts scheme is being introduced. Another major change in the pipeline is the launching of the Urban Regeneration Agency. One of the best monitors of detailed changes is the National Council for Voluntary

Organisation's (NCVO) monthly *NCVO News*. Its perspective is much broader than that of the voluntary sector. The situation over subsidies has become so complicated that individual government organisations produce explanatory booklets. The English Tourist Board has published a number of these over the years for example.

Because it focuses on the public sector, the *Architects Journal* list does not draw in the phenomenon of corporate social responsibility. This phrase is used to refer to the trend during the 1980s and early 1990s for big companies to focus resources on schemes that would not earn them conventional financial returns. The most high profile of these is sponsorship of sports and arts events. But in the inner city, corporate social responsibility initiatives manifested themselves in a variety of forms. Examples include grants to landscape specific sites, various sponsorship schemes, and paying the salary of a project officer. Nationalised industries and statutory undertakers are also involved in this activity. Business in the Community (BiC) is at the heart of it all. Limited amounts of research have been done on it. The main feature are unravelled in a Policy Studies Institute report (Fogarty and Christie 1990). The attitudes of companies vary from area to area. In many cases decisions are decentralised to local management. The value of corporate social responsibility contributions, and their potential, need investigating locally. Other sources that can be relevant in some areas are charitable foundations like the Monument Trust; and some of the bigger independent not for profit organisations of the type described in the chapter on third force organisations (TFO).

The subject of what subsidies are available on specific sites need careful research. It can be surprising what is available. Countryside Commission schemes have been exploited by policy-makers carrying out environmental improvements in the inner city for example. Including a listed building within a site may make English Heritage structural repair grants available. Leisure, tourism, heritage, recreation, and arts projects all open up different packages of funds. Obviously to be eligible for funds from specific programmes projects need to be related to the criteria of individual agencies. But some of these are linked. For example getting Derelict Land Grant (DLG) support enhances an authority's chances of getting Countryside Commission help. The essential point here is to devise strategies that make imaginative use of what is available. This can then be used as bait to attract the commitment of private sector firms.

There are important links between the subsidies that can be

exploited, and the earlier discussion on the site and the strategy. While preparing their strategy, policy-makers need to look at the range of subsidies that are likely to be available if the site is shaped in a variety of different ways, and has different mixes of projects. The available subsidies can then influence the nature of the strategy. For example, Cardiff City Council only considered including a conference element in their St Davids Centre complex when officers discovered EC money would probably be available.

Another link between subsidies, the size of the site and the preparation of the strategy is the point that the resources likely to be available will dictate the overall size of the site. Part of the point of entrepreneurial planning is to provide long-term security for private sector investors. It is thus important not to run out of financial resources three or four years into the implementation phases. It also follows that the size of the site and the direction of the strategy need to be based on a realistic assessment of the subsidies and financial resources that are likely to be available. This means not just for the first couple of years, but for the three or five or more years that implementation will require. Tactically, experience shows it is wise to base the strategy on as wide a number of subsidy sources as possible. This reduces the damage that can be done if one agency has to limit or withdraw its funds because of cuts.

Thinking in detail about the range of subsidies to be exploited takes policy-makers into the details of design. It is important at the policy-making stage to think about who is going to be responsible for the subsequent maintenance (Department of the Environment 1988, pp. 17 & 30). Most loans and grants cover capital spending. Maintenance of streets, parks, waterfronts, stretches of open water and other open spaces will largely fall to local authorities and have implications for their current expenditure budgets. It is important to think about the details of mowing grass and clearing litter out of a marina when designing projects. Poor maintenance undermines the impact of a whole scheme and private sector confidence in an authority's ability to turn an area around. Interest in investment may wane.

During the 1990s increasing importance will be attached to the ability of landscape designers to design in low cost maintenance features when preparing their contribution to the overall project. There are links here to the chapter on sustainable development and the discussion there on wildlife corridors. Properly designed these can minimise maintenance costs. Where land is in private ownership responsibility for maintenance falls outside the local authority. But policy-makers need to raise the issues of low cost maintenance and adequate resources for maintenance with the architects and others preparing private sector schemes.

There is an art to attracting subsidies. The aim here is to exploit the system of subsidies so as to be able to carry out schemes at minimal cost to the authority beyond staff time. In short, the technique developed by people in local government during the late 1970s and 1980s was *learning how to use other people's money to carry out the authority's own schemes.* At many sites there are plaques listing the number of organisations that have made financial contributions to a scheme. They stand as testament to the expertise that some authorities developed.

Spotlights

The fourth task is to attract publicity by turning the spotlight onto the growing success story of a site that is being transformed. This has several functions. It helps to reinforce confidence amongst any existing businesses. It helps attract investors from elswhere in the city, and from further afield (Department of the Environment 1988, pp. 19–20). Lock (1988, p. 28) draws a distinction between promoting an area as a whole to project a new image, and marketing specific plots on a large site. Wilkinson has looked in detail at the problems involved in creating a new image for a de-industrialising city, using Newcastle-upon-Tyne as an example (1992).

Publicity needs to demonstrate what has been achieved, and what else can be done. There are lots of ways of approaching this. One example is making play with before and after photos. Huge signs, tape-slide presentations, videos and multi-media productions can all be employed. Setting up architectural competitions for individual sites is another way of spotlighting achievement and potential. Annual reports on projects, newsletters, public meetings and exhibitions provide further opportunities. LDDC and Cardiff Bay Development Corporation are examples of agencies that have spent huge amounts on advertising to attract investment. This all needs to be reinforced by using unusual angles to generate media coverage. For example at Hull, Bellways got a sculptor to produce a set of gargoyles. They were friendly images of the councillors and others who serve on the board of the company, building the Victoria Dock village. When it goes well, as at Wigan Pier, media publicity actually saves marketing costs.

Turning the spotlight onto a successful project can also enhance an authority's ability to raise funds for a later stage of the project. Bureaucrats in charge of public sector funding programmes like schemes that make positive, imaginative use of their contributions. They feel this encourages other applicants to copy pioneering ideas, so that best practice evolves.

Skills

The final task is to assemble the staff skills needed to carry through the five stage approach. This requires a broader range of skills than town planners used in the days when economic growth was more widespread and planning applications were more forthcoming (Department of the Environment 1988, pp. 15−17; Lock 1988). The entrepreneurial approach draws broadly from established local government skills — in solving surveying, legal and engineering problems in connection with land renewal; in designing landscaping and environmental improvement schemes; in lobbying Whitehall and Brussels for specific subsidies; and in co-ordinating the public sector agencies involved in the five stages. However, if policy-makers are to take the initiative and make development happen, they have to tap into a further set of professional skills.

In particular, planners need to understand the approach of private enterprise. Companies aim at profits. If they are going to be involved in partnership schemes they will hope for as much profit as possible. This will be made easier if they exploit the partnership climate and attract as much subsidy as possible. To do this, they have simultaneously to convince the banks that the project is profitable, and to convince the local authority that it is unlikely to be, and that subsidy is needed. 'The result', as one public official, who should remain anonymous, put it, 'is that developers keep three sets of accounts. They take the optimistic one to the lending institutions; they bring the pessimistic one to us; and they lock their private ones away in their offices'.

Working closely with private sector developers means that local government officers have to be able to read company accounts, pull holes in profit and loss projections, question asset valuations, and haggle with developers over subsidy and land values. They also might be involved in helping to set up, and then possibly to run, arms-length public/private companies aiming at profits. Coping with these poblems requires accountancy, finance, valuation, management, and other skills. These are not new tasks for local government, but working more closely with the private sector has made the collective deployment of these skills more important. While they cannot be trained in all these skills, senior officers have to be able to deploy them. In the final resort it becomes a question of understanding. They have to be able to climb inside developers' heads to understand their values, attitudes and approaches. The test of their understanding comes when they negotiate over details; and try to exploit the potential for planning gain.

However, it is not just a question of assembling particular skills. There is the whole issue of what kind of bureaucratic structure the people concerned are put into. It has to be done in such a way that each profession's input is effective. It is easy to make the assumption that the assembly of skills can be done within the parameters of the local authority's established departmental structure. A common approach is to create an urban renewal team within the Planning Department. However, innovatory ideas may well challenge existing approaches and the conventional wisdom within the authority. Because of different attitudes in other departments, this can pose problems in terms of co-ordination within the authority's existing departmental structure.

The alternative is to ask what kind of organisation is most suitable for urban renewal, and to create it from scratch. Some argue innovative ideas can more easily be promoted within a specially created organisation. A variety of approaches were tried during the 1980s and early 1990s. Within a local authority it is possible to set up a new department as Manchester, Sheffield and Wakefield did in the case of Economic Development. Others drew up strategies in the Chief Executive's Department.

By the turn of the decade more complex structures began to emerge in some authorities where leading figures from industry were drawn in (Harding 1992). Some were seconded to work in project teams alongside local authority staff. Others agreed to serve on management committees overseeing renewal work. Such committees drew together the chief executive, senior politicians, and prominent people from industry, QGAs, not-for-profit voluntary organisations, and occasionally including trades unionists. Sometimes two local authorities were involved. Examples include cities with two-tier local government — the Aberdeen City Centre Project for example; and large sites traversed by local authority boundaries — like the Dearne Valley in South Yorkshire. A certain ambiguity began to enter into the situation. In some cases the broader management focus began to shift away from using the five stage model to turn a specific site around, to encompass much broader ideas about a strategy for the city as a whole.

The issue that stands out is the need for effective co-ordination. Arrangements vary from putting all the skills into a newly created unit, to much broader inter-organisational structures. With a small number of departments or organisations, liaison meetings can be kept informal. But the bigger the number of bodies involved, the greater the need to formalise things with minutes being circulated and action prompts picked out. The danger here is that the bigger, the more comprehensive the network, the more difficult it is to maintain momentum through the five stages. As a consequence self-contained action units seem to have been favoured. The underlying principle here relates to the argument in Chapter 1 about local authorities' strategic co-ordinating role. Chapter 8 on networking explains techniques for achieving effective co-ordination.

A partial alternative is to do a lot of the basic work within the authority, and to contract parts of it out. So long as clear guidelines are drawn up, specific jobs can be given to consultants. This has usually involved the preparation of strategy documents, design briefs, and the like. An alternative is to contract out specific implementation tasks. In the Salford Quays case the local authority came to an agreement with a businessman that he could have some land if he succeeded in getting, by the end of 1984, private sector investment committed for the cinema complex, the hotel site, waterside housing and some other small projects.

It has frequently been observed that, whatever the organisational context in which all the skills referred to in this section are deployed, what each project really needs is a fixer (Department of the Environment, 1988, pp. 15–6). According to the size of the scheme the project officer or manager needs to be at quite a senior level within the authority. He or she needs to be responsible for a whole range of tasks — drawing up the strategy; promoting consultations on it; getting the grant applications in; organising the various implementation agencies; negotiating with developers; reporting on the situation to senior officers, politicians, funding bodies outside local authorities, QGAs, private sector partners and other external organisations; monitoring progress against the strategy; reviewing implementation problems against the strategy's goals; and suggesting alternative ways forward. He or she needs to be everything from a clairvoyant to a juggler.

It is not just training and experience that is important here: it is personality. He or she needs not just to be dynamic, efficient and a good communicator, but able to generate enthusiasm in others, and to work positively with people from a variety of different backgrounds. Innovative, ambitious schemes often bring out scepticism in people. The project manager needs to be able to deal with this — to be champion and progress chaser, manager and trouble-shooter. It is not just the job description that needs to be right. It is the personality too.

The five Ss: complexity

The aim of the section on getting things done is to highlight the five key ingredients if the five stage process is to be carried through — picking a viable *site*, developing a *strategy*, exploiting available *subsidies*, *spotlighting* achievements, and assembling the relevant *skills*. But inevitably this categorisation oversimplifies. It does not address the fundamental issue of the design dimensions. This covers such questions as the way the schemes fit together on the site; the variety of opportunities for pedestrians to move about; the transport links to the rest of the city; and all the details of design — from seats to buildings, from public arts to trees.

This is the most difficult factor of all to convey. If an area is to be turned around, if private sector investment confidence is to be recreated, that it is not just improving the look of the place with new and renovated buildings that matters. The whole *theatre* of the place has to change, the *feel* of the place has to change. When the potential investor drives past or walks through he or she has to feel 'Yes my business will work here'. This *feel good factor* does not make further investment happen, but it is the catalyst that makes it possible, the X-factor that recreates confidence.

There are two dimensions to the feel-good factor. One dimension is the whole process of economic and social regeneration that is taking place in the city as a whole. This for example means developing training policies so there are readily available supplies of different kinds of skilled labour.

The other dimension of the feel-good factor concerns the details of design; space, ambience, and layout. There is a good summary of conventional wisdom about best practice is in *Urban Villages* (Aldous 1992). This develops the concept of creating small, mixed-use urban developments on a sustainable scale. It was prepared by the Urban Villages Group to provoke discussion and action by planners, developers and others concerned with the quality of buildings and their surrounding environment in urban areas. (The Urban Villages Group has a high-powered membership drawn from very senior figures in the house-building and property industries and related professions. It was set up in 1989 by Business in the Community at the behest of Prince Charles). Chapter 2 of the report outlines the concept of the urban village, and Chapter 4 sets out lots of detail about how to create an environment that people feel happy to be in.

It is difficult to summarise from the report because, by their nature, local materials and vernacular styles differ in different parts of the country. Getting the feel, the ambience right is the X-factor.

It helps to attract people. It transforms the site from a cold, antiseptic unwelcoming collection of buildings to a vibrant, living, stimulating, people-attracting area where individuals meet and groups like to pass the time. Many of the positive examples in the *Urban Villages* report are in fact from small towns and more prosperous parts of cities. One of the problems facing those promoting entrepreneurial planning approaches in the 1990s is to apply some of the detailed design ideas in the *Urban Villages* report to more run-down parts of cities. In that report, these ideas are developed as part of the limited concept of the urban village. They can in fact be applied to the parts of the city that need reviving.

The challenge of entrepreneurial planning

The preceding discussion of the five stage model and the means of implementing it shows why it is referred to as entrepreneurial planning. The essence of this approach is that, despairing of the lack of powers conferred on them by the post-war planning system, local authority policy-makers set out in the 1980s to create new ways of working. They used their imaginations to work out how to intervene in the market and make development happen (Lock 1988). They drew from the approaches used earlier in the Comprehensive Development Areas and new towns; and from the techniques developed in the QGAs like the SDA and the UDCs, and by some consultancies. The preceding discussion shows how the word 'entrepreneurial' is in fact used in two senses.

First, it is used in the sense of local policy-makers learning to *think* as entrepreneurs think; and understanding how business is about seeing a gap in the market, and going for it, about seizing opportunities as they become available. Intervening effectively in the market depends on getting a response from developers. This can only be done if policy-makers fully understand the values, attitudes, and perspectives of potential investors, developers, builders and their related professions (Lock 1988, p. 26). Secondly, 'entrepreneur' is also used in the sense of policy-makers *acting* as entrepreneurs to ensure development takes place. This involves taking risks with sites before private sector investment is committed.

These approaches are not just confined to partnership schemes and big flagship projects of the type this chapter has focused on. The emergence of entrepreneurial techniques has had important implications for town planners who are at the heart of it all. To make entrepreneurial planning techniques work they have to play all manner of roles acting as enablers, negotiators, facilitators and mediators. This involves intervening much more widely than in the 1950s and 1960s. Then the conventional approach was to prepare plans and wait for the market to react and produce planning applications. The emergence of entrepreneurial planning techniques marks a major development in the role of the planner. Healey *et al.*'s assessment that relationships with the private sector during the 1980s amounted to 'business as usual' (1992, p. 282) seems to under-estimate the significance of what was happening. Lock argues that this type of planning 'operates in circumstances without precedent when compared with previous decades' (1988, p. 28).

The entrepreneurial planning approach promotes the policy/action feedback where policy can be revised in the light of consultations, and of implementation problems, with developers blowing hot and cold and not committing themselves. Monitoring and review processes are there to trigger revisions to the strategy document over the several years it will take to transform a big site. The essence of entrepreneurial planning is that it is a *continuous process*, and not about producing plans. There will be many revisions over the years. This concept of process is combined with the notion of policy/action feedback for illustrative purposes in Figure 3.2. This activity still deserves the title planning because it involves strategic thinking. But it is a different type of thinking to that which dominated the 1960s.

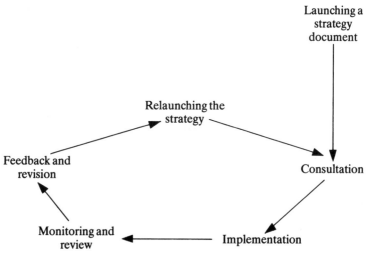

Figure 3.2:   Strategy and entrepreneurial planning

Entrepreneurial planning in the 1990s

During the 1980s the aim of entrepreneurial planning was to promote economic regeneration in the inner cities. Part of its underlying rationale was that private sector investment would create jobs which would cut inner city unemployment levels and increase real incomes for local people. They would then be able to improve their housing and other opportunities by purchasing in the market place. The benefits of private sector investment would thus 'trickle down' to inner city communities, helping to promote social regeneration. Chapter 2 discusses how, during the Thatcher era, this trickle down theory was widely criticised, particularly on the basis of what happened in the London docklands. The evidence from other entrepreneurial planning schemes indicates that the benefits to the poorest residents were not self-evident.

The core criticism of entrepreneurial planning was that the private sector was the main beneficiary of this approach of promoting private investment through the five stage model. Most of the jobs that were created went, not to local people, but to others who travelled in from outside the area. The only ones available to local people were the low paid cleaning and waitressing type jobs. Economic regeneration affected the physical appearance of the area. It produced shiny new investment projects. But it was criticised for not improving housing conditions for local people, and for having only a limited impact on job opportunities for them.

This whole 'who benefits?' question is the central dilemma facing those trying to regenerate declining cities in Britain, America and other western industrialised countries. It can be summed up as follows. Do you plan on the basis of what the private sector can be induced to deliver, letting it largely determine patterns of land-use? Or do you analyse local social conditions and plan on the basis of tackling local needs, like access to low-cost housing? The first approach aims at economic regeneration, while the second tried to focus more explicitly on social regeneration. The following discussion draws from this important distinction.

The problem at the heart of the debate on urban renewal in the 1980s and 1990s is getting a balance between the two approaches based on economic and social regeneration. This point is illustrated by the arrival of City Challenge in the early 1990s. City Challenge was introduced in 1991 to tackle not just economic regeneration of inner city areas, but social regeneration too. In the first two rounds in 1991 and 1992 local authorities were invited to compete for funds by developing strategies to tackle the whole range of inner city problems for a specific part of their area. The details are explained elsewhere (Young 1993). After two bidding rounds, a third was shelved, pending a review of the effectiveness of targeting inner city problems with Whitehall funds.

City Challenge reflected a change of attitude in Whitehall. This was prompted by the return of Heseltine to the DoE in 1990 when the departure of Mrs Thatcher meant it was no longer necessary to defend her private sector-dominated approach to inner city policy. It marked the DoE's response — developing from the winter of 1987/8 onwards — to criticisms of the failure of trickle down approaches. Although new rounds of City Challenge are not being embarked upon in 1993 or possibly 1994, the approach adopted in the scheme seems likely to colour the DoE's attitude to inner city issues in the early/mid 1990s.

City Challenge is about finding imaginative, practical, innovative, cost-effective solutions. Between them, the bid and the action plan needed to identify the economic problems, and the jobs, housing and other difficulties facing the deprived communities in the chosen area. The DoE required an emphasis on a holistic approach — on linking policy areas so that the analysis and solutions relating to the environment, jobs, training, health, education, social services, crime and so on were woven into an overall approach. The aim was a kind of mini-corporate plan for the area. The documentation had to show how the spending programmes and investment projects would tackle the problems that had been identified; benefit local people; and produce lasting change. The strategy documents needed to show how private sector interests, and public sector organisations like the police, had been brought in. They also had to set out how community groups had been consulted and would be empowered to help tackle urban decay.

This appeared to take entrepreneurial planning beyond economic regeneration, linking it with ideas about social regeneration. But two problems emerged with City Challenge. First, the DoE seemed to be going for information overkill in the bids and the action plans. Enormous amounts of detail were required from local authorities. The positive moves during the 1980s towards more flexible strategy documents — discussed above under strategies — appeared in danger of being reversed. The second problem was the level of funds coming from the public sector. Jeremy Beecham, Chair of the Association of Metropolitan Authorities, pointed out how his own authority of Newcastle City Council was gaining £37.5m from City Challenge whilst losing more than £200m from the wider process of public expenditure cuts (1993, p. 240). Such an approach seems likely to seriously undermine the attempts at social regeneration.

The City Challenge experience, and the analysis that flows from it, is important in the wider context of entrepreneurial planning. Because it has been targeted at social regeneration, as well as economic regeneration, it may, despite the overall lack of resources, have lessons for all tiers of government trying to target inner city problems more specifically.

The question at the end of this chapter on entrepreneurial planning is how can the five stage approach help local authorities trying to focus on *social* regeneration as well as *economic* regeneration. To be sure, in the 1990s many economic regeneration schemes will go ahead based around the five stage model. But a brief word is needed to explain how it can be adapted to accommodate a wider *social* regeneration approach targeted more explicitly at *local* needs and *local* problems.

The model can accommodate the wider ambitions of City Challenge-type approaches with regard to social issues if stage three is widened. In the earlier discussion, public sector investment projects were interpreted quite narrowly to refer to buildings that would enhance prospects for private sector investment. This still applies, but stage three needs to cover a broader range of projects that will help tackle social deprivation. It also needs to embrace schemes promoted by not-for-profit organisations. These include housing associations, and the whole range of community based self-help groups running their own projects. These third force organisations (TFOs) are discussed in a separate chapter. The timing of these schemes will need to be flexible to fit in with the availability of funds. Where public sector funds can be locked in — as with Housing Corporation money — they can be used at an earlier stage than that shown in Figure 3.1 to help inject confidence.

City Challenge highlights one of the main difficulties of urban planning. This is the extent to which policy-makers can relate land and buildings to local problems — rather than offer them as economic opportunities to developers with little interest in the area. Planners tend to lock themselves away when looking at a site and to think in terms of the best use for that site — housing, retail, light-industry or whatever. It is comparatively straightforward where there is a social housing problem to link a housing association to a site.

But the real issue that needs tackling — that City Challenge is trying to address — is how can land and buildings be used to focus on all local problems? This means not business parks and retail sites but training and truancy as well, and all the other aspects of the multi-dimensional problem that is the inner city. The challenge for the 1990s is to apply the techniques of entrepreneurial planning more widely so they can be used to tackle social regeneration as well as economic regeneration. Policy-makers need to work out more specific ways of focusing on the broad, diffused problems of the inner city even where there is no land available; and assembling resources to tackle them. This is the equivalent of trying to get a baked potato out of the oven when you have not got a tea-towel. The significance of City Challenge is that it may offer lessons about how to get a handle on long-established problems where existing powers and conventional approaches seem to be of limited use.

References and bibliography

Aldous, T. (1992) *Urban Villages* London: Urban Villages Group, 5 Cleveland Place, London, SW1Y 6JJ.

Beecham, J. (1993) 'Waiting for signs of hope in our cities' *Municipal Review and AMA News,* No. 734, January/February, 240–1.

Brindley, T., Rydin, Y. and Stoker, G. (1989) *Remaking Planning* London: Unwin Hyman.

Butler, E. and Moore, P. (1989) 'Sources of funding: public sector support' *Architects Journal,* 16 August, 53–66.

Department of the Environment, Inner Cities Directorate (1988) *Improving Urban Areas: Case Studies of Good Practice in Urban Regeneration* Prepared for the DoE by JURUE, a division of ECOTEC Research and Consulting Ltd, London: HMSO.

Fogarty, M. and Christie, I. (1990) *Companies and Communities: Promoting Business Involvement in the Community* London: Policy Studies Institute, 100 Park Village East, London, NW1 3SR.

Harding, A, (1992) 'Property interests and urban growth coalitions in the UK: a brief encounter' in Healey, P., Davoudi, S., Tavsanoglu, S., O'Toole, M., and Usher, D. (eds) *Rebuilding The City: Property-Led Urban Regeneration* London: Spon.

Healey, P., Davoudi, S., and O'Toole, M. (1992) 'Property-led urban regeneration: an assessment' in Healey, P., Davoudi, S., Tavsanoglu, S., O'Toole, M., and Usher, D. (eds) *Rebuilding The City: Property-Led Urban Regeneration,* London: Spon.

Lock, D. (1988) 'Planning and opportunism' *The Planner* September, 26–8.

Wilkinson, S. (1992) 'Towards a new city? A case-study of image improvement initiatives in Newcastle-upon-Tyne' in Healey, P., Davoudi, S., Tavsanoglu, S., O'Toole, M. and Usher, D. (eds) *Rebuilding The City: Property-Led Urban Regeneration* London: Spon.

Young, S. C. (1993) 'Assessing the Challenge's local benefits' *Town and Country Planning*, January, 3–5.

4 Sustainable development at the level of the city

...so far State of the Environment Reports have generally been conducted as one-off exercises. Many authorities have indeed found them difficult to turn into action, being faced with a mass of data of uncertain meaning and of little immediate application to policy.
(Jacobs 1992, p. 14)

Although 'sustainable development' has merit as a slogan, for it to be of practical value a clearer view is needed of what is meant by the term.
(Breheny 1992, p. 277)

The challenge of the 1990s is to turn the principles of sustainable development into achievable policies that lead to concrete change.
(Soussan 1992, p. 26)

The heart of this chapter is concerned with analysing what the idea of sustainable development means; and with working out a framework to operationalise the concept. Local authority interest in environmental issues grew in the late 1980s and early 1990s, but no consensus was reached about how to approach these issues. Some authorities chose quick, cheap and easy schemes. Wakefield for example opted out of 'mowing to death' regimes on roadside verges, commissioned a survey, identified 38 sites of botanical interest, and established a different management regime. This reduced costs and helped wildlife. At the other end of the spectrum some authorities had much more ambitious ideas. Lancashire County Council began to think in terms of promoting renewable energy initiatives using tidal energy, land-fill gas, and low quality agricultural land for wind-farms.

This chapter looks at the growth of local authority interest in the environment in the late 1980s. It is necessary to understand this to appreciate the watershed years of 1991/92. These were important because the Department of the Environment (DoE) instructed local authorities to take the principle of sustainable development on board; and because, as a result of the Government signing the Agenda 21 Treaty at the Rio Summit, local authorities have to develop their own Local Agenda 21s. Local authorities are thus confronted with having to take sustainable development seriously. It has thus become an important issue in its own right. This is quite apart from the benefits of focusing on this area that attracted pioneering authorities to it in the mid/late 1980s. The central purpose of this chapter is to analyse how local authorities can respond to the challenge, and make better use of the information they have assembled. Some, as the first quote above indicates, have not been helped much by the data they have collected.

The theme of the chapter is the need to get beyond tokenism. It is easy to see the environment as an 'add-on' to local authority responsibilities, as something that just needs a few gestures — some recycling schemes, reduced use of chemical weedkillers, and lead-free petrol in the authority's vehicles. It is much more complex than that. This chapter argues it needs a whole new way of thinking about the issues an authority faces. It also illustrates the need for elected councils to provide leadership at the local level.

The benefits to be gained from giving environmental issues a high profile

The main benefit is economic. Invariably the image of a city reflects its past and is out of date. But images of decline can be reinforced by the physical appearance of a city. Potential investors are deterred by swathes of derelict land and rusting machinery in car parks beside empty factories. A more positive image attracts tourists, conferences, students and others. It is not just the money that's spent that is important. Some may stay to live and work. Improving a city's environmental attractiveness can also help retain indigenous industry, skilled workers and residents thinking of leaving.

There are other benefits apart from the economic dimension. For education authorities, greening strategies help schools relate to the environmental parts of the National Curriculum. Such approaches also help promote community action. There is a separate chapter on not-for-profit organisations where green issues have played a prominent role. Environmental strategies also help create and protect informal recreation areas. In these 'Jimbob places' people, kids and dogs get up to all sorts of things — jogging, insect-hunting, mountain-biking, ornithology, blackberrying, picnicking, lolloping about, angling, courting, exploring, sunbathing. Such spots are especially important for those on low incomes as they are free and often close at hand. What appears to be a narrow issue, broadens cut to be about the quality of local living conditions for local people. Concentrating on environmental issues helps project the image of a responsible up-to-date council. It is also an area where authorities have realised that they can play a prominent and growing role — despite centralisation, the cuts and the loss of powers.

Growing local authority interest

Three significant points stand out from the sudden flowering of local authority interest in the environment during the late 1980s and early 1990s. First, it led to the publication of a variety of documents on environmental issues. Ward (1993) distinguishes between four different kinds. To begin with there were the environmental charters. These set out broad principles which guide a local authority's policies towards the environment; and aim to make its own internal practices more environmentally friendly. These charters grew from the model worked out by Friends of the Earth (1989) during its work with Kirklees Council — the authority based in Huddersfield.

Next, there are the internal environmental audits. An ordinary audit is an assessment of an organisation's economic position. Auditors examine the value of assets, the amounts owed, income forecasts and so on. An environmental audit is a similar kind of assessment focusing on the impact on the environment of an authority's internal operations. Many routine, apparently insignificant decisions have environmental implications. An audit can lead to wider use of recycled paper and envelopes; reduced spending on environmentally unfriendly cleaning agents; the elimination of peat from horticultural operations; and energy saving in the authority's buildings.

The third kind of document to emerge round the turn of the decade was the state of the environment report. These are very ambitious documents aiming at a comprehensive assessment of environmental conditions in a local authority's area. They cover such things as levels of air pollution, water quality in rivers and on beaches, the amount of derelict and contaminated land, and the extent of traffic congestion. They are sometimes called environmental audits as they are, in effect, audits or assessments of the state of the environment in a council's area. One of the better known examples of these documents is Lancashire County Council's (1991). A source of confusion needs to be identified here. Some people refer to these state of the environment reports as environmental audits. This is understandable in that they assess the state of environmental conditions. But it confuses them with the environmental audits discussed above as the second type of document. It is thus necessary to distinguish between internal and external audits.

Finally, there were the environmental action plans. A state of the environment report analyses the existing situation. It does not tell a council what policies it needs to pursue. The logical approach is to follow up the external environmental audit report with a document setting out the ways existing policies need amending. Lancashire County Council followed this sequence in the early 1990s.

Moving on from the documents, the second significant point to emerge was the dawning of the sheer complexity of what councils are trying to grapple with. The documents discussed briefly above reveal a wide range of issues. These include transport; energy; recycling and waste disposal; pollution of air, water and land; the future of agricultural land in the context of set-aside; land use planning; access to informal green recreational areas; the protection of wildlife sites and the promotion of wildlife corridors; the management of landscapes with minimal use of peat and chemicals; and the scope of what constitutes a healthy city — while not forgetting debates about the quality of life. Following the canteen trail illustrates how complex small issues are. Internal environmental audits raised issues about purchasing policy. The use of throw away plastic cutlery, paper plates and polystyrene cups adds to the demand for goods which are not biodegradable; and to the city's waste disposal problem. Using non-disposable items reduces the volume of waste.

The local dimensions of environmental policy are far-reaching. As with the inner city, the environment is multi-faceted, and concerns a complex set of inter-related issues. The authorities that really discovered the scale of this complexity were those that did the first state of the environment reports.

The third significant point to emerge during the late 1980s and early 1990s was local authorities' lack of powers in the environmental field. The documents described above had aroused the interest of many councils, and also confronted them with the scope of the issues that needed tackling. Local authority departments like Leisure and Recreation, Planning, and Environmental Health have relevant statutory and permissive powers. But in many spheres decisions are made outside the town hall. On the prominent issues of energy and transport the parameters of public policy are drawn in Whitehall. The Government determines the role and funding regime of key actors like British Rail. Quasi-government agencies (QGAs) like the National Rivers Authority (NRA) have important regulatory powers, as on river pollution for example.

Councils are also dependent, whilst promoting their ideas, on the decisions of others outside the sphere of government. Growth in public transport and waste recycling depends on individuals changing their habits. Small environmental improvement schemes frequently depend on local self-help groups or third force organisations of the kind discussed in a separate chapter. More important here is the private sector. Decisions made by companies can undermine attempts to reduce air and water pollution levels; and to increase the take up on renewable energy projects. On many aspects of the environment local authorities lack direct powers. They have to try to work with others, and to influence those that have the powers. This is a theme that will be taken up later in this chapter. It also relates strongly to the point in Chapter 1 about local authorities providing local leadership.

The strengthening focus on sustainable development

It was not just the Rio Summit of June 1992 that marked a turning point in environmental policy for Britain's local authorities. That conference of world leaders has to be seen in the context of what preceded it. The DoE's attitudes and ideas had begun to evolve around 1990 following on from the earlier introduction of Environmental Impact Assessment (EIA) approaches. After the 1991/92 period, sustainable development was taken much more seriously.

A new planning framework emerged in 1991. This was the year the Planning and Compensation Act was passed, and the year of Planning Policy Guidance (PPG) 1. PPG 12 was formally published in February 1992. These documents introduced significant changes. The first point to draw out here is the greater influence of plans in the development control process. Previously there had been a presumption in favour of development. A council only *had to have regard to* what the plan said, while judging a planning application in the context of other material considerations. After the 1991 Act there was to be a presumption in favour of proposals for development if they were in accord with the development plan (DoE 1991(a), para. 25). This attaches greater importance to the plan, which can prevent or influence development through clearly defined policies. The ambiguity that was there before — because what the plan said was just one consideration — has been removed. This has been made more important by the fact that all councils now have to prepare plans. Apart from the county council's structure plans and the metropolitan districts' Unitary Development Plans (UDPs), every district council has to prepare a local plan covering all of its area.

The other important change to the planning system in 1991/92 is linked to the greater importance of plans. This was the instruction to local authorities to take account of the environment in a much wider sense than before (DoE 1992(a), para. 5.52). Para 6.3 says that plans need to go further than they have before

> to ensure that newer environmental concerns, such as global warming and the consumption of non-renewable resources, are also reflected in the analysis of policies that forms part of the plan preparation.
>
> (DoE 1992(a))

Paras 6.4 to 6.8 argue that planners need to attach greater importance to environmental issues in the statutory plans than they had previously. 'The cost(s) to the community of many forms of pollution are more substantial than we had been accustomed to think' (para. 6.7). Here PPG 12 is referring to such things as clean air, water quality, landscape conservation, noise, and sites for wildlife. Para. 6.8 goes further, making, as the next section of this chapter shows, links to the 1987 Brundtland Report (World Commission on Environment and Development). It explicitly says 'Attention must be given to the interests of future generations'. In this connection most of the focus is on the implications of global warming for energy and transport policies. But other issues are mentioned, including the protection of ground water resources; the prevention of coastal flooding; reclaiming derelict and contaminated land; and a clearer focus on a variety of environmental health issues.

It will not be until the mid-1990s or so that the extent to which the scope of topics to be covered in plans really becomes clear. By then, when a number of plans have gone through all their stages, the DoE will have revealed the scope of policies on these wide-ranging issues that it is prepared to allow, and what it would prefer to exclude from these statutory land-use plans. But the 1991/92 changes, especially the widened interpretation of what plans should deal with, do appear to be a significant step forward.

In parallel with the introduction of the new planning framework in 1991/92, Whitehall was involved in all sorts of discussions that were changing its perception of the nature and scope of policies on environmental issues. It promoted the Pearce Report (Pearce 1989); and the White Paper on the environment, *This Common Inheritance* (DoE 1990). Also in the early 1990s came other PPGs including the coastal planning one for example; the first two annual monitoring reports on the environmental White Paper (DoE 1991(b), 1992(b)); and the protracted argument with the Department of Transport over the PPG on atmospheric pollution.

Whitehall, especially the DoE, was also having to react to new ideas from Brussels. The 1980s had produced agreement in Brussels about the environment having overriding importance; and the introduction of Environmental Impact Assessment (EIA) (Young 1993). Much of the *Fourth Environmental Action Programme* had been translated into British legislation, as with the 1990 Environmental Protection Act. In the early 1990s it seemed as if much of the *Fifth Environmental Action Plan* — entitled *Towards Sustainability* — would be too. There were discussions about launching the European Environment Agency. The Commission produced reports about the urban environment and sustainable mobility. Finally, the concept of Strategic Environmental Assessment was being developed from the experience of EIA (Therivel *et al.* 1992).

The importance of Rio

In the run-up to the Rio Summit, the UK's local authority associations were also developing their ideas about sustainable development (Local Government Management Board (LGMB) 1992(a)). This added to the pressures on Whitehall coming from Brussels, forcing Whitehall to try to analyse its existing policies, and to come to terms with the implications of adopting sustainable ideas. Unusually, local government representatives were included in the UK Government delegation. This reflected the close co-operation between central and local government before the Rio Summit. Whitehall was also pressured by British local government interest in the international local government associations' conferences during the run-up to Rio to discuss their ideas (LGMB

1992(b)). The most important part of this activity was an invitation from the Secretariat of the United Nations Conference on Environment and Development (UNCED) to the International Council for Local Environmental Initiatives (ICLEI). ICLEI was asked for a draft chapter on the role of local authorities in promoting sustainable development to go into the Earth Charter to be discussed at Rio. As a result local government across the world went to Rio with its own agenda.

This became the basis of Chapter 28 in the Agenda 21 document agreed at Rio. Agenda 21 is the name given to the global action plan for sustainable development in the 21st century. It has 40 chapters, and is divided into four sections (LGMB 1992(c), 1993). The first deals with the interdependence of environmental problems, and issues like debt, trade, population and poverty. The second focuses on the need to manage physical resources like forests, the land, the sea and so on while promoting sustainable development. The third examines ways of strengthening the involvement of organisations like industry and local authorities, and groups like non-governmental organisations (NGOs), farmers, women and the poor, in the process of working for sustainable approaches. The final section analyses implementation mechanisms and covers issues like funding, the role of technology and education, and institutional development. Agenda 21 has been widely criticised for being repetitive, and for lacking targets. Its importance is that it is the document everyone is working from.

One of the significant points to emerge from Rio was a growing and widespread realisation that much of the implementation of Agenda 21 would not fall to national governments. There is much to be done at the international level, on atmospheric pollution for example. Equally, successful implementation will depend on what happens at local authority and sub-national level. LGMB claims that two-thirds of the statements adopted by national governments 'cannot be delivered without the commitment and co-operation of local government' (LGMB 1993, p. 1). Much of Chapter 28 is written in the same vein.

The importance of sustainable development for local government

The main consequence of Rio for British local authorities is that they have to produce their own Local Agenda 21s, drawing from Agenda 21, and based in particular on Chapter 28. But this has to be seen in the wider context. In the late 1980s a number of authorities had realised there were, as discussed briefly in the introduction, real benefits to be gained from developing environmental initiatives. Others began to appreciate these. During the 1991/2 period a watershed was crossed. Apart from Rio, other pressures from Brussels and Whitehall combined to propel the wavering authorities down the path that pioneering authorities like Sutton, Kirklees and Leicester had earlier forged. By 1993 sustainable development had become much more than a trendy new idea. It was at the heart of Whitehall's overall approach, with inexorable pressures behind its promotion. The issue confronting local authorities was working out what sustainable development actually meant in practice. It is to this that we now turn.

The concept of sustainable development

Before unpacking the layers of sustainable development, it is necessary to briefly summarise what sustainable development seeks to tackle. The problem is aptly put by Stewart and Hams.

> Human economic activity is taking resources faster than the planet can replenish them and producing wastes faster than the planet can absorb them. If this continues it will destroy the planet's ability to support human life.   (1992, p. 7)

Transport provides an example of the complexities of this point. Limiting public transport and promoting cars and the movement of goods by road has long term impacts. These include, amongst others, building motorways through areas of countryside; damaging wildlife sites along the routes; quarrying for road-building materials in rural areas, often in practice in national parks; allowing cars to dominate cities to the detriment of pedestrians, bus-users and cyclists; adding to atmospheric pollution and global warming; and so on. These long term impacts limit the choices available to future generations. Oil reserves are used up; there is a loss of wildlife habitats and even species; railway tracks are dismantled and built over; the outward spread of cities is encouraged, thus generating more traffic and limiting options in adjacent rural areas; more traffic is generated; and cities are given over to cars in such a way that it becomes very expensive to get back to putting public transport first. Many other examples could be given to illustrate Stewart and Hams' point. Our present approach to land-take, transport, energy consumption and growth cannot be sustained. At present we convert resources to waste and damage the environment along the way. This is reaching the point where continuing unabated with present approaches may cause further permanent damage to the planet and limit the options available to future generations more surely.

The much-quoted definition of sustainable development comes from the Brundtland Report of 1987 (WCED): development needs to be sustainable 'to ensure that it meets the needs of the present without compromising the ability of future generations to meet their own needs' (p. 8). This definition is deceptively simple. It provoked widespread discussion. One book (Pearce 1989) has an appendix with 23 definitions in!

Six key dimensions of sustainable development

A typical criticism of the Brundtland Report is that it contained 'a series of fine statements which are impossible to disagree with, but which are too vague to be translated into concrete actions' (Soussan 1992, p. 26). It remains difficult for policy-makers in the real world to apply the concept. This section draws from a number of authors — Blowers (1992), Bosworth (1993), Breheny (1992), Elkin *et al.* (1991), Goodin (1992), Grove-White (1992), Jacobs (1990, 1991, 1992), Pearce (1989), Soussan (1992), Therivel *et al.* (1992) and WCED (1987). Rather than attempt a definition, the approach here is to try to distil out six dimensions of sustainable development. It is made up of several inter-linked ideas.

Futurity

The essential point here is that we need to consider the impact of our economic activity on the ability of future generations to meet their needs. Economic decisions have to take into account the interests of future generations as well as current generations. This means two things. First, the needs of future generations need to be incorporated into the decision-making process. Second, we need when considering new developments to examine their impact over a larger time-horizon — longer than the 15 years of a conventional plan for example. A better example concerns oak trees. They take up to 400 years to mature. This is the kind of time-scale those preparing management plans for nature reserves have to think in terms of.

Inter-generational equity

The essential point here is that future generations should have access to the same resource base as existing generations. They should have the 'opportunity to experience the same level of well-being from the use of the natural environment as the present generation' (Jacobs 1990, p. 9). From this two things follow. First the resource base has to be well managed. Second is the point that Pearce in particular has developed (1989). If finite resources are being used — like minerals for example — we need to pass on constant or improving capital to future generations. This can be interpreted broadly to cover such things as physical assets, financial capital, institutions that protect the environment, knowledge, skills, and slow maturing environmental assets like new forests.

Intra-generational equity

For the Brundtland Report sustainable development is partly about 'meeting the basic needs of all, and extending to all the opportunity to satisfy their aspirations' (WCED 1987, p. 44). There is no space here to discuss the complexities of the concept of need. Its centrality in the Brundtland Report mainly reflects its authors' concerns about internationalism and tackling third world poverty and deprivation. But equity between current generations also relates to living conditions in cities in the developed industrial world. Jacobs is just one writer who points out that 'poorer people almost always live in worse environments than the more affluent' (1990, p. 25). Intra-generational equity is thus about redistribution and approaches to sustainable development that discriminate in favour of the disadvantaged in our cities, thus promoting intra-generational equity.

The need to consider environmental costs as well as economic costs in decision-making processes

Throughout human history, particularly during the Industrial Revolution, the environmental impacts of development decisions have frequently been ignored (Ponting 1991). They have focused on economic costs and on whether schemes are financially viable. The environment has commonly been regarded as a sink for waste products. The ai , the land and the rivers have all been seriously polluted. Brundtland and Agenda 21 recognised that this could not continue, that problems like global warming were causing serious and possibly irreversible damage to the planet and to the surrounding atmosphere. The implication of this is clear in principle. When decisions about economic development are made, environmental dimensions need to be taken into account. The UK

Government's instruction to local authorities in 1992 to take account of the environment in a much wider sense than before, as discussed above, marks a recognition of this principle.

The principle of considering environmental costs when making decisions about economic development can be simply stated. But in practice it opens a Pandora's Box of problems. Environmental economists have responded to the challenge by arguing that cost-benefit techniques can be used, and that everything has a value (Barde and Pearce 1991). The result has been 'a preoccupation with the technical problems of assigning monetary values to environmental properties or goods which do not have a market price' (Soussan, 1992, p. 27, see also p. 28, and Jacobs 1990, p. 7–8). This whole topic has proved to be a minefield of assumptions, value-laden judgements, and prejudices. Grove-White has commented 'The operationalisation of sustainable development presented by economists seriously over-simplifies the meaning of "the environment"' (1992, p. 7). There is no space here to explore this issue further.

Broadly speaking the situation can be summed up as follows. There is widespread agreement on the need to consider environmental costs. The environmental economists have made the running in developing techniques to do so. They have been widely criticised — but no coherent alternative has yet emerged. Within the whole enormous subject of sustainable development, this is one of the most important and pressing areas for new research.

An approach to economic growth that stresses quality not quantity

Sustainable development is neither for nor against economic growth. It is concerned to change the nature of economic growth to make it compatible with environmental needs. Therivel *et al.* argue that the British Government's view is that 'both development and growth need to be sustained and sustainable' (1992 p. 65). Stewart and Hams put it this way, 'The concept of sustainable development is designed to reconcile the hope of growth in quality of life today with the interests of future generations' (1992, p. 27). The Brundtland Report stresses the need to think about the *quality* of growth, rather than the *quantity* of growth (WCED 1987, pp. 52–4).

There are several ways in which this can be done. First, there needs to be economic growth that does not permanently damage the environment. In practice this means reducing travel, energy consumption, polluting industries and waste. Second, economic growth needs to be sustainable. It is not sustainable if it 'depletes the future viability of the resource base' (Soussan 1992, p. 25). Nor is it sustainable 'if it increases vulnerability to crises' (WCED 1987, p. 53). An example here would be development that creates further demands on water resources in South-East England where there is already a serious long term shortage of water in an area vulnerable to drought. An important part of making growth sustainable is promoting jobs that will help improve environmental conditions (Gibbs 1991). Examples here include woodland work, organic farming, the production of pollution control equipment, and waste management and recycling. Finally, and in keeping with the earlier notion of intra-generational equity, economic growth needs to benefit underprivileged groups by providing them with educational, training and other opportunities. When economic regeneration policies are aimed at local people in inner city areas for example, they can lead to social regeneration. In this kind of way sustainable development seeks to promote a new type of economic growth with emphasis on quality not quantity. This does relate to the quality of life issue which some might say should be a separate heading here.

Environmental capacities

Jacobs has developed ideas about the nature of environmental capacities (1990, pp. 12–13, 1991, Chapter 8). Environmental capacity is about the capacity of the environment to perform its functions and to cope with human demands on it. This involves the planet and the surrounding atmosphere providing natural energy, and renewable and non-renewable resources; absorbing wastes in soil, air and water; and maintaining the natural world. What is at issue here is the capacity of the biosphere to cope with the consequences of human demands on it. This can be illustrated using the example of waste. Until the 1980s the governments and peoples of the world assumed that the environment would absorb all the wastes that were being deposited in it. As a result of the discussions surrounding the Brundtland Report and the Rio Summit, a new perspective has emerged. The environment can absorb our wastes, but only so long as the rates at which wastes are deposited do not exceed certain thresholds or limits. If the limits are exceeded, the biosphere's capacity begins to decline. The disposal of all kinds of waste has to be restricted to the absorption limits of its recipient medium. Jacobs argues that the important point here is that environmental capacities must not be allowed to slip below minimum levels. It is possible to assess what these thresholds are; to measure pollution levels; and develop policies to ensure that environmental capacities are not damaged.

Six key dimensions of sustainable development

Reducing a complex concept like sustainable development to six dimensions begs many questions. There is a lot waiting to be read by those wanting to explore the complexities. The point of this approach is to draw out the basic points before proceeding to the next section on operationalising the whole concept.

Before doing so though, a couple of broader points need making. The discussion here is focused on cities in developed industrial societies. The Brundtland Report relates its analysis to the problems of the third world. The extent to which cities in less developed countries need to be examined within a different framework, because of their different problems, needs further research, and cannot be embarked on here. Also it must be acknowledged that deep ecologists like Devall, and others discussed by Eckersley (1992) and Goodin (1992), will argue that this approach makes too many compromises, and ignores the issue of anthropocentrism, or the focus on humans at the expense of other creatures and the planet. They favour a more radical approach to the world's environmental problems. For them, even modified economic growth of the kind sustainable development envisages, is incompatible with the need to protect the planet from further damage.

Operationalising the concept of sustainable development

The previous section has tried to unpack the layers of sustainability, to get at the essence of the concept. The aim of this section is to draw from the different dimensions of sustainable development to reformulate the idea of sustainability in a way that policy-makers can relate to. This is done through the checklist of questions set out in Table 4.1. The purpose of these is to provide a set of test questions that policy-makers can ask of the issues that arrive on their desks. Initially, the questions help to tease out the environmental consequences of different respones. In addition, they should also help policy-makers to work out enviromentally friendly responses; or where impacts are inevitable, approaches which are least damaging in environmental terms.

In the discussion that follows a distinction is drawn between new proposals and continuing with existing policies. Considering a

planning application for a big out of town retail or business park is
rather different from looking at the environment consequences of a
city carrying on as before. Approving planning applications for big
developments will have new consequences for the environment in
terms of their impact on such issues as loss of land and habitats,
and additional air pollution from the traffic that is generated. On
the other hand the ageing of the housing stock affects the quality of
life of residents. The same applies to living conditions on run-down
council estates. Sometimes they are a direct threat to health. Examples include drinking water in lead piping in Blackburn; and more
widely, issues relating to asbestos, radon and sick building synd-
rome in existing buildings. Issues like these relate to the city as it is.

Table 4.1:   Getting a handle on environmental issues

1. What is the scope for reducing the impact on the environment of
    (a) a specific new proposal?
    (b) the continued application of existing policies in such spheres as
         transport, waste collection and disposal, economic development,
         housing and so on?

2. What is the scope for reducing the impact on resources of
    (a) a specific new proposal?
    (b) the continued application of existing approaches in different spheres
         of policy?

3. To what extent can demand be managed to reduce the impact on the
    environment stemming from
    (a) a specific new proposal?
    (b) the continued application of existing approaches in different spheres
         of policy?

4. What is the scope for recycling land and materials with regard to
    (a) a specific new proposal?
    (b) the continued application of existing approaches in different spheres
         of policy?

5. What is the scope for developing compensatory initiatives to tackle
    existing environmental problems with regard to
    (a) a specific new proposal?
    (b) the continued application of existing approaches in different spheres
         of policy?

The environmental problems of the existing city need to be
considered separately from the environmental impacts of new
developments. This distinction is carried through into the questions
that are designed to help policy-makers to get a handle on
environmental issues.

The first question focuses on reducing impacts on the environment — on the air, on the land, on the sea and on rivers. In the case of a new proposal such as a waste disposal site, what sorts of issues are raised? Liquids can leak from these sites, draining away onto surrounding land or into water courses. Even in the 1980s new schemes were being proposed for sites that were on the coast which would be vulnerable to rising sea levels in the 21st century. Some suggested locations are adjacent to sensitive wildlife sites. Clearly the pollution dangers from land-fill sites need to be carefully considered before the go-ahead is given for new schemes. The only safe approach is to site them where they will not be flooded and to collect and treat the leachate to ensure it does not cause any damage.

Traffic congestion provides an example of an issue where continuing with existing policies unchecked has consequences for the environment. Road vehicles pollute in two ways. To begin with they add lead, hydrocarbons and carbon monoxide to the atmosphere. Secondly, some pollutants then cause further chemical reactions in the atmosphere. In hot weather this can lead to smog. Lengthening rush hours mean that high concentrations of vehicle emissions last for longer. For those living near major road arteries this is unpleasant and can be unhealthy. The facade of buildings can be damaged by vehicular emissions. This particularly affects carving in soft stone in historic cities. If no attempts are made to control increasing amounts of traffic, then these and related problems will have a steadily worsening impact on the environment.

The second question in Table 4.1 is about the resource implications of new proposals, and of carrying on with existing policies unchecked. Our concern here is with such things as energy consumption, and the use of finite and other resources. Big new housing, industrial and other developments can have important resource implications. Buildings need to be designed in energy efficient ways, with less glass for example as this promotes heat loss. In some parts of the country special circumstances arise. In the south and east of Britain water shortages have become a way of life, rivers are drying up and aquifer levels are falling. An application for a golf course, hotel and leisure complex in an affected area would generate further demand for water, and make the local situation worse.

Sometimes the issues are very complex. For example some British and European cities have looked at the possibility of running buses on a fuel derived from rape-seed oil. But such ideas have to be set in the wider context of producing the rape-seed oil. This includes the fossil fuels used by the farmers to plough, sow and harvest it; to apply fertilisers, and to spray weedkiller. This helps create the demand for pesticides and inorganic fertilisers, which then run off into water courses. Further diesel is used to move the crop to the plant where — using energy — it is processed into fuel for buses. There is a danger of duplicating the American experience. In Nebraska a study of the attempt to substitute ethanol for petrol showed that almost as much fossil fuel was used as was saved (*Economist* 28 November 1992, p. 35). Bright ideas need to be fully analysed in the context of their impact on the planet and the atmosphere.

Next, the second question about resource implications needs to be related to carrying on with established policies with regard to the existing city. A good example here is energy. It is widely accepted that Britain's energy bill could be substantially reduced if buildings were more effectively insulated. Energy consumption remains artificially high because thousands of houses, offices, industrial premises and other structures do not retain heat. Heating bills could be substantially reduced through insulating lifts and walls and other measures. This would have important consequences for retaining reserves of fossil fuels like oil, gas and coal; and for the future of nuclear power and the need to dispose of nuclear waste. If total energy consumption was significantly reduced, the potential of renewable energy schemes would be increased as they could more easily make a significant contribution. It would thus be more worthwhile investing in wind, solar, wave and other alternative sources so as to explore their potential.

Moving on, the third question in Table 4.1 concerns the issue of managing demand. There are certain situations where an authority is able to manipulate demand to limit damage to the environment. An example here is siting a major new industrial development scheme so it can readily be plugged into the existing public transport networks. A statutory plan can identify sites with such potential by picking those which are adjacent to railway lines, and which can readily be linked into major bus routes. This makes it possible for people to travel to and from work via public transport. It may even be worth building a new station. Some of the flow of goods in and out can also be handled via the railway. Such an approach helps limit the growth of cars and HGVs. This process of managing demand limits damage to the atmosphere; restricts the noise and intrusion of the traffic for those living nearby; and contributes to the process of trying to reduce the overall growth in road traffic.

The question about managing demand can also be related, not just to new developments, but to the existing city as well. Some authorities have managed to introduce successful park and ride schemes so that people leave their cars on the outskirts of cities and take the — sometimes free — bus in. Where this goes hand-in-hand with a deliberate policy to limit the numbers of car-parking spaces in the city centre there is a strong incentive for people to use it.

When the idea of demand is pursued in detail, all sorts of issues come up. For example it is possible to reduce demand for water through the introduction of water meters, and through water recycling schemes. The latter has potential with regard to big industrial users. The privatised water companies have been widely criticised for the slow pace at which they carry out repairs to leaks. It is argued that the demand for water would be radically reduced if burst pipes were mended more quickly. Some even argue that there should be no further planning permission for new reservoirs — until water companies show that they have consistently improved their repair record.

The fourth question in Table 4.1 concerns the scope for recycling land, buildings and materials. Recycling is usually thought of in connection with waste. The aim here is to apply the principle more broadly by, for example, adopting recycling approaches to reduce the construction of new buildings using new materials. The demand for new housing and industrial development is frequently met through development on green field sites at the edge of the city. Despite the reclamation schemes of the 1970s and 1980s there is still a lot of scope for locating new development on disused and reclaimed sites in urban areas. Chapter 2 highlighted the 1990 DoE survey of such sites. This shows that in England there is land equivalent to the area covered by Cleveland County Council waiting to be redeveloped. Recycling of land means that brown-field sites can be used rather than green-field sites. This need not affect green open spaces of value to people within the city. From the traffic generation point of view, it has the advantage that it keeps the city compact, promoting the use of public transport. One of the disadvantages of developing sites on the edge of the city is that it encourages the spread of the city and the growth of road traffic.

The most ambitious approach to recycling land applies to the largest sites. The bigger urban renewal schemes discussed in the chapter on entrepreneurial planning have reclaimed huge areas — old docks or steel complexes for example. One widely discussed idea in the early 1990s was the concept of an urban village, based on sustainable principles (Aldous 1992). It would provide housing, shopping, office space, small firm premises and recreational and other community facilities like a library. The development of largely self-contained urban villages would need substantial sites. But such schemes would demonstrate the potential of recycling land, and be a high profile way for an authority to demonstrate its commitment to sustainable development.

The question of recycling land, buildings and materials also needs to be related to the existing city as it is. There are many ways in which new uses can be found for buildings. The examples are legion. Warehouses get converted into flats, schools into bus stations, mills into work spaces, and so on. This is where peoples' imaginations have to be given a free rein. Hotels and heritage centres have appeared in all sorts of unlikely buildings. In Bristol an old chapel was converted, exploiting the height of the nave, into a mountain climbing training centre. Ideas get recycled too. The early 1990s witnessed another attempt to use empty flats over shops and to convert empty offices for housing provision. Where stone buildings are demolished there is scope to re-use the stone for new building.

The fifth question in Table 4.1 is about the extent to which there is scope for using technology and lateral thinking to combat environmental degradation. The essential point here is about exploiting opportunities for compensatory action. It is possible to design schemes which tackle environmental problems while meeting other needs.

An example of a new investment project that relates to this question is the issue of closed cycles. In the context of waste management plans it is possible to develop ideas about turning waste into energy, to link the design of waste processing schemes to the heating needs of adjacent housing projects. This reduces the volume going into land-fill sites; it cuts the demand for heating from fossil fuels; and puts waste to a productive use.

Another example concerns the landscaping surrounding big new development projects on reclaimed land. It is not possible, of course, to recreate an ancient wood. But on these large sites there is considerable potential to plan not just for people and jobs and development, but for wildlife as well. The key point here is to involve ecologists in the landscape design process, so they can advise as to retaining part of what was there, and the use of appropriate indigenous plants — ranging from grasses to trees. These will then attract a range of insects for different birds to feed on, and provide the variety of host plants that likely species of butterfly need to lay their eggs on. With careful planning the landscaping can create a greater range of wildlife habitats than had previously been there. In such cases the redevelopment process improves the value of the land for nature. This all then provides benefits of a pleasant green environment for those working there. If hard paths and steps are worked into the design, there are opportunities for interesting lunch-time strolls. Also the site can be made to play a more effective role in the pattern of wildlife corridors through the city. All these are benefits that flow from a new initiative. It is so easy to surround car parks with the same unimaginative collection of non-native shrubs that are of little benefit to wildlife. Yet with a bit of thought, it is possible to compensate for some of the loss of habitats and wildlife elsewhere in the city.

Compensatory mechanisms can be developed in a variety of other ways to tackle environmental problems in existing cities away from the context of a new development. Modernising sewage works is an example. New treatments are possible where sewage sludge ends up as organic fertiliser; and the water is recycled and treated until it is fit to be drinking water. Here waste is turned into a useful product and the shortage of drinking water is alleviated. Another example is the development of community forests. Here wasteland or poor agricultural land is used to plant trees. The trees help soak up the carbon dioxide that is produced by the city, and new jobs and recreational facilities are created. Here again a scheme is developed that tackles one issue while having benefits that compensate for other problems.

The extent of the local authority's response

The previous discussion has drawn out ways in which local authorities can highlight the environmental dimensions of different lines of policy. This section focuses on the local authority's response. To act on the environmental issue it has analysed, an authority needs powers, finance, energy and determination. The key question here is the extent to which it is willing and able to act. The following discussion breaks this issue down into five questions. These 'willing and able questions' are set out in Table 4.2. They help an authority to work out whether it has the resources and the capacity to carry out the policies it wants to; and to identify the resources it needs for successful implementation.

Table 4.2:   The extent to which an authority is willing and able to act

(i)	Has it the powers?
(ii)	Has it the political will to act?
(iii)	Has it the administrative capacity to implement its decisions?
(iv)	Has it the financial resources?
(v)	Has it the energy to network effectively to outside organisations with relevant powers and resources?

Powers

The first of the willing and able questions is the one about powers. On some issues local authorities have clear statutory powers to promote environmentally sensitive solutions. For example in the transport sphere, councils can reduce the capacity of existing roads; promote lower speeds through traffic calming measures; introduce pedestrianisation and park and ride schemes; set out bus and cycle lanes; and restrict parking spaces when granting planning permission (Pharoah 1992).

But in other spheres the situation is less clear. For many years planning authorities were not able to refuse planning permission for new industrial developments on the grounds that their emissions would worsen air pollution levels. But in the early 1990s Lancashire County Council did refuse planning permission for one project on just those grounds. Another area where the extent of planning controls is not clear-cut concerns a council's ability to refuse planning permission on a site of local environmental value. These are the 'Jimbob places' described, in the earlier section on benefits, as being important to local people. Before the wider interpretation of environment introduced in PPG 12, it was difficult to refuse planning permission on these sites because they lacked a special designation. However, by the early 1990s, a number of authorities had refused permission on such sites on the grounds that they needed to protect sites of local environmental value. Even so, such a change takes place slowly as precedents have to be established.

In some circumstances central government acts to clarify a confused situation. During the 1980s, after it began to be clear that sea levels would rise and spread inland, a number of authorities continued to give planning permission for new housing and waste disposal projects on sites that are likely to be submerged. The extent to which councils could refuse permission on such sites, and uphold their decisions at inquiry, was unclear. However, clearer guidance on coastal planning in PPG 20 did clarify this whole issue. This is an example of the way in which central government can remove the ambiguity over local authorities' powers.

Political will

Promoting environmentally sensitive policies can involve difficult choices. Promoting traffic calming off the main roads in inner city areas may be popular. But outrage often greets determined attempts to reduce the number of cars in city centres through parking restrictions, the promotion of public transport and the introduction of park and ride schemes. People do not believe it will improve things until they see it. This may take months. It requires courage to take unpopular decisions and to stick with them in the belief that they will attract support.

Councillors' political will can also be tested over the jobs versus the environment issue. A common example is where an existing works is causing a pollution problem, but needs approval for its air emissions or planning permission for an extension. It may be chimney emissions into the atmosphere; or occasional dreadful smells — as with factories making glue from animal hoof and horn. In areas of high unemployment it takes a lot of political courage to argue for rejecting applications in order to improve environmental conditions for those living around the works. Such decisions can lead not just to no new jobs, but to closure and further redundancies.

Administrative will

Implementation processes can be complex and protracted in the environmental sphere. A considerable administrative commitment is needed if implementation is to be effective. For example a programme to recycle waste needs to be sustained if it is to have an impact. Officers have to work out whether it is best to get people to separate waste in the home for collection, or to expect them to take paper, bottles, aluminium cans and so on to collection points in the city. Apart from organising all of this, there is also the education dimension. People will only take recycling seriously if they understand why the issue is important. That will only happen if there is a sustained administrative commitment to the education dimension of recycling. Without this, the recycling programme will not take off — however well the collection processes have been thought through.

Mobilising financial resources

Increasingly in the early 1990s there are pressures on councils' financial resources. In these circumstances, statutory services have priority. But it is still possible to pursue green ideas, despite these commitments. The first point here is the link to the chapters on lobbying and entrepreneurial planning. There, it is argued that the art of effective lobbying is to carry out projects using other people's money at as little cost to the authority as possible — beyond staff time. This principle can apply to environmentally friendly projects.

Promoting new developments on reclaimed land is a typical example. The land renewal scheme can be prepared within the authority, but funded via Derelict Land Grant. Countryside Commission money can be used to help green the site at the landscaping stage, leaving building costs to the firms carrying out development. The same principle of financing a project from outside the authority applies to quite small schemes. English nature offers various forms of support to authorities establishing local nature reserves.

Lack of funds need not deter a local authority from pursuing environmental projects. To begin with finance is not always involved. Promoting green ideas when granting planning permission does not cost money. It requires a different way of thinking. Also there is an important link here back to the section, on the benefits to be gained from promoting environmental schemes, at the start of this chapter. Some projects are not only environmentally friendly. They also save money. Identifying the road verges with the best collections of wild flowers can lead an authority to reduce the use of pesticides and to adopt a less frequent mowing regime. This reduces maintenance costs. Some of the ways of saving money do require investment first. For example, alterations to an authority's buildings can cut energy costs.

Networking

The final 'willing and able' question concerns the extent to which an authority can network to outside organisations, with powers and resources in the environmental sphere. Networking is an important enough issue to be the subject of a separate chapter in this book. The focus of that chapter is on networking as a new way of thinking. It is based, not on co-ordinating committees, but on individuals in an authority seeking out people in other organisations who share aims and values, and who are committed to similar ideas. The processes of networking are well illustrated in the sphere of environmental policy (Stewart and Hams 1992, pp. 23–4). This is because local authorities have limited relevant powers. They can use planning permission to control development, and they can direct operations over the collection and disposal of waste. But in areas like energy, transport and wildlife their presence is more limited. Here they have to work with other agencies who have the relevant powers. This involves using networking techniques to promote environmentally sensitive policies. There are three dimensions to this.

First there are the cases where outside agencies have relevant regulatory powers. Good examples here are the National Rivers Authority (NRA) and Her Majesty's Inspectorate of Pollution (HMIP). (At the time of writing there are plans to merge these two into an Environmental Protection Agency in the mid-1990s.) To take the rivers example, polluted water kills fish, damages plant life and deters birds like the kingfisher. In the worse cases there are unpleasant smells. Local authorities become concerned for a number of reasons. First, rivers played a key role in waterside property development during the 1980s and early 1990s. Polluted rivers deter potential developers, investors and tenants. Rivers are also a key recreational resource, often running through parks and past heritage-type tourist developments. Smelly, polluted rivers affect the enjoyment of anglers, walkers, naturalists, visitors and others. In the case of canoeists, health can be affected. Ultimately poor river quality can undermine a city's attempt to improve its image.

These are issues where a local authority has a concern — but limited powers. It can use its development control powers to insist on effective water pollution control equipment being installed in new industrial developments. But here the earlier distinction between new projects and the existing city recurs. With regard to pollution incidents from water authorities' sewage works or companies' discharges, it is the NRA that has the powers. Local authorities need to network effectively to regulatory agencies with relevant powers — like the NRA — if they are to tackle pollution problems. This is especially the case where there are persistent offenders.

The second dimension to a council networking to outside organisations concerns agencies with constructive, initiating powers in spheres the authority is trying to influence. Transport provides a clear example. When a council is trying to tackle the growth in road traffic and improve public transport it has only limited powers. The earlier discussion of the adequacy of local authority powers pointed to a council having relevant powers to promote traffic-calming measures and park and ride schemes. But this needs to be part of a wider strategy. To tackle a city's overall transport problem requires the establishment of effective networking links to other agencies with relevant powers. This means building effective links to British Rail, the Passenger Transport Authority (PTA), bus companies, and neighbouring councils.

If the city involved is one of the 40 or so said to be actively considering Light Rapid Transit (LRT) schemes in the early 1990s, then other agencies become involved. The authority has to develop effective networking links to the collection of private sector interests that it will need to involve if a successful joint bid for finance is to be put to the Department of Transport.

The third dimension to networking concerns groups and not-for-profit organisations. These are discussed in the separate chapter on third force organisations (TFOs). That term is used because they provide a third force to help tackle problems — in addition to the public sector and the private sector. Part of the willing and able question on networking concerns the resources that TFOs can mobilise. In the field of greening the city and promoting nature, the county wildlife trust; specialist botanists, biologists and others from higher education institutions; community-based self-help projects; and a variety of other urban wildlife groups can all make a contribution. Collectively they have a range of resources that the local authority can mobilise — if it can network to them effectively. They can carry out surveys to help identify locally important habitats; they can clean up canals or woods; they can help create new habitats by planting trees and making ponds; they can help provide education facilities for schools; and they can take on maintenance jobs. The energy of TFOs can be encouraged through environmental grants schemes for their projects. The network of wildlife TFOs in a city is very diffused, involving individuals in a number of organisations. If the council can locate the more dynamic characters it can build useful networks. This will enable it to harness a range of resources for its wider ends.

The willing and able questions

It is possible for local authorities to tackle a whole range of issues on the environmental front. They can be ambitious or much more limited in their approach. When evaluating different policy options and looking at whether they can implement different options, they need to assess whether they have the powers; the political will to stick with unpopular decisions; the administrative capacity; the necessary finance; and the energy to network effectively to outside agencies. Each of the willing and able questions needs to be asked of each proposal. The answers will help identify future problems, and any missing resources that are needed for successful implementation.

A sustainable development ladder

At this stage of the argument the 'handle' questions and the 'willing and able' questions come together. The purpose of the 'handle' questions is to provide authorities with a toolkit to do two things. First, they are there to help an authority work out the environmental consequences of different lines of policy. Secondly, these questions are there to help work out responses that are environmentally sensitive with regard to new initiatives; and to continuing with existing approaches. The aim of the willing and able questions is to help authorities work out whether they have the resources and capacities to carry out their chosen policies.

A local authority's answers to the two sets of questions are very revealing. They display its priorities. They show the importance that the authority attaches to the environment. This is portrayed in Figure 4.1 via a ladder showing different degrees of commitment to the concept of sustainable development. This is a variation on the distinction that Pearce (1990) and Jacobs (1992) draw between weak and strong approaches to sustainable development.

Figure 4.1: The sustainable development ladder

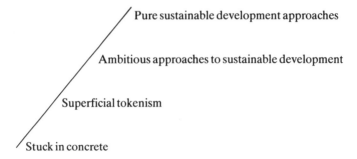

The idea of a ladder is borrowed from Arnstein (1969). She developed it in the context of participation. She had a ladder displaying different approaches to participation. These start at the bottom with notions of manipulation and therapy. They then progress through consultation in the middle, to citizen control at the top. Her ladder reveals the differing commitments that government agencies have towards the idea of participation. Similarly, the sustainable development ladder draws out the differing commitments that local authorities have to the whole idea of sustainable development.

If the authority thinks the handle questions are unimportant, and chooses to ignore the willing and able questions, then it is revealing its approach to be thoroughly negative in terms of the environment.

It is pursuing economic goals irrespective of their environmental impacts. Such business-as-usual approaches are about manipulating the environment for economic ends. Strictly speaking this position is stuck in concrete, and not even on the ladder.

At the top of the ladder is the pure sustainable development approach. This appears unobtainable in developed industrial societies. However, Pearce (1989) would argue that it can be achieved because even if a city uses up finite resources it need not close off options for future generations. It can pass on skills, infrastructure, and other forms of compensatory wealth to the next generation. Many would argue though that the development of cities cannot be environmentally benign. Whether they are growing or contracting, cities are net consumers of scarce resources. But even so, the pure sustainable development approach remains theoretically possible; and it may become more attainable in the next century. It thus has a value as a goal at the top of the ladder — in the same way that the rarely achieved citizen control rung has at the top of Arnstein's ladder.

Moving up from the bottom, the first thing is superficial tokenism. This is where the answers to the handle questions, and the willing and able questions reveal that a council has begun to appreciate the significance of environmental issues. But its initiatives are limited and self-contained. It picks issues like cycle paths and nature reserves. But it fails to address the wider issues thrown up by the handle questions about the overall impact of its policies on the environment. A council involved with superficial, token approaches sees the environment as an optional extra, as an add-on. This is in stark contrast with the next step up the ladder.

The essence of the ambitious approach to sustainable development is an authority grasping the point that the environment is not an add-on issue. Developing environmentally sensitive policies requires a whole new way of thinking. At this point on the ladder, the answers to the handle questions reveal the authority understands this fundamental issue. It demonstrates its understanding in a variety of ways. Its answers to the first two handle questions — about environmental impacts and resource implications — reveal that it realises it has to produce tough responses to minimise impacts of policies on the environment. Its answers to the other three handle questions — about the management of demand, recycling and compensatory initiatives — illustrate its ability to initiate ambitious policies to tackle environmental problems. It responds positively to the willing and able questions. It develops the political will and the administrative capacity to implement projects. On issues where it lacks powers and finance, it is prepared to network with sustained energy to draw in other agencies with powers and resources. These are the features, the characteristics of councils pursuing ambitious approaches to sustainable development. They are revealed by the answers to the handle questions and the willing and able questions.

The main prescriptive role of the sustainability ladder is to help identify what a council needs to do to get from superficial tokenism to the ambitious level. It has to develop a much more positive set of answers both to the handle and to the willing and able questions. This revolves around the central argument of this chapter, that the environment is not an add-on. The development of environmentally sensitive policies requires a whole new way of thinking. A prism takes a beam of light and diffuses it into all the colours of the rainbow, identifying its different ingredients. What emerges from an analysis of sustainable development is the idea that all policies need to be subjected to an environmental prism to analyse their impacts on the environment. The handle questions can best be thought of as that prism. The willing and able questions concern an authority's ability to mobilise resources and to develop the capacity to implement its policies effectively.

Sustainable development in the 1990s

As a result of Rio, the Government has agreed to produce regular reports about how it will be developing its contribution towards implementing Agenda 21. As a further consequence, local authorities have been strongly urged by the DoE to produce their own Local Agenca 21 documents by 1996. From the preceding discussion, a logical sequence of steps can be identified if a council is to achieve the level of ambitious approach to sustainable development on the ladder.

Building towards Local Agenda 21s

The natural starting point is a state of the environment report. This provides an authority with a detailed survey of environmental conditions. It then provides a baseline against which future changes in such things as air conditions and water quality can be measured. This can be supplemented by an internal environment audit to examine an authority's overall impact on the environment. This can lead to a local authority changing its practices. Setting an example has a certain moral force in a situation where the council is trying to persuade companies and individuals to change their behaviour.

Whether there is an internal audit or not, the essential follow up to a state of the environment report is some kind of strategic plan looking at the authority's next steps.

An environmental action plan has a number of different functions. First, it identifies the problems. Second, it sets out — drawing from the handle questions — the authority's lines of response to new developments; and the changes that can be made to existing policies towards the city as it is. Next it works out specific targets for improvements. In particular these need to be related to environmental capacities. Finally, it relates the whole range of what can be done to the willing and able questions. The point here is to work out whether it has the powers and resources to act; and to identify which organisations it needs to network to. The fundamental purpose of the environmental action plan thus emerges. It is there to determine priorities.

It may be possible to cover some of the ground an environmental action plan focuses on whilst preparing a UDP, or local or structure plan. But statutory plans tend to set out how an authority will respond to private sector development. They are less effective at setting out how a council will initiate action. There is scope for an environmental action plan to be much more positive and wide-ranging in this sphere. There is a limit to the extent to which a land-use plan can tackle sustainable development issues.

Beyond the state of the environment report and the action plan, two other steps in the sequence are important. Where appropriate, it is necessary to translate some of the ideas in the action plan into policies in statutory planning documents and other reports like waste management plans. Finally, the action plan needs to be monitored annually to assess how far its policies and priorities need changing.

Following this set of steps provides a coherent approach to producing a Local Agenda 21 document. It will be all the stronger if there has been time for monitoring to lead to revisions in the environmental action plan. This will refine the process of identifying the worst problems; and of determining the priorities in the light of the willing and able questions.

The dimension of a Local Agenda 21 that has been omitted so far is that of participation. The agreement in Rio was clear about local governments drawing up their documents in partnership with their communities and local businesses. Special mention was made of the need to involve women, young people and disadvantaged groups. Participation is especially important in the context of sustainable development because achieving sustainability will depend, in part, on people re-thinking parts of their everyday lives.

It is not just about explaining to children what they find when they go pond-dipping. It is about people turning taps off, consuming less domestic energy, separating out their waste for recycling; leaving the car at home; picking up litter; and so on. Involving people in making choices between conflicting objectives; and in the generation of ideas will help educate people about the issues, and create support for Local Agenda 21 documents. Stewart and Hams argue that, 'Sustainable development must be built by, through and with the commitment of local communities. The requirements of sustainable development cannot merely be imposed, active partici-pation by local communities is needed' (1992, p. 12). Ultimately, attempts to achieve sustainable development will be more success-ful if they have grown from effective participation programmes.

Internal policy-making processes

The process of reacting to a state of the environment report will raise issues about an authority's internal structure. The promotion of sustainable development requires a holistic approach. It needs lateral thinking and an understanding of the complex links between a variety of issues. Stewart and Hams argue that, 'Responsibility for sustainable development cannot be confined to a particular department. It is an issue for the whole authority' (1992, p. 24). It follows that it will be necessary to review the links between departments and committees, and possibly to embark on some restructuring. Almost certainly, staff retraining will be needed if a coherent, holistic approach is to be established.

Next steps

Achieving sustainable development from a standing start will be difficult. Policy-makers are only just beginning to come to terms with the concept, and it is not yet fully understood. But the issues need to be addressed now. A short-term, coping, damage limitation strategy is needed, while a more coherent long-term approach that promotes *ecologically* sustainable development, is worked out.

The handle questions used earlier provide a start to the coping strategy. We argued that when examining the environmental consequences of policies, it is important to draw a distinction between the impact of existing policies towards the city as it is, and of new developments. This distinction has implications for the next steps. With regard to current policies towards the existing city, the starting point needs to be a damage limitation exercise, a start to the process of reducing the activities that cause most environmental damage. The most serious problems in contemporary cities are probably reducing vehicle journeys, encouraging more walking and cycling, producing less waste and pollution, and cutting consumption of energy. As environmental action plans begin to emerge they will need to identify the worst local problems.

The other dimension to the handle questions was the consideration of new developments. The obvious approach here is widespread adoption of the precautionary principle as a part of the short-term damage limitation strategy. In practice this means preventing new developments unless all the environmental consequences are fully understood, can be contained, and fit in with the principles of sustainable development. Owens argues that with new developments we need to find urban forms that are robust and energy efficient in a variety of circumstances (Breheny 1992, pp. 283 and 289).

While the short-term damage limitation strategy is, hopefully, beginning to move things in the right direction, policy makers need to work out a more coherent, ecologically sustainable long-term approach. A more detailed understanding of the issues and potential instruments is needed so that a more sophisticated, coherent set of long-term guidelines is developed. Targets need to be established so problems identified in state of the environment reports can be tackled over time. Effective environmental action plans need to be developed. Local contributions to sustainable development goals at national and international levels need to be worked out. This will require a great deal of research. The extent to which local authorities can have an impact is not yet clear.

Short-term damage limitation strategies need to be developed quickly, while, in parallel, more coherent long-term approaches are devised. The most pressing need for research in the short term is on the jobs front. The earlier discussion of sustainable development drew out the idea of a new type of economic growth that relies on quality not quantity. Sustainable approaches will require different *kinds* of jobs. The detailed implications of this need working out too.

References and bibliography

Aldous, T. (1992) *Urban Villages* London: Urban Villages Group, 5 Cleveland Place, London, SW1Y 6JJ.

Arnstein, S. (1969) 'A ladder of citizen participation' *Journal of the American Institute of Planners* **35**, 216–224.

Association of County Councils *et el.* (1992) *Environmental Practice in Local Government* 2nd ed. Luton: Local Government Management Board.

Barde, J.P., and Pearce, D.W. (1991) *Valuing the Environment* London: Earthscan.

Blowers, A. (1992) 'Planning a sustainable future: problems, principles and prospects' *Town and Country Planning* May, 132–5.

Bosworth, T. (1993) 'Local authorities and sustainable development' *European Environment* 3, No. 1, February, 13–17.

Breheny, M. (1992) 'Towards sustainable urban development' in Mannion, A.M. and Bowlby, S.R. (eds) *Environmental Issues in the 1990s* Chichester: John Wiley.

Commission of the European Communities (1992) *Towards Sustainability: Fifth Action Programme on the Environment* Brussels: CEC.

Department of the Environment (1990) *This Common Inheritance* Cmd 1200. London: HMSO.

Department of the Environment (1991(a)) *Planning Policy Guidance* 1, London: HMSO.

Department of the Environment (1991(b)) *This Common Inheritance: The First Year Report* Cmd 1655. London: HMSO.

Department of the Environment (1992(a)) *Planning Policy Guidance 12: Development Plans and Regional Planning Guidance* London: HMSO.

Department of the Environment (1992(b)) *This Common Inheritance: The Second Year Report* London: HMSO.

Eckersley, R. (1992) *Environmentalism and Political Theory: Towards an Ecocentric Approach* London: UCL Press.

Elkin, T. and McLaren, D. with Hillman, M. (1991) *Reviving the City: Towards Sustainable Development* London: Friends of the Earth.

Friends of the Earth (1989) *Environmental Charter for Local Government* London: Friends of the Earth.

Gibbs, D.C. (1991) 'Greening the local economy' *Local Economy* 224–239.

Goodin, R. (1992) *Green Political Theory* Cambridge: Polity.

Grove-White, R. (1992) 'How far can market mechanisms deal with environmental problems?' in South East Economic Development Strategy' (SEEDS) *The Seeds Green Plan Process*, Harlow: SEEDS Association.

Jacobs, M. (1990) *Sustainable Development: Greening the Economy* Fabian Tract 538, London: Fabian Society.

Jacobs, M. (1991) *The Green Economy* London: Pluto.

Jacobs, M. (1992) 'Sustainability and locality' in South East Economic Development Strategy (SEEDS) *The SEEDS Green Plan Process,* Harlow: SEEDS Association.

Lancashire County Council (1991) *Lancashire: A Green Audit* Preston: Lancashire County Council.

Local Government Management Board (1992(a)) *A Statement to UNCED on Behalf of UK Local Government* Luton: LGMB.

Local Government Management Board (1992(b)) *Earth Summit: Rio '92 — Information Pack for Local Authorities* Luton: LGMB.

Local Government Management Board (1992(c)) *Agenda 21 — A Summary of Contents* Luton: LGMB.

Local Government Management Board (1993) *Agenda 21: A Guide for Local Authorities in the UK* Luton: LGMB.

Owens, S. (1991) *Energy-Conscious Planning: The Case for Action* London: Campaign for the Protection of Rural England.

Pearce, D., Barbier, E. and Markandya, A. (1990) *Sustainable Development: Economics and Environment in the Third World* Aldershot: Elgar.

Pearce, D., Markandya, A. and Barbier, E.B. (1989) *Blueprint for a Green Economy* London: Earthscan.

Pharoah, T. (1992) *Less Traffic Better Towns:Friends of the Earth's Illustrated Guide to Traffic Reduction* London: Friends of the Earth.

Ponting, C. (1991) *A Green History of the World* London: Penguin.

Soussan, J.G. (1992) 'Sustainable development' in Mannion, A.M. and Bowlby, S.R. (eds) *Environmental Issues in the 1990s* Chichester: John Wiley.

Stewart, J. and Hams, T. (1992) *Local Government for Sustainable Development* Luton: LGMB.

Therivel, R., Wilson, E., Thompson, S., Heaney, E. and Pritchard, D. (1992) *Strategic Environmental Assessment* London: Earthscan.

Ward, S. (1993) 'Thinking global, acting local? Local authorities and their environmental plans' *Environmental Politics,* **II**, 30.

World Commission on Environment and Development (WCED) (1987) *Our Common Future* Oxford: Oxford University Press.

Young, S.C. (1993) 'Environmental politics and the EC' *Politics Review* **2**, 3, February, 6–8.

5 Decentralisation and area approaches

Initiatives aimed at particular geographical areas within the local authority are a common theme of urban policy. Various area approaches came to the fore in the 1970s. Decentralisation initiatives in different local authorities dominated the experience of the 1980s. In both decades initiatives were surrounded by rhetoric about bringing local government closer to the public and adjusting action to the needs of neighbourhoods. This chapter reviews the experience of the last two decades and argues that area or decentralisation initiatives should continue to play a part in the approach of city policy-makers in the 1990s. We begin by outlining the development from the area approaches of the 1970s, largely promoted through central government stimuli, to the more local authority-driven decentralisation experiments of the 1980s. This section explores differences of emphasis in the motivation of policy-makers in the two periods. The second section examines the main arguments for and against such initiatives. It concludes that area or decentralisation approaches tend to attract unreasonably high expectations but if they are seen as one part of a wider strategy they can make a valuable contribution. The scope and limitations of that contribution are then discussed in the third section of the chapter by reference to the most comprehensive decentralisation initiatives attempted so far — the radical experiment launched by the London Borough of Tower Hamlets in 1982. The concluding sections of the chapter review the main lessons to be learnt from past experience and indicate the way forward for decentralisation in the 1990s.

From area approaches to decentralisation

Policies that discriminate between geographical areas have a long history. During the 1970s there emerged into the political limelight a group of initiatives focused on relatively small areas or neighbourhoods. Many of these policies were explicitly designed to tackle issues of urban deprivation. They constitute, for the purposes of our argument, the establishment of an area approach as a main plant of urban policy.

In the 1980s area-based initiatives continued under the label of decentralisation. A useful definition of the type of approaches we are concerned with is provided by Hambleton (1978, p. 71):

> Area approaches involve gearing the planning and/or management of policies to the needs of particular geographical areas within the local authority and may involve delegating administrative and/or political responsibility for at least part of this work to the local level.

This broad definition captures the range of initiatives of both the 1970s and 1980s.

Hambleton (1978) provides a comprehensive review of the development of the neighbourhood policies of the 1970s. Substantial programmes developed in a range of policy sectors including: education priority areas, action under the planning acts, general improvement and housing action areas under the housing acts. Many of these initiatives emerged as a result of central government legislation. There was no overall strategy. Policies in education, housing and planning emerged separately from one another. The experience of initiatives in the United States played a part in encouraging the development of the area approach. The main rationale appeared to be that concerted effort in particular areas, backed by more flexible and sophisticated management would help in the battle against intractable urban problems. A complex mix of political and managerial motivations were at play. The overall impression was of a patchy spread of initiatives in different policy sectors pursued in relative isolation from one another. Indeed this characteristic of neighbourhood policies provided for criticism and response within the 1970s.

Hambleton (1978, p. 128) notes that 'a recurring theme in the development of the various area approaches [of the 1970s] has been the need to integrate separate policy initiatives'. The Shelter Neighbourhood Action Project, which ran from 1969 to 1972, expressed a strong commitment to developing a total approach to the problems of deprived areas of Liverpool in which it was based.

The same rationale played a part in Community Development Projects, the Inner Area Studies and the comprehensive Community Programmes. Those various central government sponsored initiatives sought to focus attention of the needs of a particular neighbourhood and provide a co-ordinated government response to its problems. The Area Management trials of the mid-1970s promoted by the Department of Environment, laid an additional emphasis on changing the role of elected members and enhancing their ability to perform their constituency role. Area management involved both decentralised administrative arrangements (organised often through an area co-ordinator) which focused on the needs of a particular neighbourhood, and a system of area committees composed of local councillors (supplemented by mechanisms for consulting the public). According to the Department of the Environment, area management could be seen as 'a means of adapting local government organisation so that it can respond more sensitively and effectively to the particular needs of areas. It is a means of identifying priorities and objectives at area level, seeing their relevance locally and putting them in their district-wide context' (quoted in Hambleton 1978, p. 131). The irony of central government sponsoring area management trials, shortly after overseeing a reorganisation leading to larger local authorities, was not lost on observers of urban policy in the 1970s.

The 1980s saw continued interest in the development of initiatives aimed at the needs of particular neighbourhoods. In contrast to the 1970s much of the momentum for such reforms came from local rather than central government. Central government began to put its faith in privatisation and market-based solutions to improve the effectiveness and responsiveness of local government to its public. Local authorities continued to experiment with public service reform. The label decentralisation came increasingly to be used to describe a range of local authority initiatives. Many initiatives focused on the decentralisation of service outlets within one sector. A survey conducted of local authorities in England and Wales in late 1987 and early 1988 found housing was the service most frequently delivered from decentralised offices. Social service patch teams were also common. The greatest growth occurred at the neighbourhood level with offices providing services to populations of less than 10,000. In 1980 only 9 per cent of authorities used neighbourhood service outlets. By 1988 this figure had grown to nearly 20 per cent. In the case of metropolitan authorities the rise was even more dramatic. Whereas in 1980 just under 20 per cent had a system of neighbourhood offices. By 1988 this had increased to 75 per cent. (Stoker et al. 1988).

The decentralisation of service delivery to improve access and responsiveness to consumers was in the case of some authorities taken a step further by schemes which combined a more comprehensive cross-departmental approach to service delivery with attempts at decentralised decision-making. Up to 40 authorities in the 1980s developed plans for radical decentralisation with large scale initiatives appearing on the ground in places as diverse as Walsall, Birmingham, Glasgow, Middlesborough, Manchester, Islington, Tower Hamlets, Rochdale, Basildon, Harlow and Edinburgh. Not all these schemes survived into the 1990s.

In this chapter we will pay particular attention to the experience of Tower Hamlets. In part this is for pragmatic reasons since one of the authorities has been involved in a systematic evaluation of the Tower Hamlets scheme (see Stoker and Lowndes 1991; Lowndes and Stoker 1992(a) and (b). But the focus on Tower Hamlets is also justified by the radical nature and scope of its decentralisation which transformed not only its structures of service delivery but also its system of political control. The traditional system of centrally-based committees and departments has been dismantled and replaced by seven decentralised neighbourhoods with considerable decision-making autonomy and responsibility for most services.

The Tower Hamlets scheme expresses in a radical form the solutions promoted by the advocates of decentralisation in the 1980s. Each neighbourhood covers two or more wards. A standing committee made up of the councillors from the area has been established in each neighbourhood and has prime responsibility for policy-making and overseeing service delivery. As the process of implementation rolled forward, each neighbourhood appointed a neighbourhood chief executive, and subsequently, staff to provide a wide range of local services. Both support staff and front-line service deliverers were relocated to the neighbourhood.

Neighbourhoods are responsible for housing, social services arts and information, parks and recreation, planning, enironmental health and other environmental services. They also have their own personnel, financial, legal and property management staff. Policy and community development workers are also present in the neighbourhoods. The neighbourhoods have the character of 'mini-town halls'. They are the primary units of local government in their area. As such they were able to focus a co-ordinated effort on the needs of particular neighbourhoods.

The system is premised on the neighbourhood having considerable decision-making and administrative autonomy. Indeed immediately following decentralisation three of the seven neighbourhoods fell under Labour control. After losing a seat in a 1988 by-election the Liberals retained overall control of the borough on the casting vote of the mayor, but four of the neighbourhoods became Labour-controlled. After the 1990 elections only two of the neighbourhoods remained in Labour's hands.

A central decision-making capacity, however, has been retained. A Liberal-controlled policy and resources committee (and associated sub-committees) exercises political influence at the centre. The posts of borough chief executive and treasurer (along with supporting staff) have also been retained. Against the wishes of the Liberals, but as a legal requirement, a social services committee and director are also in place at the centre.

The emergence of such a radical initiative in Tower Hamlets requires an explanation which is behond the scope of this book. In general it is possible to identify a complex of motivations that contributed to the surge in local government interest in decentralisation. Shifts in management thinking encouraged getting closer to the public (Peters and Waterman 1982; Local Government Training Board 1987). A political momentum was given by a concern to win public support. If public services were to be defended against spending cuts and the threat of privatisation from the Thatcher-controlled central government then they needed to be reformed and improved in order to gain and cement the support of the public. In other respects the propaganda surrounding decentralisation was similar to that of earlier approaches. The claim was that by getting closer to the public the responsiveness and effectiveness of public services would be improved. Only in a few cases did a more radical political philosophy emerge. For some on the new urban left, decentralisation was part of a new system of politics which would transform relations between the local state and local interest groups. Conflict and domination would be replaced by co-operation and democratic control (Beuret and Stoker 1986).

The last two decades have seen decentralisation and area approaches become an established element in weaponry of those seeking to tackle the problems of cities. Commentaries in the early 1980s (Hambleton and Hoggett 1984) perhaps over-emphasised the differences between the experiments of the 1970s and 1980s. Central government was the prime mover in the earlier period, with local government taking on the lead röle in the later period. The language of some decentralisation advocates in the early 1980s was more political and radical than anything that emerged in the 1970s but as schemes moved from the drawing board to implementation the langauge of justification began to have a similar ring to the managerial tone and more modest political ambitions of the 1970s. Moreover there are important elements of the experience in both the 1970s and 1980s. Both decades provide important lessons for decentralisation in the future.

The case for and against neighbourhood policies

In the late 1970s critics of the early initiatives with an area-based focus made a telling argument. They pointed out that the problems of areas often have their roots outside the immediate neighbourhood and reflect wider social, economic and political inequalities. A focus on a neighbourhood might provide some minor benefits to the local community but it runs the risk of underwriting the political motive of power holders to show maximum concern at minimum cost. Indeed these criticisms found especially strong expression in the writings of those involved in the area-based Community Developments Projects (CDP 1974). We accept the limits of a neighbourhood approach on its own. Plainly neighbourhood policies only make sense as part of a wider strategy to tackle urban deprivation.

What is the particular contribution of the area approach? Hambleton (1978, p. 138) provided an answer to this question in the late 1970s.

> [T]he spatial dimension remains important and public policy makers would be unwise to reject the value of various forms of area approach for they retain considerable potential for opening up fresh possibilities for change. First, they can promote new ways of learning about problems and opportunities in the city and the efficacy of current policies. They can cut across functional patterns of thinking. Second, they can bring important new perspectives to bear on the combination of processes which coalesce to give rise to our most serious problems of urban deprivation. Third, they can, by relating policies to areas which are meaningful to local residents, assist in the renovation of management and political processes at the local level.

Reflecting on the experience of the 1980s, Lowndes (1992, pp. 62–3) offers the following response:

> [A]rea-based decentralisation can bring gains in both managerial and political terms. The setting up of neighbourhood offices can create the conditions for increased efficiency, flexibility and customer-responsiveness. The setting up of neighbourhood committees can

create the conditions for a renewal of local democracy, in terms of the increased accountability of elected members and the greater involvement of citizens in local decision-making.

We follow both writers in stressing the potential improvement in political accountability that decentralisation can bring. Management gains are possible both in the service delivery aspects stressed by Lowndes and in the ability to see issues in the round, a point emphasised by Hambleton.

Neighbourhood-focused policies are not a panacea. As Hambleton (1978, p. 114) comments, area initiatives have attracted 'unreasonably high expectations as to their likely impact'. Further we accept that a decentralised geographical focus does not automatically have a positive impact. Rather it offers a range of new opportunities which can be exploited. '[D]ecentralisation is not a cure-all for the problems of local government. Decentralisation involves trade-offs which must be confronted and resolved (rather than wished away), if a local authority is to avoid the pitfalls and exploit the potential of area-based management' (Lowndes 1992, p. 63).

The debate about decentralisation or area approaches is too often conducted in absolutist terms. No organisation can or should be either totally decentralised or centralised. The issue is the balance within an organisation and whether it is appropriate to the goals and objectives given to that organisation. Further, much of the debate about area or decentralised approaches is conducted in the absence of systematic evidence. As Gyford (1991, p. 113) comments 'much of the evidence so far is piecemeal or anecdotal and the question of whether benefits outweigh costs may sometimes be a matter of political judgement'.

Our conclusion is that an area dimension or decentralisation has proved attractive to policy-makers in the past and is likely to prove so in the future. It does carry substantial potential advantages. However, it is essential to also have a clear understanding of potential pitfalls. It is a more detailed investigation of the potential and dilemmas of decentralisation that we provide in the next section.

The scope and limitations of decentralisation: an evaluation

The disadvantages of decentralisation revolve around the difficulty of turning potential benefits into an effective practice. Some of the key issues are captured in Table 5.1. We examine issues under four headings — organisational effectiveness, relations with service users, role of councillors and resource management — drawing in particular on the experience of Tower Hamlets but referring where appropriate to the experience of other authorities.

Table 5.1: Area approaches and decentralisation: the potential and the pitfalls

Potential		Pitfalls
Area-based integrated working replacing departmental divisions	Organisational effectiveness	Difficulties in defining areas
Variety and innovation in local service provision		Maintaining specialisms and recognising non-divisibility of some services
Seeing issues 'in the round' and providing new base for learning		Managing central-local and inter-local links
Increased responsiveness and accessability to user demands	Relations with service users	Representatives of user bodies
Participation of users in decision-making		Powers of user bodies vis-a-vis officers and councillors
Increased accountability, more in touch with local needs	Role of councillors	Parochialism and populism in policy-making
Greater involvement in monitoring services and action on the ground		Proliferation of meetings
Efficiency gains via devolved resource management	Resource management	Loss of scale economies
Drawing in resources from private, voluntary and other public sector agencies in a focussed effort	Costs of reorganisation	
	Allocation of resources to decentralised units	

Source: Adapted from Lowndes (1992)

(a) Organisational effectiveness

Under decentralisation, organisation capacity may be improved by the encouragement of integrated and innovative provision and new opportunities for policy learning. In the case of Tower Hamlets many oficers found working in the neighbourhood setting a liberating experience after years of operating in a relatively centralised bureaucracy. A survey of staff in Globe Town neighbourhood suggested that communication between staff within neighbourhoods appeared to be much improved with 78 per cent of staff describing their relationship across departmental boundaries as co-operative and friendly. The 'bureaucratic' mentality had been exorcised but there was among staff a certain unease about the system that has emerged. When asked to provide a description of the neighbourhood's management style the following responses were obtained from staff:

- only twelve per cent felt the neighbourhood exhibited 'bureaucratic management which stifled good ideas';
- about half settled for a description of the neighbourhood as 'boldly experimental, but with a tendency not to consolidate good ideas';
- a third opted for the description 'crisis management in an environment of chaos'.

These responses indicate some of the tensions created by the radical nature of the Tower Hamlets scheme. Operating at its best, however, it did create a sense of patch among staff. They felt able to grasp the issues confronting their area in the round. Local knowledge gave new insights and the smaller-scale provided by the neighbourhood focus helped to encourage a view that issues could be tackled.

Difficulties exist over how to define the geographical boundaries of area initiatives. Should they reflect administrative considerations, political constituencies or public opinion about local communities? If the last option is adopted it can be difficult to ensure that the definition of an area is meaningful to the variety of residents within it: the young, the elderly, families etc. If service delivery is decentralised it is important to recognise that some services such as highways are non-divisible. In all cases some specialist services will need to be provided on a non-neighbourhood basis. The judgment about what is appropriate will vary from authority to authority.

In a decentralised system effective channels of communication between neighbourhoods and along the neighbourhood-centre axis will be required. In any system of decentralisation there is likely to be a tension between the centre and the neighbourhoods. For this tension to have a creative impact it is necessary for the centre to recognise the desirability of learning from the neighbourhoods and spreading good practice between neighbourhoods. If the decentralised units cover only part of an authority's area or responsibilities then there is a particular danger that officials in the decentralised unit will find themselves on the margins of the mainstream thinking and operation of the organisation. The various difficulties that have been identified can be tackled but when planning decentralisation initiatives the role of the centre and relationship of the neighbourhoods to other parts of the organisation needs to be carefully designed.

(b) Relations with users

Responsiveness in service delivery to users is associated with decentralisation in at least two ways:

> Local offices are more accessible in a 'practical' sense because they are smaller and closer to home. They are also more accessible in a 'conceptual' sense because residents more readily identify with one multi-service local office than a range of specialist outlets.
>
> (Lowndes, 1992, p. 54)

Many local authorities have found the idea of a 'one-stop shop' a valuable one. In Globe Town, one of Tower Hamlet's neighbourhoods its 'First Stop Shop', located in the reception area of the main neighbourhood building provided not just a first point of contact with the public for all services but took on the task of advocate for the public. Its staff were involved in solving problems and progress chasing, tasks which involved close liaison with other officers, and the neighbourhood chief executive being drawn in on problematic cases.

The smaller scale offered by neighbourhood working makes it easier for local knowledge and contacts to be developed by officers. A survey of Globe Town staff in Tower Hamlets reveals the extent to which decentralisation was seen by them as creating a new relationship with users. Some 83 per cent of staff described themselves as working directly with the public. In response to an open question about what they most liked about working in Globe Town nearly a third of all staff identified the opportunity to work closely with the public in a flexible and responsive way as a key positive attribute. Staff generally believe that Globe Town residents have benefitted from the introduction of decentralised service delivery. Of those who chose to comment on how Tower Hamlets had changed since decentralisation the majority (61 per cent) felt that their relationship with the public was now more productive for the public. Some 53 per cent felt that decentralisation had led to better quality services and given the public a greater voice in decision-making. Only 15 per cent felt that services had deteriorated and less than 4 per cent thought the public had less say in decision-making.

Surveys of consumers also reveal a positive assessment. In Globe Town 50 per cent of residents felt that the council kept them well-informed about its services; 88 per cent found getting hold of the right officer easy and 73 per cent were satisfied with their treatment by the neighbourhood office. The figures for other neighbourhoods were not so positive. Globe Town's success reflects in particular concern to turn the advantages of a decentralised structure to the benefit of users.

A further dimension of changing relations with users is providing opportunities for participation in decision-making. Several of the neighbourhoods in Tower Hamlets offered new mechanisms for public involvement. In Globe Town an open advisory committee was established as well as several user groups for particular services. Islington's decentralisation scheme involved the establishment of neighbourhood forums. Birmingham, Glasgow and Middlesborough among other authorities have long-running schemes of decentralised public participation.

Two issues tend to be raised by the experience of neighbourhood or community forums. The first is the 'representativeness' of the members of the public that become involved. A difficulty in Tower Hamlets — and one shared in other authorities — is the under representation of ethnic minority interests in participatory structures. Councillors and officers are often aware of the problem but have found it difficult to provide solutions. The difficulty in this area may reflect a broader problem with decentraliation which has an exclusive neighbourhood focus. People's sense of effective community may not be based on locality but on identities relating to age, ethnicity or gender, for example. Equally, service-use may form a basis for community identity and organisation. Concerns may be as much borough-wide and shared as neighbourhood-focused and particular. This is not an argument against opening up a neighbourhood channel of communication but it does suggest that there should be an awareness of the need to also provide other routes for those interests not readily organised and expressed through the neighbourhood. The option of working with third force organisations discussed in Chapter 6 may be relevant here.

A second issue relating to neighbourhood participation has a familiar ring to it — uncertainty about extent and degree of power that is on offer to the public. Reflecting on neighbourhood schemes of the 1970s it was common for critics to challenge the extent to which real participation was on offer and how the result of neighbourhood participation led to the co-option of deprived residents 'into irrelevant talking shops bereft of real power' (Lawless 1981, p. 198; cf. Dearlove 1974). Such criticisms have not disappeared. Referring to the 1980s decentralisation schemes Cochrane (1991, p. 296) argues:

> They offer a way of integrating and better managing the troublesome classes left in the residual welfare state...It is accepted that these groups need to be given representation within the system, but their position within the hierarchy is clear. The key decisions about resources are taken elsewhere...

Table 5.2:   Requirement for successful public participation

1. Both the council and the public need to be clear about the purpose of the exercise from the outset; are the public being informed, consulted or more actively involved in decision making?

2. It is necessary to identify in advance exactly who is to be involved from amongst the public: are there specific target groups and do they have particular problems with attending meetings or understanding procedures?

3. A variety of methods need to be used to reach the public from large meetings to informal groups to opinion polls.

4. Where groups are being regarded as spokespeople for a wider constituency, agreement should be reached at the start of a 'test of representativeness': what counts as representation and who is authorised to act in that fashion?

5. Both the council and the public must accept that public involvement will add to the time taken, not only for policy-making but also for implementation.

6. Advance agreement should be secured on mechanisms for reporting back to those taking part.

7. The role of council employees must be clarified to all concerned, especially when they are involved in helping groups to formulate their views and to present their case.

Source: Manchester City Council (quoted in Gyford 1991, p. 74)

There is little point in denying that the power offered to residents through neighbourhood participation is limited. It is important to recognise too that there may well be a considerable amount of suspicion on both sides of the officialdom/public fence. The dilemmas are real and the best advice is to be clear and honest about what is intended. A checklist of useful questions and criteria drawn up by Manchester City Council's neighbourhood service committee is presented in Table 5.2.

(c) Role of councillors

The role of councillors varies in different decentralisation initiatives. The area management trials of the 1970s were unusual in offering new opportunities for councillors to operate in their ward constituencies. Many initiatives offer very little in terms of a new role for councillors but, in some cases, councillors have been given substantial area or neighbourhood-based decision-making powers. The Tower Hamlets case, as we have already noted, involved substantial political delegation and profoundly affected the role of its councillors.

For councillors in a Liberal-controlled area the system of neighbourhood decentralisation delivered:

- A sense of patch, so that councillors felt that their knowledge of issues in the area and policy options they faced had been considered enhanced.
- A sense of control, they saw more opportunities to direct and control the bureaucracy. The system was one that they could manage and in which they could establish a culture to guide decision-making.
- A good relationship with staff providing not only an opportunity to work with senior managers but also a wide range of more junior officers. Both councillors and senior managers comment on the closeness of their working relationship based on a shared understanding of local issues.
- An ability to take initiatives. Councillors were able to identify a particular concern or priority and ensure that the neighbourhood took action on it.

Councillors formed policy in informal exchanges with each other and with officers. Globe Town's Liberal Democrats found it unnecessary to maintain group discipline through pre-meetings prior to committees, so that the committees became arenas for debate and discussion. However, in general, policy was developed in more informal and mixed settings over a drink or lunch. In addition there were a series of working parties examining particular issues which involved officers and in some instances members of community, voluntary or other external organisations. Each councillor maintained a general interest in the affairs of the neighbourhood while the working parties and other mechanisms provided an opportunity to pursue an issue of particular concern.

Something of the style of Globe Town's concillors can be illustrated by reference to their approach to performance review. Detailed performance figures for various services were presented at each meeting of the neighbourhood standing committee. In addition, at annual 'away weekends' with senior officers, longer term service priorities and targets were established. However, a more informal monitoring system was also developed. One councillor undertook regular tours of inspection by bicycle with an officer alongside him, tape-recorder in hand, to note problems and service failings. Their findings were passed on to an appropriate senior officer who was required to remedy the situation or take action of some sort.

As these examples indicate, decentralisation can help councillors break from the treadmill of the formal committee cycle. Councillors' time and initiative can be freed, with the result that a range of new ideas and ways of working can develop. Decentralisation can encourage councillors to develop an approach which is outward looking towards residents as customers and citizens.

There were some costs involved in operating through a neighbourhood. The prime among these from the perspective of the councillors is the time and effort that is required. The strain of undertaking such an active political role while still facing work, career and family demands are considerable. Only one of the four Globe Town Liberal Democrats put up for re-election in May 1990. Turn-over was high in other areas.

For the lone Labour councillor in Globe town the experience of neighbourhood government was not as positive as that of his Liberal opponents. While access to information, officers and support for casework were adequate, the Labour councillor inevitably was excluded from a full involvement in decision-making. When Labour controlled the neighbourhood committee their councillors found themselves in the position of being both 'in government' and 'in opposition'. They recognised the opportunities available to take initiatives, but equally feared being co-opted into a system not of their making. The opportunity for Labour neighbourhoods to undertake service initiatives and develop policy preferences has been constrained by interventions from the Liberal-controlled centre (especially over land-use planning issues) and through having to work within Liberal-dictated resource allocations (which are viewed by Labour as favouring Liberal-controlled neighbourhoods).

To the outside observer other tensions within the neighbourhood system also emerge. First the neighbourhood system enhances the influence of councillors as individuals. They can become policy entrepreneurs and forces for change but equally the system allows them to pursue their own particular concerns or prejudices. At times the politics of Globe Town neighbourhood was overwhelmed with multiple initiatives competing and conflicting with one another. For some officers (especially those at a more junior level) the system encouraged overpowering political interference and resulted in confusing and conflicting demands from competing political masters and a changing political agenda. The very creativity that the system unleashed was in danger of leading to haphazard and unrestricted decision-making.

Naive populism is one threat. Parochialism is also likely to rear its head. In many respects healthy parochialism was what Tower Hamlets neighbourhood system was trying to encourage. However as Lowndes (1992, p. 60) comments:

> The danger of parochialism arises when councillors are determined to defend the interests of 'their' neighbourhood at the cost of a planned and equitable distribution of resource across a wider area. In Tower Hamlets there is a long-standing paper commitment to redistribute budgets between the seven neighbourhoods in the recognition that some areas are more seriously disadvantaged than others. However, the plan is being blocked by an unwillingness on the part of councillors to give up even part of their area's money to another neighbourhood.

The dilemma is a real one and of course finds an echo at the various levels throughout the political system, from community to international settings. One person's freedom may potentially be another person's constraint — a well understood dilemma of political philosophy.

Resource management

Decentralisation offers the prospect of increased 'value for money'. Local councillors, officers and people can use their detailed understanding to identify local needs and define priorities in a way that is both cost-effective and consumer responsive. The former

Chief Executive of Stepney Neighbourhood, Tower Hamlets comments:

> Flexibility in the use of resources was a major gain. Once the annual budget was fixed by policy and resources committees it was up to neighbourhoods as to how they spent that money — no references to a central committee were needed to move money between budget heads. Similarly the fixing of establishments and the filling of vacancies was for neighbourhood decision. This allowed money to be moved to meet locally determined priorities and posts, to be filled that were considered priority from a neighbourhood point of view. Flexibility even extended to allowing a carry forward of underspends from one year to the next, unheard of for departments in a traditional local government set-up. (Stoker *et al.* 1991, p. 375)

Decentralisation offers the potential of efficiency gains where neighbourhood units are given a substantial degree of autonomy. The centre allocates budgets and therefore has a role in monitoring expenditure but local offices need flexibility.

As Lowndes (1992, pp. 61–2) points out different possibilities exist for establishing such flexibility:

> Local offices could be given complete power of virement within their overall budgets; this would ensure that they were not tied to detailed budget sub-headings which reflect historic assumptions about spending patterns in an area. They could also be given the right to raise their own finance, perhaps through the managment of assets within their area.

All neighbourhoods in Tower Hamlets benefitted from powers of virement and extensive local control but the disposal of capital assets was a policy pursued with more vigour in Liberal-controlled than Labour-controlled areas. Labour neighbourhoods also found that other schemes aimed at raising additional finance were blocked by the Liberal-controlled centre. A former Labour councillor in Stepney comments:

> Our initiatives were hampered by the Liberal-controlled centre. Our major enironmental improvement on Stepney Green involved putting together a multi-funding package, dealing with three landowners, and trying to use planning gain money from an office development scheme. The Liberals who were councillors in the neighbourhood, [but a minority] abstained from supporting the initiative, rarely attended public consultations and tried to frustrate a local annual summer festival on the green. Finally, those Liberals ensured that the planning gain issue was taken to the centre on the basis that it had

'borough-wide implications. This undermined the initiative and our autonomy as a neighbourhood.

Other Labour neighbourhoods also found that, with respect to developments on which they expected to raise planning gain (in order to siphon into improvements or develop housing for rent), the system operated against them. Bow could sell wholesale, Globe Town could auction most of its high street shops to pay for estate improvement, but Stepney, the Isle of Dogs and Wapping had projects plucked out of their hands for 'borough-wide reasons'. (Stoker *et al.* 1991, p. 378)

The political tensions of the Tower Hamlets scheme might well find reflection in other areas yet the benefits of decentralised resource management in terms of flexibility over current budgets and the use of capital assets are clear.

A further dimension where decentralisation can offer potential benefits is by drawing together resources from various sources to provide a focused effort to tackle the problems of a particular area. Neighbourhood units can demonstrate a capacity to bring in funding from other public agencies and co-ordinate the activities of various voluntary and private sector organisations. Sponsorship or joint-financing of particular initiatives is possible. More generally there is the possibility of bringing together the effort of public, private and voluntary sector agencies in shared focus on the issues of concern to the residents of a particular neighbourhood. Health services, police, education responsibilities and social services may, through a neighbourhood focus, establish new and productive collaborative relationships.

In a full-scale, across the authority, decentralisation, the costs of decentralisation may come to the fore in the minds of policy-makers. The costs of reorganisation may include: new buildings or alterations to existing establishments; the appointment of new staff with relevant skills; the setting up of new communication systems, etc. Costs may also be incurred where decentralisation involves the loss of scale economies. It may take more staff, especially those with specialist skills, to provide services through a decentralised system. Numbers of administrative and managerial staff may also increase, although it is not necessary to see this as an inevitable consequence of decentralisation. Finally, in a full-scale decentralisation such as Tower Hamlets the allocation of budgets to the neighbourhoods can be a source of political tension and administrative argument. Should allocations be based on the historic cost of providing services in different neighbourhoods or should it be on the basis of need? Is the information available to facilitate the development of a fair allocation system? Dilemmas in relation to resource allocation are inherent in any organisation. Decentralisation does, however, provide a new set of challenges which can present considerable problems to councillors and officers alike.

The debate over resource management is such that evidence and technical argument only get you so far. Whether decentralisation is desirable or not depends ultimately on a political judgement. Are the potential benefits of efficient and effective service delivery sufficiently attractive that they outweigh the potential costs involved in reorganisation and the disruption of established patterns of service delivery? Comparing the costs before and after the decentraliation of Tower Hamlets provision is irrelevant given a wider concern with efficiency and effectiveness. The issue becomes more than input costs and expands to include the benefits delivered to local residents. Once expanded, the debate is very difficult to resolve by resort to evidence alone. Referring to the competing claims of the districts and counties involved in the reorganisation of non-metropolitan government in the 1990s, a Rowntree funded project concluded, after a careful review of the evidence, that it was not possible to suggest a straightforward and consistent link between population size, costs and effectiveness (Jones *et al*, 1993). This conclusion is valid for decentralisation within local authorities as well as the wider debate about reorganisation.

Decentralisation in the 1990s

The argument of this chapter has been that the benefits and pitfalls of decentralisation are contingent and not fixed. Decentralisation, or a neighbourhood focus, should be seen as strategy, as a means to a range of possible ends rather than a goal in itself.

First the choice is not between a centralised structure or a decentralised structure. It is important not to think in terms of absolutes but rather in terms of the overall balance that is within an organisation. The radical decentralisation of Tower Hamlets was flawed by its failure to clearly define the role of the centre and romantic notions of local power prevented a serious consideration of those issues that should have been reserved for the centre. It is essential to recognise that certain issues are of such strategic policy concern that the centre should assume borough-wide responsibility for their resolution. These issues would concern matters of economic development, race relations, large-scale land development, and revenue-raising in most authorities, although the mix will vary. It is important, to avoid tensions within the organisation, that the role of the centre is specified as well as the roles and responsibilities of neighbourhood units.

As well as having the strategic role outlined above the centre could in a decentralised structure have the following roles:

- a regulator, ensuring that neighbourhoods took into account appropriate legal, value for money and other considerations;
- a policy adviser, forming policy and then exporting policies to the neighbourhoods;
- a promoter of learning, drawing on the best practice of neighbourhoods and offering opportunities of learning between neighbourhoods.

In performing these roles it is essential for the centre to be sensitive and responsive to the autonomy of the neighbourhoods. The challenge is to achieve a balance between effective monitoring and unsympathetic policing, policy advice and dictat, and promoting good practice and recognising the scope for diversity. This balance was not achieved in Tower Hamlets and remains a central challenge to those committed to decentralisation.

What of the roles and responsibilities of neighbourhood units. What should they do? In terms of decentralised service delivery the following checklist of questions might apply:

- Are the problems of economy of scale overwhelming?
- Does the service have a neighbourhood focus that would lead it to benefit from increased local knowledge and an ability to 'manage things in the round'?
- Does the service involve overwhelming strategic concerns that require borough-wide handling?
- Will appropriate and qualified staff for this service be sustainable at a neighbourhood base?

Improving the quality of service is a complex issue. Decentralisation is one of the tools that a local authority could consider using but it needs to be assessed alongside other options. It may well be possible to encourage knowledgeable, accessible and customer-oriented staff without physically relocating them to smaller neighbourhood structures. On the other hand decentralisation does provide new opportunities to improve the responsiveness of services.

It seems unlikely that many authorities in the 1990s are going to take the Tower Hamlets route. The radical and comprehensive nature of that reform means than the number of full-scale emulators is likely to be small. Yet decentralisation issues remain close to the surface in local government circles. Reorganisation with its wider debate about the size and structure means that decentralisation remains on the table. Decentralisation may be already embroiled in this larger debate. For some regions, counties or districts, decentralisation may be a way of suggesting that they can achieve 'smallness within bigness' and match their structure to diverse local histories and cultures of their area. In other cases efforts at creating inter-authority co-operation may centre around a decentralised focus. A larger authority may offer to provide a neighbourhood platform in which it can work alongside districts, community or parish council and other statutory and non-statutory providers. In a city where the district authority is seeking new responsibilities and extended boundaries as part of its bid for unitary status, then decentralisation offers one way of managing change in an acceptable manner.

Beyond these pragmatic forces the broad appeal of decentralisation remains strong. It can improve service delivery. It does provide new mechanisms of political accountability. Above all it does enable policy-makers to see issues in the round and provide a focused attack on issues of concern to the residents of a particular neighbourhood. This last feature of the area approach came to the fore in the 1970s but was perhaps neglected in the 1980s. In the 1990s perhaps it will come to the fore again. The problems of cities, as we have argued, require multi-dimensional solutions and decentralisation can provide a strong encouragement to multi-dimensional thinking and action.

A final issue is the management of change. The Tower Hamlets approach might be described as the 'Big Bang' where everything is thrown in the air in the hope that it will land in a new, better order. Part of the explanation for Tower Hamlets' success in achieving change may well lie in the simplicity of the idea that drove many of the councillors and senior officers to pushing forward decentralisation. Their view was that by physically relocating staff into small-scale neighbourhood structures the problems of the authority were going to be largely resolved. The simplicity of this vision helped them to cut through doubts, obstacles and resistance from some in senior management, the trades unions and other sceptics. From the arrival in power of the Liberals in 1986 it took only two years for most of the main features of the new system to be put in place. Other authorities have adopted a more measured approach to achieving change either through a rolling programme or a number of pilot projects aimed at demonstrating that things can be done differently.

We support that few policy-makers will have the bravado or foolhardiness of the Liberals in Tower Hamlets. If what is envisaged is a process of experimentation or a flexible programme of decentralisation then it is crucial to learn one of the most important lessons of the past: the need for an embedding strategy (*cf.* Barnes and Wistow 1992). Experiments, pilots or partial reforms run the risk of being marginalised within the established service delivery and political structures of the authority. Once the initial enthusiasm has gone it may be difficult to sustain the commitment to innovation and change. A well-designed embedding strategy can tackle some of these issues by ensuring that changes become established within the incentive structure and cultural framework of the organisation. The strategy may require: changes in people's job descriptions; the creation of new co-ordinating posts; the championing of the scheme in the higher and lower ranks of the organisation; and a process of external review and publicity which reinforces to those within the organisation the value attached to the reform. The details are best evolved to meet particular circumstances but an embedding strategy will be an important part of the 'toolkit' of reformers in the 1990s.

References and bibliography

Barnes, M. and Wiston, G. (1992) 'Sustaining innovation in community care' *Local Government Policy Making* **18**, 2, March, 3–10.

Beuret, K. and Stoker, G. (1986) 'The Labour Party and neighbourhood decentralisation — flirtation or commitment' *Critical Social Policy* 17, 4–22.

CDP (1974) *Gilding the Ghetto: The State and The Poverty Experiments* Community Development Project Inter-Project Editorial Team, London: CDP.

Cochrane, A. (1991) 'The changing state of local government: restructuring for the 1990s' *Public Administration* **69**, 3, Autumn.

Dearlove, J. (1974) 'The control of change and the regulation of community action' in D. Jones and M. Mayho (eds) *Community Work One* London: RKP.

Gyford, J. (1991) *Citizens, Consumers and Councils* London: Macmillan.

Hambleton, R. (1978) *Policy Planing and Local Government* London: Hutchinson.

Hambleton, R. and Hogget, P. (eds) (1984) *The Politics of Decentralisation* WP 46. Bristol: School for Advanced Urban Studies.

Jones, G. *et al.* (1993) *The Impact of Population Size on Local Authority Costs and Effectiveness* York: Joseph Rowntree Foundation.

Lawless, P. (1981) *Britain's Inner Cities* London: Harper & Row.

LGTB (1987) *Getting Closer to the Public* Luton: Local Government Training Board.

Lowndes, V. (1992) 'Decentralisation: the potential and the pitfalls' *Local Government Policy Making* **18**, 4, March, 53–63.

Lowndes, V. and Stoker, G. (1992(a)) 'An evaluation of neighbourhood decentralisation: customer and citizens perspectives' *Policy and Politics* **20**, 1, 47–61.

Lowndes, V. and Stoker, G. (1992(b)) 'An evaluation of neighbourhood decentralisation: staff and councillor perspectives' *Policy and Politics* **20**, 2, 143–152.

Peters, T. and Waterman, R. (1982) *In Search of Excellence* New York: Harper and Row.

Stoker, G., Baine, S., Carlyle, S., Charters, S. and Du Sautoy, T. (1991) 'Reflections on neighbourhood decentralisation in Tower Hamlets' *Public Administration* **69**, Autumn, 373–384.

Stoker, G. and Lowndes, V. (1991) *Tower Hamlets and Decentralisation: The Experience of Globe Town Neighbourhood* Luton: Local Government Management Board.

Stoker, G. Oppenheim, F. and Davies, M. (1988) *The Challenge of Change in Local Government: A Survey* Birmingham: INLOGOV.

6 The contribution of third force, not-for-profit organisations

There are dangers that arise when the local authority...moves in, with its big boots and its grand intentions, to support local initiatives. An important part of the potential strength of initiatives and organisations at the base...is their independence from management or the state, and their dependence on, and accountability to, the people whose needs they express.   (Wainwright 1985, p. 7)

The aim of this chapter is to outline the growth, roles and value of organisations operating in British cities on a not-for-profit basis. It starts by setting out their emergence. It then examines the advantages and disadvantages of working through them. The heart of the chapter is an analysis of how they operate. This leads on to a discussion of how policy-makers can promote and support them. The argument is that beside conventional public and private sector organisations these public/private partnerships are, in effect, a third force. Many perceive these organisations as only operating in the context of social services. But they have a much wider, potential and are an unappreciated and underdeveloped resource that can be used to tackle urban problems.

The growth of third force organisations

During the late 1970s and the 1980s a number of changes took place around the boundary between the public and private sectors. Different, but inter-connected processes were at work. First there was the contraction of the public sector. One of the Conservative's main aims throughout the 1980s was to reduce the role of government. At the local level the impact of this strategy was clear. Limiting the role of Direct Labour Organisations; selling off run-down tower-blocks; deregulating the buses; and promoting Compulsory Competitive Tendering are all examples of the contraction of the public sector and of new market opportunities created for the private sector.

The second process followed on as a consequence. The contraction of the public sector created a vacuum, and led to the emergence of public/private partnerships. There were two distinctly different forms of partnership. To begin with there were private sector companies looking for opportunities for profit. Where prospects were uncertain they entered into public/private partnerships of many kinds with councils and quasi-governmental agencies. These urban renewal projects involved some kind of public subsidy to attract private sector interest. This reduced the net cost to firms, making it possible for them to develop projects on unlikely sites and earn conventional profits. Chapter 3 on entrepreneurial planning contains many examples of these urban renewal flagships and partnership schemes.

More important for this chapter though is the other kind of partnership, created as a result of the contraction of the public sector. This is the emergence of organisations running projects and providing services of their own devising. These organisations operate on a not-for-profit basis. This form of partnership involves charities, development trusts, community groups, voluntary sector bodies and a variety of other organisations. These partnership bodies bring together resources from the public and private sectors, and from various other sources. They represent a new breed of organisation that became increasingly common from the late 1970s through to the early 1990s.

As a breed these organisations represent a kind of cross between pressure group and a quasi-governmental agency (QGA). Briefly, a QGA can be taken as an agency set up by Act of Parliament, funded and steered from Whitehall, and directly accountable to ministers. In essence a pressure group is an organisation that stands outside government while seeking to influence it — without running candidates at election time.

The new breed of organisations we are interested in in this chapter are independent and outside government like a pressure group. But instead of trying just to influence policy-making processes, they get involved in implementation, in carrying out projects. Examples range from tenants management co-ops, through organisations running multi-purpose community centres, for pre-school playgroups, youth clubs and as OAP drop-in centres, to environmental improvement projects. They have access to public sector funds like a QGA, but they can raise finance from a variety of other sources and do not rely just on the public purse. They are detached from Whitehall like a QGA, but are not subject to ministerial direction.

Three particular trends stand out from the experience of the period from the late 1970s to the early 1990s. First, the model of the not-for-profit partnership organisation was used to channel resources to ethnic and other special needs groups like women and the disabled. This incorporates a basic underlying principle — letting local people define what is needed, and control the way services are delivered within their neighbourhood. Secondly, in cases like nature reserves and canal improvement schemes, the organisations involved shouldered long-term maintenance responsibilities. Thirdly, some of the more adventurous partnerships tackled a mix of local problems. Examples of these neighbourhood developers are the Eldonians in Liverpool, and Coin Street and the North Kensington Amenity Trust in London. The model was also followed in the spheres of the arts, training and community care.

These public/private partnership organisations take many different forms, but broadly speaking they have five features in common:

- Most register as charities and as limited companies. Being a charity brings particular benefits, like eligibility for some grants. Being a company also allows an organisation to trade, to earn income to help finance its activities. The key point here is that, in overall terms, these organisations operate on a not-for-profit basis.
- They tend to have a common structure. A management committee is formed. It appoints a full-time director and meets periodically to provide strategic guidance. This leaves the day to day work to employees and volunteers.
- They secure finance from a wide variety of sources. There are membership fees and earned income. There are grants and loans for capital and revenue spending from a range of bodies — the European Commission, Whitehall departments, QGAs, local authorities, companies, parish councils, charitable trusts and other voluntary bodies. Companies help in a number of ways: giving materials, seconding managers and sponsoring projects.
- In terms of geographical coverage some operate at the national level, but most focus on the local level. Some

partnership bodies relate to one or two local authority areas — like a Groundwork Trust. However most concentrate their efforts below this at the level of small local community or neighbourhood, like a housing estate for example. It is this kind of not-for-profit organisation that this chapter mainly focuses on.
• These public/private not-for-profit organisations have some degree of operational freedom. They function outside, and apart from all three levels of government — Whitehall, QGA and local authorities. However they are influenced by their links to governmental bodies and other sponsors. As a result the extent of their autonomy and independence varies.

These public/private organisations operating on a not-for-profit basis had become steadily more significant by the early 1990s (there is no comprehensive presentation of all that has happened. Warburton and Wilcox (1988) give a number of case studies. They operate across the increasingly hazy boundary between the public and private sectors as a kind of third force, supplementing the public and private sectors. The term third force organisation (TFO) is used here to refer to these public/private partnership organisations operating on a not-for-profit basis. The phrase the 'voluntary sector' is often used. This may cover housing associations, welfare groups and active environmental organisations. But the public/private not-for-profit model also fits lots of other organisations — the Groundwork Trusts, and the Business in the Community projects for example. So TFO is used here because it is more all embracing and less vague than voluntary sector. It also stresses the notion of a third force which can be brought to bear on urban problems.

Before moving on to discuss the advantages and disadvantages of promoting TFOs, an important distinction needs to be drawn between two types of TFO. Some emerge as a result of spontaneous initiatives at the level of a small local community. The neighbourhood developers and the housing co-ops are typical examples. Others begin as a result of government initiative — at Whitehall, QGA or local authority level. We are interested not just in how policy-makers can support the former; but in how they can act in a sensitive way to promote and stimulate the latter.

The advantages and disadvantages of promoting TFOs

This section looks at what TFOs can achieve and at the problems that working with them can lead to, arguing that the balance is in favour of the benefits. The benefits and disadvantages are summarised in Table 6.1.

The benefits

The first benefit that they can offer policy-makers, the first reason for supporting them, is that they can help tackle problems facing a local authority. To begin with they can be used to bring about one-off transformations or building schemes. These include building new or renovating existing housing; making wildlife areas, conducting clean-up operations, planting trees and carrying out a range of environmental improvements. TFOs can also be used to set up new projects in such spheres as channelling resources to minority groups, training, community transport, drugs, homelessness, the arts, recreation, and community co-ops. Tourism is another area where TFOs can be used to run information centres or museums. Beyond the one-off transformations and setting up new projects, TFOs are also useful because the management of schemes like those just mentioned can be handed over to them. This approach is most widely used in the social services as part of the mixed economy of care. In that situation, the council, TFOs and firms all contribute part of the service. It is there, too, with the tenants management co-ops and the maintenance of newly land-scaped areas.

Some of the most interesting projects are the ones that are not sector based, but neighbourhood based. These are the spontaneous, bottom-up TFOs emerging as a community response to local problems. It starts perhaps with a housing project, but people find that there are other difficulties facing the local community. This can lead on to the provision of a creche, to attempts to set up a training scheme and draw teenagers away from drugs into more constructive activities.

What is involved here is a lot of small projects. They can be carried out individually, vaguely supporting council policy; or for or on behalf of the authority. Individually as with the recycling of buildings, they are of limited use, but collectively they can have an impact of value to policy-makers. The creation and running of projects and the maintenance of schemes can be handed over to TFOs. Projects designed by local people to meet local needs can have an innate advantage over council designed services. Also if services are run by their users they can be delivered more effectively. The number of TFOs tackling problems faced by ethnic groups have grown considerably during the 1980s partly because of this factor.

Table 6.1: A summary of the benefits and disadvantages to councils that come from promoting TFOs

---

Benefits

---

1. TFOs help tackle problems facing local authorities:
   - through one-off transformations;
   - through setting up new projects;
   - through taking on maintenance jobs.

2. TFOs can help to change the investment climate:
   - through training schemes;
   - through environmental improvement projects.

3. TFOs help stretch a council's financial resources:
   - by bringing in a range of resources that are not available to local authorities.

4. TFOs help promote participation:
   - by mobilising people;
   - by getting people involved in implementation;
   - by creating a sense of pride in an area.

5. TFOs help with community development in deprived areas:
   - by drawing communities together;
   - by carrying out positive schemes;
   - by reducing the social costs of unemployment.

6. TFOs help create work:
   - through full-time and part-time jobs;
   - through training opportunities;
   - through voluntary involvement.

Disadvantages

---

1. TFOs experience unexpected problems:
   - some fail or have financial problems;
   - work can need re-doing;
   - they can overlap with other agencies;
   - they can promote divisions within communities.

2. TFOs can take up staff time:
   - on aftercare support;
   - on drawing up and managing contracts.

3. The benefits of TFOs can be difficult to measure:
   - the problem of justifying expenditure against conventional criteria.

Moving on from the way they tackle problems, the second benefit that TFOs can bring policy-makers is the way they can help change the investment climate. The St Helens Community Trust was founded in the early 1980s by Pilkingtons when it was conducting a rationalisation and investment programme. The money that was spent on training and small firms advice helped to make the town a more attractive place for small firm start-ups and inward investment.

The work of enterprise agencies, the Neath experiment, and the Business in the Community, One Town Schemes at Blackburn, Halifax and Finsbury Park are all similar examples. In these and other places, private sector resources were drawn into a public/private partnership organisation which tackled issues that were beyond the local authority's ability to confront. The Civic Trust has been building up similar experience in small towns like Wirksworth, Ilfracombe, Calne and Todmorden.

Sometimes a locally based TFO can fit into a big urban renewal project of the kinds analysed in the chapter on entrepreneurial planning. There are examples in places like Exeter of a TFO running a heritage project adjacent to a range of new private sector investment schemes. In that context it can also, by helping to lead, contribute to a more positive investment climate. The third benefit that TFOs can offer local authorities is financial. There are constraints on the sources of finance available to a council, and problems about getting Whitehall's permission to borrow. However, TFOs can draw from a wide range of organisations — approaching firms for sponsorship or groups and charities for grants for example. Also they can draw in public sector funds that might not be available to a local authority. In practice TFOs can save councils money. The local authority is making a small or nil contribution to the service that is being provided. Either that service would not have been provided, or the local authority can spend the money it would have spent on something else. So TFOs help stretch a council's financial resources. A council can provide services which it wants to, but which it cannot afford to.

The promotion of participation and community development is a fourth benefit that councils gain from supporting TFOs. Despite all sorts of approaches during the 1970s and 1980s, lack of response from the public to council attempts to promote participation by the public has remained a perennial problem. Some of the worst apathy is in areas of high unemployment and the inner city. This reflects people's view of 'the council', based on their years of experience of it.

TFOs can be used to mobilise people. Groundwork Trusts, for

example, liaise with local groups and sometimes galvanise them into action. The experience of TFOs in the 1980s suggests that people are more likely to get involved themselves if they are doing things themselves and seeing results — than if they are asked to a meeting or to fill in a form. Involving people in implementation helps overcome apathy and alienation.

Participation is also promoted where TFOs emerge spontaneously from communities. In these circumstances local people seek greater control over conditions in their neighbourhood. Local authorities can promote such participation by supporting environmental improvement TFOs by, for example, making grants available to encourage such activity. The spin-off here is that projects help create a sense of pride. People care about what they create and look after it, especially when it is close to where they live. Vandalism can sometimes be tackled in this way.

The fifth benefit that can come from supporting TFOs is the contribution that they can make to community development, particularly in demoralised communities ravaged by recession and job loss. Setting up TFOs in such areas to address local needs can help draw people together in response to the problems of decline. They can help unleash the skills, enterprise and enthusiasm of people who are not experts (Wates and Knevitt 1987). The skill base of the local community widens. People develop a stake — the pride factor — in their local area.

Part of the contribution that TFOs make to community development is the way that they can help alleviate some of the social costs of unemployment. TFOs involve people in projects. Projects can provide a structure for people's lives, a place to go, a reason to get up in the morning. There is some evidence that involvement in schemes, even on a part-time basis, can give people a sense of worth, of value, and help them come to terms with re-building their lives. It can help people get through the stages of recovering from a trauma like the loss of a job: the shock, the anger, the seeking and yearning, and the depression phases, all have to be gone through, before lives can be rebuilt and self-respect regained. There are many unquantified costs of unemployment — heavier smoking, debts, broken homes, depressive illness, suicide and so on. These create knock-on costs to the NHS and extra work for social services departments. Reducing a small proportion of the social costs of unemployment is of wider benefit to an authority, and to society at large.

Finally, TFOs do offer the benefits of jobs. Not vast numbers of jobs, but some full-time and part-time jobs are created — apart from the voluntary, unpaid involvement. Part of this is people acquiring new skills, whether they relate to practical conservation tasks or running electronic offices. Even if they are involved with TFOs for a short while, they take their new skills on into the wider labour market.

The disadvantages

However, it has to be acknowledged that the growth of TFOs has brought with it a number of problems. Some simply fail, become unreliable, and close down because of lack of support. Some can have unexpected problems. They might fail to become self-supporting, have funding difficulties and come back to the council for more support. In some cases the quality of the work is not very good. Some of the landscape projects or building renovations that were carried out for TFOs by the old Manpower Services Commission in the 1980s were criticised because they were not very well done and required further work. In some cases TFOs have taken on the maintenance of sites but have not done it adequately, or have dissolved leaving the local authority to step in. Some TFOs duplicate the work of others. This can lead to embarrassing conflicts. Some have been criticised for promoting divisions in local communities by providing facilities for one group of local people but not others.

The second disadvantage that can arise is the cost to the local authority because of the work that TFOs can generate. There is the staff time involved in helping to launch them, and then in providing aftercare where needed. Also officers have to draw up contracts where these are the basis of a TFO's contribution. Community care, for example, saw the development of a contract culture at the turn of the decade. Such contracts also need monitoring and enforcing. Yet, in the wider context of the development of the 'enabling authority', where councils are working with private companies and not-for-profit organisations, local authorities are developing the skills of managing contracts anyway.

The final disadvantage is that it is often difficult to measure the benefits that TFOs can bring. The above discussion highlighted the arguments about the benefits they can bring. But government likes figures. It is fairly straightforward to quantify the benefits that will flow from a City Grant Scheme — the private sector investment, the leverage ratio, the jobs and so on. Some TFO activity can be quantified along similar lines — housing association starts, or the numbers attending a community centre. But others are more intangible. It is much more difficult to measure the value of environmental improvment schemes, or of children learning about nature and animals from a city farm or a school wildlife garden. Equally it is difficult to put a value on involving unemployed school leavers in community woodland or building work. Yet it may help give them skills, self-respect and worth, and keep them off drugs and out of trouble.

The conventional approach to justifying public expenditure — used by the Treasury, and promoted by Whitehall departments — is that represented by the Audit Commission's three Es of economy, efficiency and effectiveness. The problem for local authorities is that TFOs bring benefits which can be difficult to measure against these criteria. For example, they channel resources to minority groups, they help change the investment climate, they involve local people, and they promote community development. The prevailing approach to public expenditure does not allow us to put a monetary value on such intangible, but positive, contributions. Meanwhile the three E's approach is being used by policy-makers to assess conventional local authority schemes with which TFOs are competing for funds.

The final disadvantage here is thus that TFOs offer benefits which are difficult to measure against the standard criteria promoted by Whitehall. There is a long term challenge here — to broaden those criteria and change Whitehall's conventional approach.

TFOs: an assessment

There have been examples of TFOs for more than a century. What was important about the 1980s was the growth in their numbers. In these circumstances there was bound to be a learning curve for local authorities trying to develop the skills of working with them. Some of the disadvantages discussed above come down to lack of experience at dealing with them. The discussion now returns to the principle of using them.

One of the central points of this chapter is to stress the *flexibility* of the TFO model. It can be applied to an area as big as an urban authority, or cover two or three, or even a county. On the other hand it can be adapted to quite small neighbourhoods or estates in a suburban or inner city situation. It can be used to channel services to ethnic, disabled and other groups neglected by more universal approaches. Authorities can take advantage of the model to help plug the gaps left by market-based approaches. Glasgow and Salford have used small housing associations, for example, to help provide low-cost housing to fill the gap left by the private sector and the shortage of the council's funds.

Another dimension of the model is promoting advisory TFOs that do not run their own projects. Their function is to help aspiring groups work out how they can launch their own schemes. The Community Technical Aid Centre in Manchester is a typical example of this type of TFO. It provides, usually free, architectural, planning and landscape advice to community groups that lack resources but have ideas about projects. For councils these advisory TFOs are worth supporting for two reasons. First, their dialogue with aspiring groups helps to identify the schemes that will take off thus weeding out the non-runners. Secondly, they develop expert knowledge which they use to help lever in grants from public sector bodies, charitable trusts and others. Their reputations for doing effective appraisals facilitates the involvement of outside funding bodies. It is cheaper and more effective for councils to support an advisory TFO than to try to fund lots of separate projects.

The ability of a TFO to supplement market-based approaches is what attracted policy-makers at all levels to the model in the 1980s. The TFO fits into the wider context of a city needing a balanced strategy — as discussed in Chapter 2. It can be used in situations where the market will not provide solutions and where the public sector cannot stretch its funds. It also fits into the broader concept of local governance, of councils having a central strategic role in drawing the contributions of all locally-based organisations together. The discussion now analyses the significant features of TFOs that policy-makers need to understand. Towards the end of the chapter the focus shifts to notions of empowerment and how TFOs can be promoted.

Understanding TFOs

The most fruitful way to look at why some TFOs achieve more than others is to examine the variety of resources available to them, and their most important features. The aim is to provide an overview of the resources and characteristics that all successful TFOs have in common. The six headings, shown in Table 6.2, that this approach provides can be used as a checklist to help identify the precise needs of individual organisations. These will vary according to the TFO's aims.

Table 6.2: Significant features that policy-makers need to understand

---

Key ingredients or resources
- people with a variety of skills
- physical assets of the right kind
- adequate finance

Key characteristics
- a formal structure that works for the TFO involved
- an efficient internal management system
- the TFO concerned is able to develop its own independence

Key ingredients

Firstly a successful TFO needs committed people with a variety of skills. An essential ingredient is strong articulate leaders capable of supporting each other, and of providing some form of collective leadership. Paradoxically enough, entrepreneurial skills seem to be important in running non-commercial organisations. Falk has neatly summed this up with the concept of 'social entrepreneurs' — people who use their entrepreneurial talents in organisations where the aim is not profit, but community benefit (Falk 1986). Many have observed that leaders need not only to have some kind of vision about the importance of the projects they are aiming to set up, but be able to convey their enthusiasm and sense of excitement. This helps attract supporters who, in their turn, become committed to the organisation. All organisations need members. Local support is especially important if it is a bottom-up, community-based TFO. Breadth of local support impresses funding agencies.

Between them the leaders and the more active members need to have a certain amount of political experience. They need not just have knowledge of how the political system operates, but experience of working with others to achieve common goals. This may come from the tradition of collective action, from involvement inside the unions, in ethnic politics, or in the peace or women's movements. It would be wrong to suggest that radical causes provided the only relevant experience. Involvement in more conventional or middle-class organisations can also be important. People who have campaigned in environmental groups against local planning authorities to protect their patch also have a wealth of experience to draw on, just as those who have been involved in the unions do. Similarly, involvement in apparently apolitical groups like the Scouts or Guides, Rotary Clubs, church groups or voluntary welfare organisations can be relevant. Donnison stresses the importance of the education provided by social and political movements (1988, p. 13). They:

> teach more than the techniques of collective action: they teach generous loyalties, capacities for self-sacrifice, scepticism about established authority, and the ability to handle conflict.

Whatever the scope of its support, a successful organisation also needs adequate skills. Different kinds of skills are needed to direct untrained enthusiasts, to manage staff, to organise the ordering of materials, to supervise building work, to let contracts, and to carry out other jobs. There is also a need for adequate professional skills, for example, to set up accounting systems, to advise small firms or other groups, or to design and carry out community architecture and landscape renewal projects. The skills needed will vary according to the nature of the organisation, but some — like financial expertise — are essential to all TFOs.

The core of full and part-time staff will be able to cope with running a project on a day-to-day basis. But when a TFO starts to expand, there will be temporary periods when a lot more people are needed. If the organisation is involved on a permanent basis with environmental improvement or similar work, it will always need extra pairs of hands. Members and sympathisers can be supplemented by volunteers, or people on working holidays with the BTCV. Survey work can sometimes be organised by teachers or lecturers from local colleges. This can have several pay-offs. It can identify or monitor local problems; it can be relevant to the students' work; and it can generate support for a local TFO.

The second resource concerns physical assets. These usually come in the form of land and property. One of the commonest examples is refurbishing a building no longer required by its owners. A disused church can be transformed into a multi-purpose community centre; or an industrial building into small units to let, and a training centre.

However it is not always necesary for groups to own assets. What is critical is getting *access* to land and buildings so that projects can be carried out. Tenants on run-down council estates can carry out housing and environmental improvement work; or provide social facilities in local authority owned buildings. Similarly, wildlife groups can establish and manage reserves on sites they do not own.

The third resource is money. A TFO needs capital finance to establish a project for building or renovation work; and revenue income to pay salaries and running costs. There are grants and loans available under many headings from organisations at every

level of government from the EC, through the Whitehall departments and QGAs, down through two tiers of local government to
the parish councils and their equivalents. The discussion of finance
in Chapter 3 is relevant to TFOs. There are also a range of national
and local charities that make money available.

Another source of finance is the private corporate sector. Big
companies make grants, offer secondees and give gifts in kind.
Discarded furniture or even computer equipment can save the
TFO having to pay for things it needs. Those running TFOs and
advising them need to understand companies' changing attitudes if
they are to exploit this resource.

There is thus a great variety of different sources of finance. TFOs
can tap into these in different ways. The skill is to mix and match,
according to different circumstances, taking advantage of what is
available. It is usually necessary to raise large amounts of capital at
the start to buy a site or a building. Some of the most successful are
the wildlife groups. They raise money from statutory organisations
including the Countryside Commission, English Nature, and local
authorities; and from wildlife charities like the Worldwide Fund for
Nature. Increasingly during the 1980s they were able to get
sponsorship from companies who were becoming anxious to be
seen to be green. Conservation groups have many members who, in
their turn, respond generously to appeals. TFOs in the arts field
also found that large sums could be raised from statutory bodies,
charities, companies and individuals.

There is always a dilemma with a TFO's initial project. Outright
ownership of some assets creates the need to raise what can seem
insurmountable amounts of money. Yet outright ownership of a
site may give greater freedom over the nature of the scheme. If a
building is bought with grants and there is no loan to service, then
ownership gives a TFO an asset against which it is possible to
borrow further money from a bank. This can help raise funds for
renovation. On the other hand, the advantage of renting or leasing
land and buildings, is that the hurdle of having to raise large sums
at the outset is removed. The disadvantage of rent or lease is that
the TFO has regular payments to make. It may also find there are
constraints imposed on what it is allowed to do with the assets.
Renting part of a building can provide useful revenue income for
example, but this option may be closed by a legal agreement.

Once a TFO carries out some of its capital projects it needs
revenue income to manage them — money to pay salaries, the
'phone and other running costs. One of the problems that emerged
in the 1980s was the need for financial security. Many TFOs put in
annual bids to the MSC or under the Urban Programme. However,

the point of some of these schemes was to get projects launched. To this end the money was available for up to three years. Therafter, projects were said to be 'time-expired', and were expected to have found alternative sources of income. This, together with the cuts affecting local authority expenditure, created a great deal of uncertainty. Many TFOs regularly spent the weeks at the end of the financial year dissipating valuable energy in a panic search to avert the threatened cut-off of public funds.

What successful TFOs manage to arrange is adequate supplies of revenue income to cover running costs. Sometimes it comes from one main public sector source, like the local authority. Frequently it comes from a combination of sources. There are annual grants from statutory organisations and charities. Perhaps there is a secondee from the private sector whose salary is paid by the firms concerned. Often there is regular income. Property can be let to other TFOs or small firms. Bought in items can be sold where there is a shop. A TFO's own goods can be sold, where there is a working museum for example.

Key characteristics

Adequate resources of people and their skills, the relevant assets, and necessary amounts of capital and revenue finance are not enough on their own to create a successful TFO. Those that ach-ieve their aims seem to have three other characteristics. The first of these features is some kind of formal structure that works for the organisation involved. Before discussing the ways in which the structure needs to work, the variety of TFOs needs to be stressed. The structure may be based on the concept of a democratically run co-operative, with everybody involved in the decision-making. In many cases there is a more hierarchical structure with a board making decisions and full or part-time staff carrying them out. In the case of big housing associations this may be very formally organised, almost like a private company. In the case of bottom-up or community-based TFOs there is often more democracy with members being elected to the management board. Sometimes sympathetic individuals are co-opted onto the board, and usually funding bodies appoint representatives to keep an eye on things.

What these structures have in common is that they work for the people involved. They provide a decision-making process that is acceptable to the leaders, members, supporters and others in a specific body. Next these organisational structures operate in an accountable way. Sometimes, in the more democratic ones this means the leaders are directly accountable to, and controlled by, the members. Sometimes it is a case of the leaders and the board being seen to be accountable, even though in practice they are left to make decisions and get on with leading. An important part of accountability is internal financial accountability. This involves regular financial reports to the management board or general meeting so that all members and staff can see what money is coming in, what money is going out, and what the forcasts of income and expenditure are.

One of the tests of an organisation's decision-making system and its accountability is whether the leaders can be controlled so they do not get carried away. TFOs just starting on their first projects need to base their decisions on the resources they have, or are likely to get. Leaders embarking on over-ambitious schemes and taking unrealistic decisions based on fantasies will create conflict and possibly the collapse of the organisation.

Apart from providing acceptable decision-making processes; operating in an accountable way; and being able to control leaders with unrealistic ideas; the organisational structure needs to be resilient enough to resolve conflict. At some stage there are bound to be arguments — between the management board and the members, between the management board and the staff; or between factions at all levels. Disagreements about accepting sponsorship, what to include in a project, or about whether to go for growth or consolidation, can all raise fundamental principles. Some leading figures may leave, or the organisation may even break up. The structure has to be resilient enough to allow the personalities involved to work through the arguments to agreed compromises.

The final point about organisational structures that work, is that they also have to work for outside agencies. Funding bodies for example look for formal kinds of organisation with secretaries, treasurers and other conventional offices. This is antagonistic to those advocating collectivist or more anarchic approaches. Members of a TFO may be happy to start without leaders or minutes and just have spokespersons and a collective memory. But companies, charities and councils tend to look more favourably on more conventionally run organisations. One of the reasons why outside agencies take this line is that if they give money to a TFO they will only do so in return for regular financial reports, and possibly a place on the management board. Financial accountability operates externally to funding bodies as well as internally.

The second characteristic feature of successful TFOs is having an efficient internal management system that ensures that decisions are implemented. Charismatic leaders who motivate others and attract support for their enthusiasms are often not good at the finnicky details that need attending to if their ideas are to be carried through. This creates the need for staff to oversee the development of projects and to set up and run management systems that work. This is necessary if a TFO's initial project is to be a success. An ambitous strategy will only succeed if it is well managed. The necessary mix of skills in an organisation will vary. TFOs running museums, or training centres, or landscaping, or housing renewal projects will need a variety of different skills. But this will always revolve around a core of organisational, project management and accountancy skills. Having staff is not sufficient by itself. The essential point here is that TFOs need efficient, reliable management systems if they are to achieve their aims and thrive.

Well-run organisations attract talented, committed people, often from within the local community. Successful TFOs need to be able to turn up new leaders when key people move on. The feature of an efficient internal management system thus links back to the resource of enough people and the relevant mix of skills. This avoids the situation where lack of people leads to deteriorating morale. It helps a TFO to grow and prosper, to evolve and cope with crises and not just to exist.

The third characteristic feature of successful TFOs is that they become independent and operate on their own account. Independence is difficult to measure. It is revealed by a TFO's ability to determine its own priorities and the pace of its development. Over-reliance on one source of finance can mean that a TFO becomes the pawn of some public sector body. On the other hand, raising money from half a dozen separate sources seems to help generate independence as the organisation has more scope to make decisions on its own. Less tangibly, independence can be seen by the respect given to a TFO by other local organisations, the local media and statutory bodies. This adds up to them becoming, in Donnison's phrase, 'a political force in their own right' (1988).

Independence has to be earned over time. It is not a resource, or something that can be bought. It emerges from an accumulation of factors. It comes from a way a TFO uses its resources to achieve its goals; from whether it has a structure that works and how it behaves; and from having an efficient management system so that it is seen by outsiders to be well run.

A TFO's independence is also related to the way in which it was set up. Some projects start as a result of spontaneous initiatives at the level of a small community. In contrast, other TFOs begin as a result of government, QGA or local authority activity.

The experience of the 1980s suggests that strong local roots are profoundly important, and that having them is a significant aspect of independence. When TFOs emerge spontaneously there tend to be leading figures who know each other, who are compatible with each other, and who have, to some extent, already established their reputations and authority in the area. TFOs emerge spontaneously, partly because there is already strong local support. This was identified above as an important aspect of the resource relating to people. This grows from strong local roots. It seems to help these TFOs become more independent more quickly than the top-down ones. The manner of an organisation's creation thus exerts a continuing influence over its ability to act independently and control what happens to it.

TFO's stages of development

When not-for-profit organisations are set up they do not stand still. They go through a series of stages. If local council policy-makers are to support TFOs they need to understand these processes. They are summarised in Figure 6.1. The first stage is the launch. A number of people come together, or are prompted to co-operate by some outside agency. They develop their ideas; they identify their aims; they register their organisation; and they make the necessary internal appointments. Big projects may require feasibility studies. The TFO's ability to move on from the first stage will then depend greatly on positive reactions to the feasibility report from potential funders.

The second stage is tackling the first main project. It may be the renovation of a building into a multi-purpose community centre. Inevitably there are difficulties, but this is when the excitement and the enthusiasm are at their height. With big schemes the work may have to be done in phases: these are often dictated by having to complete one part of the project before the cash for the next can be raised.

The third stage is the critical one because options arise. Serious differences of opinion frequently emerge. There will already have been disagreements. Some may have left before the action really started. Those that remained will have been united by their objective: their first main project. The first option at the third stage is to go for quiet consolidation: a city farm has been established, or a housing co-operative is a reality. The difficult part has been done. All that remains, if the project is viable, is the process of managing it.

The other option at the third stage is to go for growth. Some organisations, having carried out their initial ideas, begin to look around for second and third rounds of projects. It is often not realised when the decisions to expand are taken that the process of growth will change the organisation itself. This is because additional tasks have to be carried out. New projects lead to more day-time meetings with local authority officers and people in funding organisations. Getting money from a variety of sources means there are applications to write and redraft. Employing people, and perhaps getting involved with training projects, creates more and more paperwork. Accountancy skills become essential. Outside agencies require regular reports to monitor progress. Flocks of inquiring visitors have to be shown around. Leading figures will be asked to address conferences.

Fig. 6.1:   Stages of growth of third force organisations

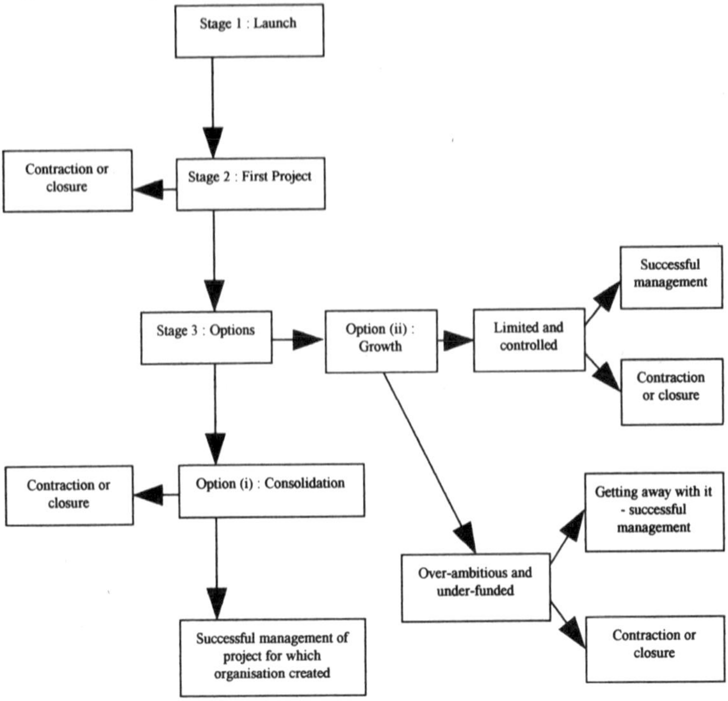

Nothing is certain: declining revenues, or lack of finance in a new financial year can lead to closure at any stage — even though it appears a project is being successfully managed.

The time pressures on the main characters, who still have to fit families, shopping and ironing, and possibly work, into their lives as well, can become acute. A group of friends swapping roles is replaced by full-time staff, the emergence of hierarchy, unclear roles, and the need to manage people. The originals, who revelled in getting their jeans on and getting their hands dirty, have to take on a new range of tasks, for which they may not be equipped. The nature of the organisation is thus transformed. Often this means that the flair, the imagination, the drive and the unorthodox approach that made the whole initiative possible, will die, stifled by internal bureaucracy and the formal, conventional approaches of public sector organisations.

There are other dangers with taking the growth option at the third stage. If the expansion strategy is too ambitious, new projects are taken on so quickly that the programme becomes underfunded and the organisation itself overstretched. In these circumstances there may be arguments rather than discussions. The result, as the consequences of over expansion become plain, can be broken nights and personal traumas, with external agencies moving in to reclaim buildings and to assert control. What is needed, if the growth option is taken at the third stage, is skilful leadership and effective management. These make controlled, step by step expansion possible. It is then more likely that the TFO will have followed the growth options through to running further projects, rather than be facing failure and contraction.

The chart sets out these stages of growth that TFOs go through. A model like this inevitably oversimplifies. The point of it is to draw out the main problems inherent in the expansionary process. But nothing is certain. A project that earns income may unexpectedly find that the revenue from its project is drying up. The cuts in local authority expenditure may suddenly mean more limited funds for the new financial year. Putting up entry fees as with a museum or sports facilities may lead to a drop in use and thus in total revenue. The model outlines what happens as an organisation grows. But each stage can end in contraction and a lower profile; or in closure and failure.

At any stage a TFO can be rocked to its foundations by conflict. It may be internal, as discussed above at the growth option under stage 3. It may be conflict with local people offended by the loss of some amenity so that a project can proceed; or disappointed by the services the organisation provides. Donnison argues that the leaders of TFOs are especially liable to be criticised (1988):

> Impoverished communities are normally oppressed by frustration, failure and powerlessness...They therefore contain a permanent charge of rage, waiting to be unleashed upon any available target. Their own more successful citizens are often amongst the more readily available.

Finally there are conflicts with a TFO's funding bodies. This may be because of conflict with local people, or because of disappointing progress and worries about commitments not being met.

Strategies to promote TFOs

The essence of the problem facing policy-makers is identified in the quote at the start of the chapter — how can they create conditions in which TFOs can prosper, even though the process of creating them is done in a top-down way? Policy-makers need to empower local groups. They need to feed in some of the missing ingredients to help release resources that are there, latent in the community. This will help to remove constraints on the emergence of TFOs. In order to follow this strategy, it is necessary to carry out a series of tasks, as shown in Table 6.3. In essence this is about relating the area concerned to the earlier discussion of key ingredients or resources that followed Table 6.2.

Relating to the key resources that a successful TFO needs

Identifying the area

First the area in which a TFO is going to be based needs to be identified. An outer estate is comparatively easy to identify. It is more difficult to decide what is a neighbourhood in an inner city area. The knowledge of ward councillors and officers will provide a starting point. But, if policy-makers are going to help bottom-up TFOs to emerge, it is important that they do not impose predetermined boundaries. Consultations with existing groups, attitude surveys, public meetings and other means can be used to help local people identify a suitable area.

Table 6.3:   The sequence of steps to be followed when creating a TFO

Relating an area to the key resources that a successful TFO needs
- identify the area
- define the needs of the local community in the area
- draw up an inventory of indigenous resources
- measure the available resources against the needs of the area: the emergence of priorities
    - people with skills ⎫
    - physical assets ⎬ See Table 6.2
    - adequate finance ⎭
- timing the launch for an opportune moment

Where organisations are being created to cover bigger areas than a small local community, different approaches will be appropriate. If a Groundwork Trust, or a canal improvement trust is being established for example, more than one local authority may be involved, and a range of other statutory organisations and existing groups will suggest themselves.

Defining the needs of the local community

The next step is to identify the needs of the local community in the area. Policy-makers may have ideas like lack of jobs or lack of training facilities. However, it is important at this stage to bring local poeple together in church halls or clubs, or in special meetings, for them to discuss their perceptions of what the area needs. They will be aware of local dimensions like the lack of facilities for teenagers. These are the kinds of details that will elude officials working in a town hall miles away and living in a quite separate area. It is also important to let local people define their needs, as it is the first step towards their creating something themselves. In some circumstances the process of identifying the area can go hand in hand with identifying local needs.

Drawing up an inventory of the indigenous resources

The third step is to make an appraisal of what there is in a neighbourhood, and to draw up an inventory of the resources that are available. These can conveniently be examined here by summarising the earlier discussion of the key ingredients that successful TFOs have. First, it needs a core of committed people with ideas about what they want to do, and supporters. If an organisation is claiming to be representative of the local community then it needs to be able to show it is. Secondly, a TFO needs access to buildings or land. Thirdly, it needs finance, and possibly goods in kind that save having to buy them.

Again policy-makers in a local authority can draw up an inventory of a neighbourhood's resources. But they will carry out their empowering role more effectively if the survey is organised and carried out by local people. This involves them in thinking about what their neighbourhood needs; and it is part of the process of the project becoming theirs. It will have stronger roots if local people *own the process.*

In this kind of situation officials need to act sensitively in providing support. This can come in the form of leaflets with suggestions. This approach needs to be supported with community workers or outreach officers being available to offer advice on publicity, organising meetings, and so on. General facilities can be useful. Bradford established a community arts centre, offering skills and facilities such as duplicating, print-making, photographics and video to local groups.

An alternative is to try to reach local people via other organisations. Many sports clubs are respected locally. Millwall FC is an example of a league football club involved in a variety of projects for local people. This has the added advantage that the resources of a big club are made more widely available. Other routes into the community are via local churches; and existing groups. Again these offer other advantages. Churches have buildings which are frequently multi-purpose or capable of conversion. As well as the part of the building set aside for worship, there is usually a hall for socials, for a nursery or youth club; a meeting room; and toilet, storage and kitchen facilities. In inner city areas such buildings are often the only place where people can get together outside their homes. Churches often have many links into the local community. Similarly, officials can exploit indigenous resources and attract support from local people when working through existing groups. Greening approaches in cities can be built around existing environmental groups. Finally there are the advisory TFOs described in the earlier section on the TFO model. These organisations do not carry out projects directly themselves. Instead they help groups of local people to design and construct their own solutions.

Measuring the available resources against the needs of the area: the emergence of priorities

After examining the resources that are there, the next step is to set them against the needs of the area, as perceived by local people. This is the difficult bit. There will be limited resources and lots of ideas. The job of the local authority is to look in great detail at how — directly or indirectly — it can help an aspiring TFO to identify its priorities and bridge the gap between its resources and its main ambitions. Run-down, demoralised communities need to believe they can achieve things again. One way that the local authority can support them in this is to get some extra manpower in: a British Trust for Conservation Volunteers team for example. They can be put in touch with advisory TFOs.

When it comes to assets, a local authority or government agency may own a building or a site that could be used by the community group for its project. Alternatively a local authority might be able

to buy it from a third party. It can be sold to the group for £1 as in
the Coin Street case, or leased at a commercial or subsidised rate.
A lease means that the public sector owner has ultimate control if
things go wrong.

Finance is obviously critical. Access to finance is also a maze. A
local authority can play an important role here in helping groups to
find their way to the specialist guides that are published. The best
way of locating up to date guides is to examine the latest
publications lists of the National Council for Voluntary
Organisations (NCVO), and the Directory of Social Change (see
p. 150 for these addresses). Also, officers can encourage groups to
apply for money. A number of authorities set up funds in the late
1980s and early 1990s from which they dispense environmental
grants. There are similar examples in connection with community
arts, housing, training and other policy spheres. A local authority
can also make its knowledge and contacts available. It might know
of commercial sponsorship opportunities in the area for example,
or the potential interest of a charity, or the Church Urban Fund.

One of the important features of finance for TFOs is the
complexity of it, and the way it has all become so specialised. If a
group wants to create a housing co-operative, a swimming pool and
leisure complex, an urban wildlife area or a training centre, then
there will be specialised sources available under each of these
headings. In these cases the Housing Corporation, the Sports
Council, the Countryside Commission and the European Social
Fund will all be of relevance, as will various other little known
organisations. It has all become so complex that some local
authority staff specialise in the process of fund raising from outside
sources. What local authorities can do to support aspiring TFOs is
appoint staff to liaise with groups as they are getting started. They
can then help the group review potential sources, co-ordinate the
grant applications and handle much of the paperwork.

Timing the launch for an opportune moment

Related to the process of creating and launching a bottom-up TFO
is the question of timing. This is an important issue for policy-
makers playing this empowering role. A straightforward example is
a planning authority giving a developer permission and trying to
impose a Section 106 agreement to get community benefits
included in a scheme. A not-for-profit trust may be needed to help
run facilities, like a creche or playgroup in a big retail development.
Here the moves to create a TFO would have to grow out of the
consultation procedures on the application. The local authorities

sometimes play a crucial role helping local community-based development trusts acquire land. Such projects would probably not proceed without the local authority getting the timing right.

Another example of getting the timing right concerns the need to act before a major closure takes place. Such a decision leaves the local community in a state of shock and disbelief. But one stage of the reaction process is a determination to fight back. After a big employer like a pit, has shut, local purchasing power is reduced and families are concentrating on surviving and adapting. It is difficult to take positive steps and create something when a community is demoralised. The same kind of problem is there in many inner city areas where the need to feed children and to survive leads to apathy.

The point about timing is to exploit whatever enthusiasms there are when an opportunity arises. There is a parallel with a town winning some sports trophy in a dramatic fashion. People smile at each other. They are more positive. Officers have to look for local equivalents. It may be pride in a successful arts festival or a local band. A TFO in one part of a city, doing well in a national competition for community projects, may inspire other groups in different suburbs to get their ideas together. Officials need to look for success and enthusiasm not just at the level of a city, but at the level of a neighbourhood too. Part of getting the timing right is exploiting opportunities like these. Local successes often throw up social entrepreneurs which helps tackle the difficult problem of finding leaders in demoralised communities.

There are also links here to the spin-offs that can be created by profit-oriented partnerships of the type described in the chapter on entrepreneurial planning. The ubiquitous water-side and urban regeneration schemes create frameworks which can be exploited to set up not just profit-oriented projects, but museum trusts, training centres, small housing associations and all the rest. In their turn, these add to the confidence being injected into the area by the profit-oriented schemes. Part of getting the timing right is thinking broadly and creating opportunities that can then be exploited.

It is more difficult to get the timing right if conflict is already there. There are more hurdles to overcome if a local authority is perceived by local people to have acted insensitively in trying to bulldoze ideas through in a top-down fashion. An authority bearing an olive branch with a cheque book in its back pocket will cause suspicions. There will be disagreements within the community, and probably between key local opinion leaders, about how to respond. There will be links from the wards affected into the local political parties, and perhaps into the controlling group within the town hall. In such circumstances the principle of letting local people determine priorities remains paramount. It is important that the authority steps back and lets local people own the processes — in particular identifyng their needs and determining their priorities. The emergence of a viable TFO can be smoothed if capital and revenue finance are put in, and perhaps some land. In the bargaining situation that arises new staff, unaffected by previous conflicts, may have more success at selling compromises or finding third parties to do so.

Reaching the launch stage

It is necessary to go through all these steps before deciding whether to create a TFO — identifying an area; defining its needs; listing the resources that are there; and appraising them in terms of local needs. At this point, a decision to go ahead would take those involved to the launch stage — the first of the stages in the development of individual TFOs discussed earlier on page 136. However, before a commitment is made a local authority should pause and consider a broader issue of tensions in the community.

The presence of rival organisations can sometimes complicate the approach of officials trying to promote TFOs. Clashes between key personalities in a community can become negative factors. The energetic, go-getting kinds of people who become social entrepreneurs can be abrasive and tactless, and alienate some people, even though they attract the support of others. The consequence for policy-makers is that in run-down estates, and amongst local arts groups and other not-for-profit TFOs, there may be rival organisations. It is often revealed by harsh language in the letters columns of local papers. This is a potentially dangerous situation. If each of the rivals receives support; resources are dissipated. If 'a winner' is picked and resources concentrated on it, the local authority will be abused in the local media for interfering. If the favoured TFO later runs into trouble or folds, the empowering authority is in a very embarrassing position. Even if things go right, there will be a legacy of mistrust in the area, which might affect community support for other things the council is trying to tackle.

Coping with this is difficult. The politics of the neighbourhood, and of the local authority; and the kind of personalities that are clashing, make every situation different. This is an important point for the local authority to look out for when a community's resources are being appraised.

Relating to the key characteristics of successful TFOs

The discussion so far on adapting ideas to local conditions has focused on the resources that successful TFOs need — people, assets and money. The analysis now turns to the key characteristics of TFOs identified earlier. First there is the need to create a resilient, accountable, organisational structure that can cope when things go wrong. An empowering authority can offer draft constitutions or legal documents on which to base the TFO. But, essentially people within the organisation have got to do this for themselves. The second feature is a reliable management system so that the TFO is well organised and run. Local authorities can insist on particular aspects of this as a condition of making money available — regular financial reports for example. They may also be able to act as brokers and persuade a company looking for places for secondees to send one to a specific TFO to act as project officer, accountant or site manager for example.

The third key feature of successful TFOs is independence. The essence of this is that the local authority or government agency has to let go. Independence is then earned as a result of a number of factors, and the way the people running the organisation behave over a period of time. It is not something that can be given like a grant. A local authority can make a limited contribution here. It can offer support and aftercare when the TFO runs — as it surely will — into choppy waters. This may happen if it goes for growth at the third stage of its development, for example. The council can pay its bills promptly too. There are some terrible stories of local authorities being as slow to pay as multinationals. Just as small firms need their bills paying promptly to avoid cash flow problems, so TFOs need their grants to be paid on time.

Other approaches to empowerment

The preceding discussion applies to attempts by local authorities to create TFOs based in their communities while acting in a top-down way. There are other kinds of TFO which need to be related to the principles outlined above. First, there are the genuine bottom-up, not-for-profit organisations which do emerge spontaneously from their neighbourhoods, and from communities of like-minded people. Helping them is much easier than trying to create something out of nothing. Much of the work of identifying needs and appraising resources has already been done. The principles outlined above can be used to help them grow through.

However, policy-makers will also want to create TFOs that do not need to be based in their communities. Organisations like the Groundwork Trusts, do not need to be as strongly rooted in their neighbourhoods as the community-based TFO. Such TFOs need to relate themselves to local people, but they are more specialised and operate across a bigger geographical area — a whole local authority and even beyond. Another example would be a trust to implement a study focusing on re-opening a canal. The principles involved in setting up TFOs like these are similar to those outlined above. It is necessary to go through essentially the same steps — defining the area and its needs; appraising the available resources; and identifying the missing ingredients that the empowering agency needs to inject to help get the emerging TFO to the launch stage. However, these organisations are more free-floating, and less attention needs to be given to plugging them into local communities. It will be necessary though, to consult closely with some pressure groups. Similarly, future conflict might be avoided, and resources might be deployed more effectively if there are discussions with existing county and city wildlife groups before an urban wildlife trust is created. With specialised TFOs covering a wide geographical area it is more difficult to find social entrepreneurs and people with time and knowledge to give, than is the case with organisations based at the neighbourhood level. Consultations with groups can help locate collections of like-minded people who may be interested in being involved — or a 'community of fellow-feelers' as it was once put on a live local radio programme.

Aftercare

One final point applies to all kinds of TFOs created or supported in an empowering fashion by a local authority. This is the question of aftercare. Not-for-profit organisations have benefits to offer, but many face a precarious existence. A common problem is lack of financial security. Guarantees that the wages of key workers will be paid for say, three years, are an enormous boon. Other problems will arise as well, and it is important for empowering agencies to retain close links with the TFOs in their areas. The conventional approach is to put councillors on the management committee. But they are busy people and the committee's meetings are unlikely to be a high priority for them. The papers for the meeting may not be studied. Even if they are, they may mask a problem which is becoming serious. It is thus more effective to keep in touch via officers developing personal contacts and getting regular reports which can then lead to discussion. Informal methods may be especially appropriate where TFOs are jealous of their freedom. In theory, effective aftercare support can be given without impinging on an organisation's independence. The important point is that it can help avert crises before they happen. Total withdrawal may be unwise.

Adapting the TFO model to local conditions

The local context provides the external environment within which each TFO has to start, and then to grow and adapt, if it is to survive and prosper. The local conditions consist of political, economic and social elements. They reflect the wider socio-economic changes taking place in cities. These local conditions influence the kinds of organisation that emerge, their relationships with funding bodies, the resources available to them, and their ability to put down strong local roots. The TFOs that survive in an area where pits are closing are different from their cousins in suburban or inner-city areas. The local context exerts a strong influence over the kinds of TFOs that are successful; and helps explain why they thrive in some places and not others.

The implication of this is that policy-makers need a detailed understanding of local conditions if they are to promote TFOs, and reap the benefits that this chapter has argued they have to offer. The problem for policy-makers is how can they create TFOs where they have not emerged but where they could be relevant and useful. The theme of this section is complexity and the need for local knowledge. It is not just the dynamics of how TFOs work that need to be understood. It is also the way that they fit into their economic, social and political environment.

The natural responses of policy-makers where initiatives are appearing in some places but not others is to take ideas and transplant them in other spots. In the 1980s the MSC, local authorities and others tried to promote ideas by transplanting them in a top-down fashion. A good example here is the interest shown in Mondragon in Northern Spain in the early 1980s. Local economic growth there had been promoted from 1956 onwards by the establishment of a series of industrial and service sector co-operatives, funded by a banking co-operative and strongly backed by the Catholic Church (Campbell 1977). This series of interlocking co-ops fed off each other and reinforced the whole process of growth in the area. It achieved a great deal of attention in Britain, but little came of many visits and much discussion. This reflected the fact that economic, social and political conditions in Mondragon were special to it, and that there are enormous problems with transplanting ideas into alien environments.

Gardeners know that two conditions have to be fulfilled if transplanting is to be done successfully — the soil conditions have to be right and the timing has to be right to get favourable climatic conditions. Azeleas like acid ground. If one is planted in limed soil outside in January it will not thrive. If the soil conditions and the climate are right, the plant will respond and grow, and put down strong roots. Policy-makers have to act sensitively. If they are to transplant ideas successfully they have to understand the local economic, social and political conditions which exist in an area. Only then will they stand a chance of getting a positive response from the public.

Important clues come from an inter-disciplinary study of economic and social responses to problems of industrial decline. Thompson has looked at how people in six different parts of Britain responded to the decline of the fishing industry in the twentieth century (1983). As it was a staple industry in the areas concerned its contraction led to growing unemployment and to other economic problems. He examines in detail the reactions over many years of six communities, varying from unionised ports to isolated, smaller settlement in North-East Scotland and the Scottish islands. He shows how differently these communities responded to the decline of the fishing industry. The result was that some areas coped better than others. The people of the Shetlands and the small ports of North-East Scotland for example diversified their economies far more effectively than the people of the Isle of Lewis or Aberdeen. He argues that this was not because of North Sea oil, but because of the resources and talents and attitudes latent within each community.

In trying to find the explanation for the different responses he stresses the influence of their different local histories. He points to the impact on each community of history, religion, geography, class, trades unions, and the extent to which the economy had a small firm base, or had been overtaken by the processes of concentration leading to a small number of big firms each controlled from right outside the area. He argues that the explanation for the different responses lies not just in the different economic circumstances, but in the local social, cultural and political traditions. He is pointing to the way in which responses to decline need to reflect local conditions and be rooted in them.

It follows from this that policy-makers need detailed local knowledge if they are to understand the local conditions in which they are trying to promote TFOs. People who know their patch well understand the extent to which local conditions vary in different parts of a city. The implication of the Mondragon and fishing examples is that successful TFOs can only grow from their natural base if they are able to develop strong roots and thrive.

This chapter has been constructed so as to help policy-makers relate their ideas for TFOs to their local conditions. The discussion on pp. 129–39 explains the dynamics of a TFO — the key resources and characteristics, and the stages of growth. The analysis on pp. 139–44 sets out a sequence of steps for policy-makers to follow. The aim of this section is to stress the importance of setting those steps in the context of a detailed understanding of local conditions.

TFOs in the 1990s

TFOs are likely to go on growing in numbers during the 1990s for a variety of reasons. To begin with the previous discussion has shown how they can produce tangible and intangible benefits for local people. Local authorities are also attracted by the financial benefits TFOs offer them. They help councils stretch their resources more broadly. The City Challenge schemes of 1991 and 1992 encouraged the wider application of the model. The establishment in 1992 of the Development Trusts Association to support and promote what this chapter calls TFOs should also encourage their growth.

The TFO model is also attractive to councillors of all parties. Conservatives like the idea of groups of people getting together to help themselves. It is also a fairly low-cost flexible approach. These aspects appeal to pragmatists in the Labour Party. The participatory dimension particularly attracts those on the left of the Party. TFOs make it possible for people to take control over parts of their lives so they are not dependant on an inflexible, paternalist state. In such cases, the spirit of the New Urban Left of the mid-1980s lives on. These dimensions of community and participation also reflect the values of the local government end of the Liberal Democratic Party. The Association of Liberal Councillors is more radical than the parliamentary wing of the Party.

The challenge of the 1990s is to explore the limits of empowerment. TFOs remain much discussed, but we need to find out more about what they are best at, and what their limits are. For example, the focus of this chapter has been on the links between the empowering council and individual TFOs. But one way to tackle problems in declining areas is to support a variety of TFOs. The argument here is that if neighbourhood development trusts, small housing associations, credit unions, a city farm, a multi-purpose community centre, environmental groups and others are supported, then they can trade, barter and interact with each other. This broader approach could help restore confidence to run-down communities, improve opportunities, and promote social and economic regeneration.

Despite their growth in numbers up to the early 1990s TFOs remain a largely unappreciated and under-developed resource. The extent of their contribution to the balanced city has yet to be revealed.

References and bibliography

Beesford, P. and Croft, S. (1993) *Citizen Involvement* Basingstoke: Macmillan.

Campbell, A. (1977) *Worker–Owner: the Mondragon Achievement* London: Anglo-German Industrial Society.

Donnison, D. (1988) 'Successful trusts' *New Society* 29 January, pp. 11–13.

Falk, N. (1986) Synopsis of address to 'Building Communities — First International Conference on Community Architecture, Planning and Design' unpublished mimeograph.

Thompson, P. (1983) *Living the Fishing* London: Routledge and Kegan Paul.

Wainwright, H. (1985) 'Sharing power: popular planning and the GLC' *Going Local?* No. 2, April, 6–7.

Warburton, D. and Wilcox, D. (1988) *Creating Development Trusts: Case Studies of Good Practice in Urban Regeneration* London: HMSO.

Wates, N. and Knevitt, C. (1987) *Community Architecture* London: Penguin.

Very little is written directly about how to promote TFOs. A number of groups promote participation and community development. The National Council for Voluntary Organisations (NCVO), Regent's Wharf, 8 All Saints St, London N1 9RL and the Directory of Social Change (DSC), Radius Works, Back Lane, London NW3 1HL, publish detailed studies of relevance. There is also an important role for the national umbrella body to play — the Development Trust, Association, 20 Conduit Place, London W2 1HZ.

7 Lobbying Whitehall and Brussels

It's all very well journalists and academics pointing to increasing centralisation. That's only half the story. The relationship between central government and local authorities is also about *dialogue*. We need the dialogue to get government policies carried out.

(Overheard in a lift in Whitehall)

Officials like to be pushed. It enables them to put pressure on ministers.

(Experienced lobbyist at a conference)

Lobbying is used in this chapter as a term to cover the attempts by local authorities to influence the detailed nature of government policies. In the 1960s and 1970s local authorities' main focus was on the Whitehall departments and their regional offices. In the 1980s their approach evolved, partly because Conservative ministers did not want to be bothered with attempts at special pleading. They also began to develop relationships with QGAs, and, increasingly, with the European Commission (EC) in Brussels. As an activity, lobbying consumed growing amounts of local authority resources during the 1980s. The facts that much of it is located in Chief Executives' departments, and that most authorities have European officers, are testament to the seriousness with which this job is taken. This chapter examines the whole subject from the perspective of the individual local authority, drawing mainly from interviews. The extent to which an authority works with other organisations — like the local authority associations — is incorporated into the discussion as it develops.

The aim of this chapter is to look at why some local authorities achieve more than others. Much of the writing about central-local relations is focused on the rhetoric of conflict between the centre and local authorities. This is understandable and indeed it does tell part of the story. Yet behind the most politicised and controversial aspects of inter-governmental relations lies a different, calmer and more consensual world. For those interested in broader academic debates this chapter deals with data that relates to the details of central-local relations, and in particular to the exchange of financial, political and informational resources in Rhodes' dependency model (Rhodes 1981). Implicit in the argument is the nature of the interdependence. There are also links to the writing about policy networks (Rhodes 1988).

The central message of this chapter is about complexity and the need for dialogue with the centre. So much of central-local relations *appears* from the media to be about confrontation. But in reality there is an intricate decision-making system involving a variety of people in a range of bodies, with the added complexity of different people in offices within a single organisation. Yet below the waves crashing on the rocks — where the media seldom penetrate — are the unseen waters. Here, as in the wild, there is a separate ecological system. Creatures are in competition. They fit into niches and co-exist. Things are worked out and a balance is achieved. Similarly much lobbying is unseen. At its heart is a complex dialogue between Whitehall on the one hand, and senior councillors and officers on the other. At any one time thousands of proposals, applications and other correspondences are being dealt with. This chapter aims to get at the complexity behind the headline-making exchanges.

The scope of lobbying

Local authority lobbying is mainly concerned with the details of implementing existing policy. There are some examples from the 1980s of local authorities lobbying to try to influence the policy-making process in Westminster and Whitehall — as over the abolition of the metropolitan counties, and the legislation that flowed from the Griffiths and Widdicombe Committees' reports. However, in general during the Thatcher era there were very limited opportunities for consultation over policy-making. The emphasis may have shifted in the post-Thatcher era but local authorities, on the whole, remain on the margins of policy formulation. The emphasis of this chapter, therefore, is on the implementation side. It deals with three aspects of lobbying.

Amending existing policy

This category relates to the situation where Whitehall departments and quasi-governmental agencies (QGAs) have schemes which only apply to some parts of the country. Local authorities lobby to try to get the boundaries changed. Typical examples here are the boundaries of the Assisted Areas which get regional aid, and of the areas where authorities are eligible for Derelict Land Grant (DLG). A second way in which authorities lobby to get existing policy amended concerns the detailed rules that govern some programmes. There have been many attempts since the mid-1970s to change the criteria by which DLG is made available to local authorities. One successful example concerns Hull. In the mid-1980s that council succeeded in persuading the Department of the Environment (DoE) that it should allow DLG to apply to water, as well as to land, so Hull could use DLG to help regenerate part of its docks.

Public sector finance

The second approach to lobbying involves the process of local authorities bidding for funds to finance all manner of projects — usually on the capital, not revenue, side. There are attempts to persuade central government departments to bend mainstream spending programmes, like housing and transport, towards areas where the scale of the problems is worse. Next, there are a number of government programmes targeted specifically at authorities coping with problems of decline, as with City Grant. The Government's aim here is to channel public funds to specific problems. For example, the £190m in the Estates Action programme in 1990/91 was targeted at improving the worst housing estates in the country. Some lobbying is aimed at QGAs like the Urban Regeneration Agency for example.

By the end of the 1980s some of these programmes were focused on very specific aspects of government urban policy. A scheme was introduced by the Department of Health in January 1989 to combat AIDS. Local authorities were invited to bid for funds to carry out projects to try to restrict the spread of AIDS. In July 1991 the Department of Education established a programme to tackle problems in inner city schools. This was not aimed at all inner city education authorities. Instead it was focused on schools where government promoted City Action Teams and Task Forces were operating. These were small geographical areas with some of the worst levels of deprivation and truancy in the country.

Opportunities in Europe

Lobbying in Brussels can also lead to amendments to EC programmes and help secure funds. Cities like Glasgow and Birmingham have done well out of Europe. Much of the finance relates to capital programmes. However the Objective 3 and the Objective 4 programmes on, respectively, combatting long-term unemployment and promoting jobs for young people involve revenue spending. These two programmes are available to all authorities. However, maps are attached to the Objective 1 and Objective 2 Structural Funds programmes. In early 1993 Northern Ireland was the only part of the UK included in the Less Developed Regions Objective 1 programme. The Objective 2 Industrial Conversion Areas programme is of greater relevance to British cities. In the early 1990s many authorities got involved in trying to influence the review of the Structural Funds and of the boundaries of the Objective 1 and Objective 2 areas. The EC has many detailed schemes and an acronym language all of its own. This is explained in a useful Audit Commission publication (1991).

The significance of lobbying for local authorities

The central point about lobbying activity is that it offers a legal way around the cuts. In the expenditure climate of the 1980s and early 1990s local authorities have found it difficult to fund projects and deliver services. Lobbying is about drawing extra resources in from outside. *The art is to devise schemes that use other organisations' funds at as little cost to the authority as possible,* beyond staff time. The Wigan Pier project received some private sector input and some finance from Wigan Council, but it was mainly launched with money from a variety of public sector sources — Greater Manchester County Council, the Countryside Commission, English Tourist Board, North-West Tourist Board, the Museums Service of the Arts Council, North-West Water, the Urban Programme, Urban Development Grant, DLG and the European Commission's ERDF. This chapter complements the chapter on entrepreneurial planning which explains how to promote major projects of this type.

But lobbying is also important in the context of combatting social deprivation as distinct from economic regeneration. For example, a local authority can use some of its money to attract extra resources from outside to improve run-down housing estates, as with the Estates Action Programme and housing association moneys, and the more controversial Housing Action Trust (HATs) scheme. There are important links here to the chapter on not-for-profit third force organisations (TFOs). It outlines ways in which community groups can be encouraged to get involved in landscaping schemes, training projects and so on. TFOs can draw on funds which are not available to local authorities. Working with and through TFOs thus extends the local authority's net as it trawls for finance.

The catch for local authorities lobbying for extra resources in the 1990s is that they have to largely go along with government priorities. The Thatcher and Major administrations have tried to limit general spending and to set up a variety of programmes to steer local authorities in new directions — like working more with the private sector. In this situation the more resourceful local authorities can reap rich rewards. Some are much more skilful at lobbying than others. Just ten authorities, including Dudley, got about half of the first 180 Urban Development Grants to be approved in the early 1980s. In the mid-1980s pragmatic councils like Oldham set out to develop programmes of projects that maximised the use of all these programmes. By the early 1990s left-leaning councils like Manchester changed tack and began to work more closely with the private sector. As competition for funds increases the development of successful lobbying techniques becomes more important.

The importance of dialogue

Whitehall's perspective

While it is true that the Thatcher and Major eras have seen a trend towards centralisation, the overall situation is more complex. Ministers know that central government implements very few of its policies directly itself. The private sector, QGAs, and not-for-profit organisations like the housing associations are all increasingly involved. But within the public sector, and in overall terms, local authorities still have an important role in carrying out urban policies. Their involvement stretches from the high profile issues of housing, education and social services, through developing ones like leisure and the arts, to less publicised functions like waste disposal and planning for the needs of women. They also have a central role in the push towards sustainable development and increased prominence for environmental issues discussed in

Chapter 4. Despite the limitations placed on their role in spheres like housing in the 1980s and education in the early 1990s, they still, in overall terms, retain significant responsibilities. They act as providers of services — as over environmental health. They act as regulators — as over homes for the elderly. They also act as enablers, enabling private companies and a variety of voluntary, not-for-profit TFOs to deliver services — as in the field of community care.

In this climate of change, central government relies on local authorities to play their role effectively. They have a big responsibility for the implementation of government policies. Local authorities are directly responsible for some policies and work in partnership with a variety of organisations to deliver others. Ministers know that the government can be damaged politically if policies it is promoting via local authorities do not work. Whitehall thus has a vested interest *in promoting a dialogue* so that it knows what is happening on the ground. Central government needs feedback to help smooth implementation processes. Powers can be clarified or even enhanced. This was the case in 1991/92 with the changes introduced to the planning system to meet the challenge of sustainable development. These are outlined near the start of Chapter 4. Schemes that face problems can then be amended, while programmes that are working well can be expanded. Sometimes good ideas can be picked up and applied more widely — as with Wigan's One-Stop Shop idea for high quality support service for local firms. Heseltine developed it further in 1992/93.

Dialogue is also important where there are controversial issues of high political salience. With the poll tax, and with measures to reduce homelessness in the late 1980s and early 1990s, the Cabinet was committed to particular approaches. Yet it needed to iron out the implementation difficulties in order to try to limit the political damage that was being caused. It tried to improve implementation by amending policy and funding more resources. Local authority lobbying, especially from Conservative authorities, was part of the wider process whereby information was fed back to government.

The Thatcher and Major administrations have both tried to involve the private sector in urban renewal. This has not been restricted to profit-making activities like house-building. In such fields as environmental improvements and training with the Groundwork Trusts and the City Technology Colleges, ministers have tried to encourage industrialists to take on a wider role (Fogarty and Christie 1990). Leading figures from business have become involved in public/private city leadership teams, as in

Aberdeen, and Bristol. Industry has its conventional links with Whitehall, as via the House Builders Federation. But the attempts to widen industry's involvement in tackling inner city problems has led to the involvement of private sector interests in lobbying Whitehall on these issues. Ministers are anxious to know how their policies need amending if their wider aim of extending industry's involvement in urban renewal is to be achieved. The private sector has thus become involved in working with local authorities in lobbying Whitehall during the late 1980s and early 1990s.

The perspective of local authorities

There are four reasons why it is worth a local authority's while to commit staff-time and resources to lobbying activity. First, there is the obvious point about finance. Local authorities can — as the Wigan Pier example above illustrates — extend the resources available to them by spending other organisations' money on their own schemes.

The next benefit is that lobbying can lead to an improved framework for an authority's own policy-making. Although local authorities often get nowhere, it is possible to persuade central government departments to alter the administrative arrangements for handling specific schemes. A good example concerns DLG in the early 1980s. This was aimed at improving degraded land so it could be sold or redeveloped, thus helping to generate further confidence. But local authorities found it was difficult to operate the DoE system within the rules. These necessitated preparing and completing schemes within a year. Local authorities were able to show the DoE that it could take two or three years to design schemes; to get the DLG applications submitted, amended and approved; to finalise the contracts; and to complete the schemes. As it stood, the administration of the DLG system was a discouragement to councils thinking of applying. Government attempts to promote private sector investment were thus being undermined. The DoE responded to this case by introducing a rolling programme for DLG applications for the big sites — like the Garden Festival ones. The more flexible rules made it easier for local authorities to retain staff; to develop a more even workload; to apply in advance for DLG; and to develop a rolling programme. In cases like these, lobbying provides feedback to the government which amends the administrative arrangements to create a more predictable and manageable policy-making framework for local authorities. By the early 1990s nearly a quarter of all DLG money was being processed through the rolling programme. This is a typical example showing how both sides benefit in cases like this. Also, of course, situations continue to evolve and Whitehall always wants further feedback. By 1992 it had agreed to allow DLG to be used for canal restoration projects, thus encouraging further applications for funds.

The third reason why it is worth local authorities lobbying Whitehall is that it is sometimes possible to amend controversial policies over the longer term. In the early 1980s the LDDC, with its emphasis on market-led planning, was widely criticised by local authorities and in the media. Chapter 2 discusses how the Government took no notice of all this until after a Parliamentary Committee report in 1988. Thereafter it began to appreciate some of the limits of the market; and the extent of inner city problems that were not touched by private sector led approaches. As a result LDDC was instructed to include a greater proportion of social housing in new developments; and attempts were made to steer the later UDCs away from controversy. The City Challenge scheme was created partly to take account of the criticism of market-led approches that they did not tackle many inner city problems. It remains true that City Challenge is only part of government policy towards the inner city, and that the emphasis remains on the contributions of the private sector. But the point here is that local authority lobbying did contribute to the process of amending government policy.

Focusing on Brussels

The final reason why local authorities commit resources to lobbying is because of the benefits to be gained in Brussels. To begin with, grants and loans can be obtained. However, there is the additionality problem here. Whitehall tries to prevent *extra* cash from Brussels from reaching a local authority whose scheme has been approved. A sum equivalent to what the authority has been awarded by the Commission is deducted from the overall amounts the authority is due to get from Whitehall. Next, the criteria relating to financial programmes are sometimes changed as a result of pressure. In the late 1980s some of the Coalfield Communities Campaign authorities persuaded the EC to amend the rules with regard to funds from the European Coal and Steel Community (ECSC) programme. Money was approved for housing associations in ECSC areas where less than half the households had working miners.

Lobbying Brussels also enables local authorities to bring indirect pressure to bear on Whitehall. There is a range of possibiities here. In 1991 Lancashire County Council tried to use the European Court to get the British government prosecuted for the sewage on Blackpool beach. Its aim here was to persuade Whitehall to get the National Rivers Authority to use its powers to get North-West Water to act. Other approaches had failed. The British government responded by committing itself to rectifying the situation by 1996. Meantime, the case was left pending as an implicit threat. The Coalfield Communities Campaign was more ambitious. In the late 1980s it tried to persuade the Commission to give coal a higher priority in its energy policy. It reasoned that this could have beneficial knock-on effects for British Coal and the economies of mining areas.

A final benefit to local authorities from being actively involved in lobbying Brussels comes simply from being there. Regular contacts and visits lead not just to getting to know people, the committees and the processes, but also to a familiarity with the changing debates, and the kinds of arguments that are likley to be successful as new policies emerge. This helps an authority lobbying for funding, and trying to get criteria amended. It also helps authorities promoting new ideas. For example by 1992/93 some authorities were starting to push the idea that the contraction of the defence industries could be assisted and diversification promoted if there was an EC scheme to address the issue. After all, they reasoned, there had previously been schemes to restructure local economies hit by redundancies in mining, steel, textiles and shipbuilding. For these authorities, intimate knowledge of evolving discussions in Brussels was of great value.

The nature of the lobbying process

Lobbying is carried out through the submission of papers to the EC, and to government departments and QGAs. The papers that are submitted fall into two broad categories. Some are straight-forward grant applications. Others are more ambitious papers making out a case for amending government policy in the kinds of ways discussed above. Lobbying papers come in all shapes and sizes. They can be less than ten pages, or, on complex issues, very lengthy. They can be cheap and cheerful; or they can be presented in a very glossy fashion. The emphasis in the discussion that follows is on those papers that are making out a case for amendments to policy, and not on the grant applications. The more complex of the latter do get drawn into this analysis though. The process of putting together a City Challenge application for example, raises issues that have to be considered when trying to amend government policies.

There is a lobbying process that is common to all situations. It begins with local authority submissions to QGAs, government departments or Brussels. The reply may be followed by a revised submission. In many cases this leads on to meetings between the local authority and the agency concerned. Such meetings take a variety of forms and are discussed at the appropriate point as the argument develops below. The lobbying process encompasses infinite variety, but the basis of the whole process is the lobbying paper.

The use of statistics in lobbying

A persistent theme since the growth of lobbying in the mid-1960s has been the importance attached to the use of statistics. The crux of the regional assistance case for example is the way local authorities use statistics to compare their situation with that of neighbouring authorities and others in a higher category. Part of this is showing how badly the authority is suffering when compared with the regional average. Comparisons help present the argument that an authority's needs are not being met and that it deserves better treatment. Arguments such as these earned new Assisted Area designations for some West Midlands authorities in the 1980s after their severe loss of manufacturing jobs in the 1970s. This would have been unthinkable in the 1960s, when the West Midlands was widely regarded as one of the most prosperous parts of the British economy. It was achieved partly because of the effectiveness of the lobbying papers in drawing out statistical comparisons to show the extent of the region's decline. In the early 1990s authorities like Luton tried a similar approach.

Statistics are also used by authorities to get across the details of a particular case. Proposals for housing schemes, for example, draw from the range of deprivation indicators. Bids for Estate Action money may be presented in a comparative way to show the needs of an estate even though that authority has already carried out renewal schemes on other estates. However, the main use of statistics in these situations is to get across the detail of the scheme being put forward. Using Enumeration District data it is possible to focus not just on specific wards, but to draw out the most deprived parts of individual wards. The principal concern of authorities mounting City Challenge bids in 1991 and 1992 was to use statistics to convey the detail of the groups being empowered; the number of people to be trained; the number of houses to be improved; the projections for a growth in home ownership; the amounts of private sector investment to be levered in; and so on. In the context of City Grant and similar applications, the ration of public to private investment, and the detailed figures surrounding that, have been particularly important since 1979.

Two specific problems arise with the use of statistics. To begin with they get disputed. One example of this is population levels in inner city wards. One of the side-effects of the whole poll tax saga was the way in which residents did not fill in poll tax registration forms or register themselves on the electoral roll, in the hope of avoiding having to pay their poll tax. When the figures from the 1991 census began to come through, some authorities tried to boost electoral registrations in order to prove that population levels had not declined by as much in some wards as the figures suggested. This is important because the population figure is one of the factors used by the DoE to work out how much RSG to give local authorities. The poll tax-depressed figures meant that authorities got less income even though their real population figures were higher than the statistics suggested. Manchester is but one example of a council that tried unsuccessfully to prove to the DoE that it had more residents to deal with than the figures suggested. This is typical of the situation where a bid does not work because the two sides cannot reconcile their different interpretations of the statistics.

Another difficulty that arises is the situation where some of the benefits of a proposed scheme are intangible and difficult to quantify. Landscaping and environmental improvements are a good example. It is fairly easy to argue for them where they are clearly part of a wider scheme — to improve an old industrial quarter or regenerate a run-down estate for instance. But the benefits from environmental improvements to disused canals are rather diffused. They can provide an extra leisure and recreational facility for local people. They can promote tourism which will have certain, rather hard to forecast, benefits for the local economy. If a circular link is completed, it is possible to attract extra numbers of boats. From the mid-1970s onwards policy-makers in Rochdale and Calderdale, the authority based on Halifax, were trying, step by incremental step, to reopen the Rochdale canal that goes from Manchester via Rochdale, Todmorden, Hebden Bridge, Sowerby Bridge and Brighouse to reach the River Calder, making round trips possible using the Leeds/Liverpool Canal and the Huddersfield Narrow Boat Canal. Part of the long-term goal of opening a canal up is to improve canal-side land values, and attract private sector investment. The end result of many private sector schemes is a clear contribution to the local economy. But it depends on progress building up over a number of years. It is difficult to translate this step by step argument into clear statistics.

Is lobbying a rational process?

The whole lobbying process is based on the assumption that White-hall is a rational society, that it will respond to a proven case. There are two particular sets of circumstances where this is the case. First, there is the case where local authorities are arguing that implementation problems are undermining the impact of a policy. The criticisms of DLG and the consequent move to a rolling programme cited above is a typical example. Second, there are the situations where a local authority argues it is being unfairly dealt with compared to other authorities. A good example here is the case of Bury's revenue spending for 1993/4. The DoE had worked out a figure for that authority using its Standard Spending Assessment (SSA) formula. The point here is that the SSA system is applied to all authorities nationwide. If it is to work it has to be seen to apply in the same way to all authorities. Bury argued that the DoE had done its sums inaccurately and that it had been dealt with wrongly within the rules of the system. It was not arguing that the system was unfair. It was arguing that the DoE had failed to apply its own rules to Bury's case. As a result Bury's figure was revised upwards.

But politics is politics of course. There are cases where the assumption that Whitehall will respond rationally falls down. This is particularly the case where proposals are judged in a vacuum, on their merits. In the SSA case there is a national set of 'rules' which can be seen to be applied. But in a situation like Light Rapid Transit (LRT) this is not the case. In the early 1990s about forty cities were trying to persuade the Department of Transport to help fund their schemes. Following the earlier success of the Tyne and Wear scheme, Manchester and then Sheffield were successful, but Birmingham's case was rejected.

Sometimes apparently good cases are turned down while weak cases attract Whitehall support. Here one explanation is that a political rationale comes into play. In the mid-1980s it was alleged that Birmingham attracted government and EC aid for its concert hall and other schemes partly because of the marginal West Midlands Parliamentary seats, which were to be important in the 1987 election. In a similar way critics argued that, once its closure had been announced, the Urban Programme was killed off in 1993 as quickly as possible with cash limits. It was alleged that the cases being advanced for a more sensitive approach to the damage being done to projects on the ground counted for nothing because they were electorally unimportant to central government.

Lobbying strategies for cities

Having looked at the nature of the lobbying process, the focus now shifts back to the local authority's perspective. Here it is taken as given that its strategy is to try to attract more resources from Whitehall and Brussels; and to lobby for policies that are more sympathetic to its needs. The aim of this section is to discuss how to marshall a good case and present it at the right place at the right-time.

Tactical considerations

The obvious initial point to make is to play the game by the rules. Applications for funds need to fit the criteria. This is not always straightforward. The criteria relating to flagship schemes like the Chatham or the Hull docks or Wigan Pier are more difficult to define because part of the point of helping schemes like these is to make an impact by changing the investment climate. The DoE looks at factors like leverage ratios, but retains some room for discretion.

A second tactic is to work out ways of involving private sector funds. In declining urban areas the dominating theme of the 1980s was that of extending the role of the private sector and limiting the role of the public — especially the local authorities. When Major took over from Thatcher this continued though perhaps not quite so prominently. Private sector investment is a critical feature of such schemes as City Grant and City Challenge. In effect there are criteria that applications have to fit. However there are other opportunities for involving private sector finance in infrastructure schemes — as distinct from conventional investment projects. Two transport examples stand out. First are the LRT schemes in Manchester and Sheffield. Second there are the cases where transport authorities have negotiated a contribution to a new road scheme from big retail firms. As the 1990s develop there will be plenty of scope for imaginative local authorities to lever funds out of private companies as contributions to infrastructure projects. This will enhance their ability to lever contributory funds out of Whitehall.

Promoting pioneering approaches is a third tactic in its own right. The Regional DoE encouraged Salford City Council from the start with its Salford Quays project. The Regional DoE knew that, from Whitehall's perspective, there was a particular value in a local authority carrying out such a scheme. It would be an example for other authorities to follow. The same was true of the first Simplified Planning Zone (SPZ). Derby achieved this — and succeeded in landing a £3m DLG to go with it. The council knew that the DoE would be anxious for it to make a success of the SPZ because it was a pioneering project. Experimental approaches of this kind carry a cost in that the authority involved is amongst the first into the situation and has a lot to learn as it goes along. But the flip-side of the coin that can be worth going for is official DoE approval. This can be useful when unexpected problems crop up.

The fourth tactic is to highlight arguments and figures that embarrass ministers. An example of this is homelessness in the late 1980s. The Thatcher government had virtually put a stop to building new council houses for rent. But the number of families who were in bed and breakfast accommodation was rising. The Government was accused of spending money without tackling the causes of the problem. Critics argued it was guilty of what it used to criticise Labour governments of — throwing money at a problem without producing a solution. In addition the numbers living rough on the streets in British cities were rising. This attracted criticism from the left that the Government would normally have disregarded. But in London, MPs, local authorities and others argued that the presence of the homeless on the streets, with the attendant threats of begging and theft, was alienating tourists and depriving London of money it could not afford to lose.

As a result of cases like this being put, the Government brought forward several schemes to tackle homelessness in 1988 and 1989. In the Autumn Statement of 1989 it also approximately doubled the amount of money available to housing associations. It had realised that providing low-cost housing was a positive way in which to answer the critics of the money spent on bed and breakfast accommodation.

Another way of embarrassing ministers is to focus attention, not so much on information about things they are trying to ignore, but rather on implementation problems over things that they are proud of. In the early 1980s ministers made much of the increased amounts of finance being put into the DLG programme. But local authorities succeeded in pointing out to ministers that the funding was not being spent as effectively as it might be. Ministers were embarrassed to find the DoE entangled in red tape at a time when they were preaching greater efficiency at local government. They were also keen to take the credit for the expanded DLG programme.

'Better targeting' and 'spending money more effectively' became insistent themes in ministerial statements in Parliament, at conferences and in the media. It follows that ministers are likely to be sympathetic in cases where local authorities are organising more effective ways of targeting the money that is being spent. Ministers will be attracted by the idea that the money on a particular programme can be made to go further. Whitehall is thus likely to be at least initially sympathetic to cases presented from this perspective.

The fifth tactic is to avoid asking for things that set precedents. These can present impossible problems for governments. The sale of council houses provides a useful example. It was aimed not just at urban authorities, but at rural ones. When the policy was being introduced in the early 1980s and authorities like Norwich were opposing it at all stages, there was a lot of opposition in rural areas. There, housing authorities argued that the sale of council houses would lead to a reduced stock for those needing to rent; and that the cost of the cheapest houses on the market would climb, putting them out of the reach of first-time buyers. This was especially the case in tourist areas where the second-home phenomenon would add to the demand for houses. But it was politically impossible for Whitehall to make exceptions to such a prominent policy. If it had exempted some authorities from selling council houses other authorities would have leapt in with all sorts of reasons why they too should be exempted.

There are two points to draw out here to illustrate the argument about avoiding asking for things that set precedents. First, if a precedent is created, it becomes administratively very difficult to hold the line and enforce the policy. This was why Whitehall steadfastly refused all the claims from Merseyside in the 1970s that its unemployment problems were so bad that it deserved to have a regional policy status on a par with Northern Ireland. Civil servants knew that if the precedent was established on the mainland, there would be a rush of similar claims.

The second problem for Whitehall about agreeing to something that sets a precedent is that it can involve ministers in serious climb-downs and loss of face. Councillors, Opposition MPs, and the media then use this to attack the Government. A good example here is the UDC in the London docks. In the early 1980s the local authorities affected by the LDDC complained bitterly about the way it was run. But this was a high profile government initiative and it would have caused acute political embarrassment if the Government had clipped LDDC's wings.

There may appear to be a contradiction between the fourth and fifth tactics. The fourth is to try to produce information that surprises and embarrasses Whitehall. The fifth is to avoid asking for things that set precedents because of the administrative problems that this can create, and the loss of face it can cause ministers. These are in some respects opposite sides of the same coin. In the case of a Conservative local authority that is pointing to potential embarrassments, the fourth is more likely to be relevant as there will be more pressure on ministers to respond.

On the other hand, asking for things that set precedents is deliberately used as a tactic by some authorities. First it was used during the 1980s by Liberal and Labour controlled councils as a means of attacking Conservative central government. Such authorities regularly made demands for more funds in order to avoid cuts in services, and to enable them to build new houses and improve the council's housing stock. This was used as a tactic to blame central government for the cuts and to attract votes at local elections.

The second reason for asking for things that set precedents is more complicated. Some authorities do it not so much because they hope to win concessions in the short term, but in order *to change the whole climate in the longer term*. They realise they are asking for things that will set precedents and cause problems for ministers in the short-term. But they do it because they hope — over a period of years — to change Whitehall's view. So the balance of the potential conflict over the fourth and fifth tactics can come down in favour of asking for what appears to be — in the short-term at least — the impossible.

An example of this from the 1980s is the Coalfield Communities Campaign (CCC). After the miners' strike of 1984/5 a number of the local authorities in the coalfields came together to form an organisation to pool ideas and experience, and to campaign for a better deal for the mining areas. On one level their demands were not too controversial: CCC authorities pressed for such things as more money for economic regeneration, retraining and environmental improvements, different policies from British Coal Enterprise and so on. But at another level they were asking for things that were politically impossible in the late 1980s: things like a higher priority for coal within a coal-oriented energy policy, keeping pits open, reductions in the imports of cheap coal, an ending of the subsidies to the nuclear industry, and a retreat from the moves towards privatising the industry. While Mrs. Thatcher was in Downing Street there was going to be little give on such issues, though the moves towards more nuclear power stations had been put on ice. But the CCC's long-term aim was to try to change the terms of the debate about the future of coal.

By the start of 1993 Major had replaced Thatcher. The Conservative strategy to close down more pits had been met with a public outcry led by Conservative backbenchers and supported by demonstrations in such unlikely places as Cheltenham. The aim of privatisation remained, but in March 1993 Heseltine announced a bigger regeneration package, and subsidies to help a dozen of the pits to stay open. Although a number of factors were involved, the amending of Conservative energy policy happened partly because of CCC attempts to change the nature of the debate over a period of years. What started as politically unrealistic demands were taken more seriously later when circumstances had changed.

A persistent theme of this chapter, elaborated earlier, is the point that lobbying can be at its most effective when a dialogue is established between a local authority and the centre. Now it may not have been the aim at the start, but with hindsight it can be seen that opposition to the LDDC led, in later years, to a dialogue about the issues concerned. The approach of the LDDC provoked a discussion about the role of UDCs that involved many others beyond the local authorities concerned. It reached out into parliamentary select committee reports and local government circles. When the subsequent rounds of UDCs were announced in the late 1980s civil servants spoke of creating 'benign UDCs' in order not to replicate the conflicts in the London docks. The LDDC was also instucted to work more co-operatively with the local authorities and to include a proportion of social housing in each scheme. The initial opposition with impossible demands helped spark off a wider debate about the nature of inner city policy. Despite the ministerial rhetoric, the later UDCs were rather different creatures from the first two. The demands had led to a dialogue, and a debate had emerged. The long-term result was an amending of government policy, with less controversial UDCs, and ultimately City Challenge.

Channels for lobbying Whitehall

The previous sections have focused on the content of lobbying documents. The main consideration, once one has been prepared, is to work out who to send it to. The choice is between concentrating on a direct approach, or using third parties to put your case.

The direct approach will usually be to the regional office of the government department the issues involves. Often this will be with the DoE but it may involve an industrial or employment matter for example. Regional offices have some delegated powers from the centre — ability to approve small DLG schemes for example. The initial contact may be with Whitehall if it is a big scheme. (For Scottish and Welsh authorities subsequent references to the Regional DoE should be read as being to the Scottish or Welsh Office.) In some cases the direct approach may be to a QGA if the issue is its responsibility.

The role of the regional DoE is slightly ambiguous. It is meant to be the objective advisor of the DoE in London, interpreting the seriousness of issues and the scale of problems in different authorities within its region. It is also meant to come to a view over competing claims from different authorities within its area — where the worst housing is, which are the best City Challenge schemes and so on. It is also meant to be able to compare conditions within its region with those in other parts of the country so there is a balance to its recommendations. However, there have been times when Regional DoE civil servants have been accused of 'going native' — of championing the cause of their region and forgetting the need to balance their recommendations with a consideration of comparative problems in other regions.

That criticism of 'going native' was levelled at the Regional DoEs in the 1970s. In his first period at the DoE in the early 1980s, Heseltine oversaw a number of appointments to the regional offices designed to remove the ambiguity. The aim in appointing these 'Heseltinies' was to resolve the ambiguity, and get the Regional DoEs back to providing objective advice. However, by the early 1990s, as the recession developed, unemployment climbed, and inner city conditions worsened, some detected a re-emergence of the previous approach.

The Regional DoE's role has two implications for local authorities. First, if it is convinced of the merits of a particular case it will argue those merits within the system. Its views will be taken very seriously in Whitehall. But the second point is that the lobbying authority needs to make itself aware of the wider politics of its Regional DoE's role. If it is seen to be going native at all, then an ear at court can be something of a mixed blessing.

These few paragraphs on the Regional DoE's role need to be related to the theme of creating a dialogue with central government. In reality an authority would not take a complicated lobbying document to its Regional DoE without discussing it informally beforehand. Contacts over the years build up. With the preparation of a revised structure plan or Unitary Development Plan (UDP) there are regular meetings discussing alternative strategies and different drafts. With major schemes too, informal meetings are used to test the water and discuss drafts before they are finalised. A typical example here is the Salford Quays case — cited in the preceding section under the pioneering experimental schemes tactic. The essential point here is that an authority's Regional DoE can be a very useful sounding board, a potential ally; which is why some authorities cultivate positive relationships with local civil servants.

The discussion now moves from the direct approach to using third parties to help bring pressure to bear. The way in which local authorities lobby the EC to try to persuade it to discuss new approaches with Whitehall was mentioned earlier. In some cases the two tiers of local government join forces. In some parts of the country there are strong regional groupings of local authorities — the North-East for example. The CCC, discussed earlier, is another case of authorities working together to press for more resources and different policies to address difficulties they each face.

The local authority associations (LAAs) do not take up specific issues relating to their members, but they do lobby Whitehall on problems their members are already dealing with. There were many examples in the 1980s concerning the details of the Poll Tax and revenue spending programmes. Another channel of influence is to try to seek wider support on a topic amongst other local authorities to argue a rational case so Whitehall will take the issue more seriously.

Another channel of influence is Parliament. MPs representing a lobbying authority in the Commons can be useful allies, particularly if they are backbenchers on the government side and sitting for marginal seats. Their links into the Whitehall machinery can be fruitful. Select committee investigations also offer lobbying authorities opportunities to develop their case and attract further support. The select committee reports that were critical of the first two UDCs in the mid 1980s link back to the earlier discussion of that controversy. Lancashire County Council took its concern about sewage on Blackpool beach into this arena.

What often happens is that what was a dialogue between an individual authority and the DoE evolves into a wider debate on an issue within a policy community. During the 1980s for example, a policy community on urban renewal emerged. It involved not just DoE civil servants and active national politicians, but planners and senior councillors from prominent authorities, managers from development companies, people from the UDCs, the LAAs, and Businesses in the Community (BiC); and others from academia, and from a variety of organisations and groups around the fringe like the churches and the Civic Trust. They debated the problems about who is benefitting from urban policy; and how it can be improved in specialist journals, at meetings and on the conference circuit. Some of the policy community debates seeped out into the national media. Questions about the future of run-down inner city housing emanating from the urban part of the housing policy community are an example. That was a fairly open policy community.

Some policy communities are quite specialist and closed. An example of this is the one dealing with urban ecology and the future of wildlife in urban areas. In the late 1980s, a number of authorities complained over cases of sites of wildlife interest being damaged by developers. Such sites were not Sites of Special Scientific Interest (SSSI) and of national importance, but were significant in a local context. However there was no means of protecting them. In 1992 the Association of County Councils drew from the policy community the concept of an order, like a Tree Preservation Order, which could be applied to such sites by local councils. In the same year Sutton persuaded the Association of Metropolitan Authorities to carry out a survey of its members on the same issue, and pushed a similar scheme of nature conservation orders. The complaints and the lobbying had widened into a debate which produced a constructive proposal to put to the DoE.

The point that comes out of this brief discussion of policy communities is that it is worth local authorities investing time to feed ideas into them, despite the problems with the lack of staff time. It may distract an authority from its own specific concerns and from developing a dialogue with the DoE but, if an authority is trying to amend Whitehall's view, this is the channel most likely to lead to change, albeit incremental change, over time. This links back to the earlier discussion about setting precedents and asking for the impossible. Local authorities can influence wider debates and promote change over a period of years by building contacts with people well placed within policy communities.

Moving back to the position of a local authority concentrating on lobbing the centre about its own case, the question of local support needs analysing. During the 1970s Whitehall seemed to lay quite a lot of stress on lobbying authorities developing broad-based local support for their strategies — cross-party support, county/district support, and some voluntary sector support.

That all changed in the 1980s. Government policies gave the private sector a more prominent role. As a result it became important for local authorities to build links with the private sector locally, lobbying them for their support. Harding puts it well. 'In contrast to the 1970s, pump-priming and infrastructural grants are more and more tied to the effectiveness with which local actors can present themselves as potential economic winners to Government' (1992, p. 231). The implication is that economic regeneration strategies need to be developed with private sector support so that they are taken more seriously by Whitehall. Government departments will be more likely to listen if they are convinced that local authorities are asking for what private sector firms need in their particular areas. A typical example is the private sector support for Blackburn's case for an improved link to the M6 and the motorway network. Other more detailed examples are to be found in such cities as Hull and Birmingham. In places like these, local authorities have developed structures for drawing private sector leaders and their views into policy-making processes (Harding 1992). Part of doing this is also to draw in the TECs, UDCs, Task Forces and other government agencies active locally, because they have already developed strong links with the private sector. Support from BiC has also been important in some cases.

The role of the private sector in supporting local authority lobbying is probably most advanced in the North West where the Business Leadership Team (BLT) emerged in 1989 to promote the long-term prosperity of the region (including Cumbria). It is made-up of the chief executives of major firms in the North West, comprising 30 business leaders. It is backed by a wider forum to which a range of companies, government agencies, local authorities and groups belong. Apart from helping to attract inward investment, it aims to address the infrastructure needs of the region; to help lobby for environmental and urban regeneration projects; and to develop an economic strategy for the region to put not just to Whitehall, but to Brussels. It has close links with the North West Regional Association of Local Authorities.

In the 1990s private sector support remains an important factor. Local authorities need to lobby private firms to draw in their contribution. But this is not universally the case. The final section of the chapter on entrepreneurial planning in the 1990s analyses the impact of City Challenge on participating authorities. The discussion then draws a distinction betwen *economic regeneration* aimed at new investment projects; and *social regeneration* aimed at training, housing and other problems facing local people.

In the City Challenge context the support of the private sector has remained central. But the DoE has also pushed the concept of empowering local community groups. The successful bidding authorities had to draw in local tenants groups, churches, schools, and neighbourhood based organisations. The DoE was trying to get away from the 1970s approach of consulting the local Council for Voluntary Services and having a voluntary sector representative on a committee. City Challenge has involved the bidding authorities reaching right down into communities at the neighbourhood level. Breadth of local support has also been looked for in cases where cities lobby for resources made available by organisations outside government. An example here is the competition to be Environment City that was established in the early 1990s. Leicester and Middlesborough were among the first winners. The central role of local authorities here reflects the argument in Chapter One — that elected councils are the only local organisations able to speak for all local interests.

European Dimensions

Before relating the principles underlying tactical considerations and channels of influence to lobbying the European Commission, it is necessary to pause briefly to draw out the salient features of the politics of the European Community. Mazey and Richardson have written about the processes involved where pressure groups lobby Brussels (1992(a), 1992(b)). Some of their findings are relevant to this discussion. The 1986 Single European Act strengthened the Commission's power to initiate policies. The scope and frequency of lobbying in Brussels by local authorities, groups, and industrial interests grew during the late 1980s and early 1990s in what became an 'unstable and multi-dimensional environment' (Mazey and Richardson 1992(b), p. 110).

Final decisions in the Community are taken in the Council of Ministers by ministers from member states, backed by their officials. Behind the Council though, is a rather diffused policy-making system. Power is dispersed within the Commission, with little horizontal co-ordination between the separate Directorate-Generals. This means local authorities have to link in at different points. Also the Commission is still developing regular procedures for consultations with interested parties. Several changes since the 1986 Act have made the Parliament more significant, giving the MEPs potentially a more influential role. The result of these developments is a more open policy-making system with multiple access points. The agenda-setting process is unstable. Also the Commission publishes proposals at an earlier stage in the policy-making process than the British government does. It is not as committed to its ideas at that stage in the way ministers are. There is more scope for discussion. If the policy-making process is well understood, there is scope to exploit it. The neatest way to learn is to follow the example of Strathclyde and Bradford and second people to the Commission.

Several of the earlier arguments about tactics are relevant here. The distinction made between applying for funds for projects and trying to influence the details of policies, transfers across to discussion about lobbying Brussels. Applications for funds obviously have to meet the criteria governing different Commission schemes. Part of that can involve private sector moneys. The EC is keen on pilot and experimental schemes, like those designed to achieve better co-ordination between economic and environmental goals. After being submitted to the Regional DoE, applications are passed to Brussels via Whitehall. In practice this means they can only go forward if they have government approval. It has to be remembered though, that, because of Britain's approach to additionality, successful applications 'save' Whitehall money.

The real significance of local authorities lobbying Brussels lies in relation to their attempts to influence the wider parameters of policy. During the late 1980s a growing number of local authorities developed direct links with Brussels. By 1992 about a dozen had opened offices there. Their aim is to try, over time, to change the details of draft regulations, the rules surrounding funding schemes, and the development of new ideas. Here too the theme about the importance of dialogue recurs.

On the processes involved in lobbying Brussels the Audit Commission has identified four main precepts (1991, pp. 32–4). These are repackaged here so they can be related to the previous discussion about channels of influence. With the direct approach to Brussels there is the starting point, not just of the need for officers to find their way round the small but complex Commission bureaucracy, but also of the need to learn the relative significance of the contact with regard to the issue being discussed. Mazey and Richardson stress the importance attached by officials to lobbying style, to the absence of the confrontational approaches sometimes adopted by groups (1992(b), p. 110). If a long-term relationship — and thus a dialogue — is to be established, an authority needs to acquire a reputation for expertise, reliability and trust.

A number of third parties can be used to bring pressure to bear on Brussels. The first to mention, paradoxically enough, is Whitehall (Audit Commission, 1991, pp. 28–34). This is important when an authority is involved in competitive bidding for European funds, as bids need government approval. Whitehall also has a reputation for being influential at the draft stage when regulations are being drawn up. The Audit Commission argues that it is important to spend more time lobbying in London than in Brussels. It develops a complex argument about optimising the use of staff time.

A prominent theme in discussion of lobbying via third parties is the importance of networks. This links to one of the main themes running through this book — and illustrates the arguments of the chapter on it. Some sub-regional groupings of authorities and transboundary links between them have emerged spontaneously. Also DG16 have actually sponsored the creation of twelve networks to develop different kinds of programmes. Two networks of particular relevance to this book are the Eurocities network, and the Quartiers en Crise network (Audit Commission 1991, pp. 38–40). MEPs become part of these networks, especially the most prominent in a sub-region. One particular problem for British cities is that in other countries there are actors at the regional level for the Commission to relate to. It was the lack of such an institution that led the Business Leadership Team in the North-West to develop the regional strategy discussed earlier. There is clearly a role, not just for cross boundary links between cities, but for regional groupings of authorities within Britain. Networks like these help generate policy communities. As the Commission is promoting networks, it is likely to be interested in what they have to say about its developing role to the local level. There are opportunities here for the more entrepreneurial cities.

Timing

Where authorities are trying to get policies changed, timing can be all important. Authorities are more likely to make an impact if they lobby when a policy is being made or reviewed, as for example consultations over the Assisted Area boundaries. Otherwise Whitehall has a position to defend. In the European context the Audit Commission stresses the need for authorities to get involved early on, not just when trying to influence new schmes, but especially where draft regulations are involved. The other point about timing relates to general elections. Apparently Parliamentary journalists constantly muttered 'chink, chink' during the couple of months before the 1992 election was called, such was the queue of ministers coming to the despatch box to announce further spending plans. In the same period a number of commitments were made to authorities in Greater Manchester, not all of which were dependent on the Olympic bid being successful. Opposition politicians argued this reflected the significant cluster of marginal seats in the conurbation. It certainly seemed strange in the context of the previous arguments between Manchester City Council and the DoE.

The approach and attitudes of Whitehall departments

The aim of this section is to look at what local authorities are doing from the perspective of those in Whitehall. It has been argued that while Whitehall needs the lobbying process to see how its policies are working out, it does not like to be caught out or embarrassed. Civil servants have to police government policy and control expenditure. Whitehall thus has a vested interest in maintaining existing policy. Bids for funds are judged by the criteria of the relevant scheme. Attempts to amend government policies are met by stone-walling tactics. But it has to be remembered there is a dialogue going on. Concessions are limited, but they are made in the kinds of circumstances described above.

During the 1980s and early 1990s a number of Whitehall techniques for containing lobbying activity emerged. Underlying these there is the key role of the Regional DoEs as the eyes and ears of the DoE itself. First, there is the process of announcing a programme, and inviting bids, as with the enterprise zones. Second, there is the process of hiring consultants to collect information and to come to an initial judgement about which authorities face the worst problems in a particular scheme. This was used in the Housing Action Trust (HAT) case for example.

Third, there is the trend towards setting up new schemes that reflect the Government's priorities. All through the Thatcher years, from the Urban Development Grants to the City Technology Colleges and the opted out schools, there were many examples of finance being available to councils submitting schemes that fitted in with changing Whitehall priorities. The general purposes money became less important. This was all part of redirecting authorities towards new ways of doing things, with the implication that, if they did not co-operate, there would be less money available. In some cases local authorities tried to ignore the scheme hoping they could get the money under another heading. The HATs were a good example of this when they were first introduced at the turn of the decade. The tenants, often with council support, conducted strong campaigns against them, voting the initial proposals out. Undeterred, the DoE kept money allocated for them in its spending programme. It reasoned that, as time went by, authorities would realise that money for modernising particular estates would not be forthcoming and that councils would put in applications. In 1991/2 tenants in Hull, Waltham Forest and Liverpool voted to endorse proposed HATs, and in early 1993 three other authorities were actively preparing schemes.

The DoE's fourth way of trying to control and direct all the energy that goes into local authority lobbying activity is competitive bidding, with the money going to the successful at the expense of unsuccessful authorities. This was at the heart of the first round of City Challenge in 1991 when 15 authorities were invited to bid against each other. Ministers liked what they saw. They felt that the competitive edge produced better quality bids. Increasingly in the late 1980s, people in Whitehall and the Regional DoEs had felt that there was a certain sameness amongst the Urban Programme submissions. Consequently, the second round of City Challenge in 1992 was opened up to all 57 authorities in the hope it would encourage a more original approach and more innovative ideas. It seems likely that this use of open competition as a means of managing local authority lobbying will continue during the 1990s. In 1991 the technique was used with some of the housing moneys (*Planning* 8 November 1991, p. 6).

Local authority reactions

Local authorities are faced with a steady restructuring of the ways in which discretionary finance is distributed. Apart from bearing in mind the tactics mentioned above, their response needs to encompass other points. Getting respected consultants to do evaluative studies and prepare schemes can add a touch of objectivity in Whitehall's eyes. Another factor that councils have considerable control over is processing the finance they get. Government departments and QGAs are sympathetic to authorities that establish a good record for getting money spent.

Of greatest importance during the early 1990s though, is demonstrating private sector support. The 1980s saw moves away from the 1970s approach of allocating funds on the basis of social indicators. In some circumstances — as with some of the housing money — they are still used. Similarly, broad community support for an authority's lobbying approach can still be important — as with City Challenge. But Harding (1992) is right to argue that private sector support for discretionary infrastructure type money is the most significant factor. For bidding authorities, building links and creating structures that help generate such support is becoming increasingly significant.

The lobbying process is largely handled by officers and civil servants, but ministers get involved in judging the details of big or controversial projects, taking over discussions where official channels break down. The idea of allocating a friendly minister to each major city also encouraged the process of issues being taken from the official onto the political network. Authorities have to be ready to handle the shift in gear that this involves.

Contact with ministers comes via visits and delegations. Increasingly it seems ministers are helicoptered in to open projects, and to have their photos taken against the background of successful schemes that their departments have funded. People involved say these visits can be very useful because of the informal contact with officials as well as ministers. There are opportunities to talk about the chance of funding a second phase; or about the development of a new project. Delegations on the Intercity 125 to London do not often win concessions. But they can still be valuable in terms of publicity. Also those with experience say it is well worth meeting ministers with closed minds because it is then possible to see whether the minister is in command of the issues, or relies on his or her officials. That is useful intelligence to gain which helps determine future tactics while that person is a minister. To make that approach work though, the members of a delegation have to make sure they do not talk too much. This ensures the minister has space to reveal the extent and limitations of his or her knowledge and ideas.

Lobbying in the 1990s

Visits and delegations are also part of the central argument of this chapter — the need to establish a dialogue. Major changes are only rarely achieved, as in 1977 over inner-city policy. The inner-city White Paper named five partnerships as authorities due to get extra resources. Urban councils from all over the country objected. As a result of this lobbying, Whitehall created two more partnerships and named 15 programme authorities and 14 designated districts. Suddenly the lobbying process had widened the number of specially favoured authorities from 10 to 43. But major change is an untypical Whitehall response.

Dialogue is used in this chapter in two situations. First, there are examples where policy is amended over time because of pressure from many quarters. A new decision-making climate is created.

Second, there are the specific concerns of an individual authority. Trafford's case illustrates what can be achieved. In the early 1980s that council bid for an enterprise zone, and for partnership status with Manchester and Salford. It was refused the latter. It complained to Mrs Thatcher and to ministers, presenting its credentials as working towards government priorities. Following the loss of manufacturing jobs in the early 1980s, it set up a study of the local economy with the participation of local private sector interests. It argued for a development agency. Throughout a dialogue had been maintained with the centre. When the second round of UDCs was announced in 1986, Trafford was ideally placed to receive one. It came because of the dialogue, although that goal could not have been foreseen as the dialogue was continuing. Barnsley was the only authority to win in both rounds of City Challenge. This reflected the successful establishment of a dialogue with the Regional DoE.

Lobbying is at its most effective when a dialogue is established and maintained. It sometimes produces concessions. But more important is its impact over time when it leads to a changed framework within which authorities make decisions. In the environment sphere, the creation of the Central and Local Government Environment Forum in 1992 marked a recognition of the value of dialogue, and its institutionalisation. Whitehall had recognised it needed to learn from the experience of local government. The political rhetoric and the media headlines about conflict will continue. But with regard to discretionary finance and the evolution of policies it is what happens where the media seldom penetrates that matters. This chapter has provided some new insights into this hidden world of lobbying.

References and bibliography

Audit Commission (1991) *A Rough Guide to Europe: Local Authorities and the EC* London: HMSO.

Fogarty, M. and Christie, I. (1990) *Companies and Communities: Promoting Business Involvement in the Community* London: Policy Studies Institute.

Harding, A. (1992) 'Property interests and urban growth coalitions in the UK: a brief encounter' in Healey, P., Davoudi, S., Tavsanoglu. S., O'Toole, M. and Usher, D. (eds) *Rebuilding the City: Property-Led Urban Regeneration* London: Spon.

Mazey, Sonia P. and Richardson, J. J. (1992(a)) 'British pressure groups in the European Community: the challenge of Brussels' *Parliamentary Affairs* **45**, 1, 92–127.

Mazey, Sonia P. and Richardson, J. J. (1992(b)) 'Environmental groups and the EC: challenges and opportunities' *Environmental Politics* **1**, 4, 109–128.

Rhodes, R. (1981) *Control and Power in Central–Local Government Relations* London: Gower.

Rhodes, R. (1988) *Beyond Westminster and Whitehall: The Sub-Central Government of Britain* London: Allen and Unwin.

8 Networks: the new driving force

> In every area there is a network of relationships between the local authority and the public, private and voluntary sector agencies which operate in the area...through them the enabling authority will influence the welfare of its area often in fields beyond the confines of its statutory services — and in its turn be inflenced.
>
> (Rodney Brooke 1989)

Throughout this book it has been suggested that local authorities can make a major contribution to tackling urban problems if they succeed in developing a new style of governance. We have explored various dimensions of this style of governance. In discussing entrepreneurial planning, greening the city, decentralisation, third force organisations and lobbying, one theme has been constant: the need for local authorities to work through and alongside other interests. In this chapter we reflect on the nature of this new style of working.

The first section of the chapter argues that what is emerging is a third way of co-ordinating the complex social and economic activities in which local authorities are engaged in — the network mode. The network method stands in contrast to models of hierarchy that have traditionally driven local government management. The network method can also be distinguished for the market mechanisms heavily promoted by central government over the last decade or so. It is concluded that in future local authorities must enhance their capacity to network alongside their ability to operate through hierarchy or markets. Networking provides the key to the new style of governance we advocate. It involves the pooling of resources in a co-operative manner to adhere to shared purposes.

The second section of the chapter explores how networks work — what makes them 'tick'? We look at the core components of networks. The third section examines the key dilemmas in operating through networks from the viewpoints of local authorities and their citizens. The concluding discussion looks at the potential and limitations of networks.

Beyond hierarchy and markets: working through networks

Co-ordinating complex social and economic activities presents a considerable challenge in the modern world. One helpful way of thinking about the different ways that this challenge is met is to identify three models — hierarchy, market, network — which offer different solutions to the problem (Thompson *et al.* 1991). Each model emphasises a distinctive driving force. Hierarchy works through a chain of command. Market models achieve co-ordination through price signals which bring together demand and supply. Networks create a shared outlook which allows the pooling of resources to achieve a common purpose.

Hierarchical modes of organising will be familiar to anyone involved with local government. Hierarchies operate on the basis of tasks defined by those at the top of the organisational pyramid. The task is then broken down into a number of subprocesses and performed by paid employees under a system of supervision. A chain of command ensures that subordinates carry out their functions and enables those at the top of the hierarchy to receive reports about the achievements of objectives. In many respects hierarchy was the key organising principle of post-war local government. It is undoubtedly the image of local authority organisation that is most prominent in the public mind.

The hierarchical method of organising has considerable strengths — especially in ensuring the delivery of routine services — yet it also has considerable limitations. Four key problems can be highlighted. First, it does rely on all the appropriate resources to achieve a task being within the ambit of a hierarchical chain of command. However as we have seen many of the problems confronting cities cannot be resolved from input from one organisation or interest acting alone. Second, hierarchical systems can be slow to respond to new demands and circumstances. Flexibility and an ability to adapt would, however, appear to be key factors in meeting many of the challenges facing cities. Third, hierarchical systems can tend to be inward-looking, driven by their own rules and regulations, rather than the needs of consumers and citizens in the wider environment. The careers of employees are driven by the ability to win the approval of their superiors rather than their impact on the problems confronting the users of cities. Finally, learning capacity in hierarchical systems can be limited because subordinates do not always find it desirable or possible to bring their experience of problems on the ground to the attention of their superiors.

The recognition of some of these problems has encouraged experimentation with another model of co-ordination: the market model. Since 1979 the Conservatives have promoted this model and many local authorities would accept that it has heavily influenced their way of organising and thinking. Market mechanisms involve organisations or interests acting independently of one another with co-ordination achieved through competition regulated by the price mechanism. The supply of a service matches demand because the price given to the service reflects competition among service providers and the willingness (ability) to pay among those customers demanding the service.

Applied to the public sector the market approach involves establishing surrogates which parallel the market dynamics of the private sector (Le Grand 1990). Government defines itself as a funder rather than as a provider of services. The supply of services may come from a variety of public, private and voluntary producers, all operating in competition with one another. The competition is governed not so much by a pricing system as by a system of contracts. The contracts lay out what is to be supplied and the price to be paid. Compulsory competitive tendering has played the major role in encouraging this contract culture within local authorities but other reforms in housing, education and social services have also played their part. The contractual basis of relations extends to relationships with the private sector and voluntary organisations in the local environment. It also finds reflection within the local authority as clients (those who define the needs of users), contractors, (those involved in direct service provision) and support services (those providing back-up services such as computing, those responsible for defining users needs, buildings) separate into a series of units relating to one another not through hierarchical control but the terms of negotiated contracts.

The success of the introduction of the market model is difficult to judge given the relatively recent nature of the experimentation with the method. It has undoubtedly achieved some refocusing in the efforts of local authorities. Short-term savings in the cost of provision have been claimed. In some instances it has provided a catalyst for remotivating staff and an opportunity to reconcentrate on the needs of service users.

Yet from the viewpoint of this book the market method is of little use in developing the corporate and community dimension to local authorities, which we see as essential to tackling the problems of cities. Strategies for entrepreneurial planning or greening the city rely on a much closer, intensive and developed set of relationships than can find full expression in any contract. The commitment to decentralisation or working with third force organisations cannot operate on the basis of formal contracts but requires a more fluid, informal set of relationships. Area approaches or community-based third force organisations allow a deeper and more rich expression of need from the locality than either hierarchy or market models can claim. Finally the relationships with central government or Euro-officials described in the chapter on lobbying could not be reduced to the dimensions of a contract. A formal contract may form part of the relationship but it does not capture the richness of the processes we describe.

Most of the activities we examine in this book involve a break from both hierarchical and market models. The network model captures much more the kind of processes we have been analysing. Indeed as a model it also captures important dimensions of the way that firms in the private sector operate.

> Many firms are no longer structured like medieval kingdoms, walled off and protected from hostile forces. Instead, we find companies involved in an intricate latticework of collaborative ventures with other firms, most of whom are ostensibly competitors.
>
> (Powell 1991, p. 269)

Case studies abound of companies developing 'value-adding partnerships', moving beyond competitive market-based relations to more collaborative relations. Alongside the larger, vertically integrated companies — eliminating or engulfing competitors — 'are sets of independent companies that work closely together to manage the flow of goods and services along the entire value-added chain' (Johnston and Lawrence 1991, p. 193).

This way of working — the creation of a shared outlook allowing a pooling of resources — we describe as a network approach. It stands separate from hierarchical and market models. Local authorities are likely to continue to find use for those two models but if they are to achieve the new style of governance we consider essential for meeting the challenges of our cities then their capacity for networking needs to be enhanced.

Networking emerges as a key activity along three dimensions. First as discussed in the chapter on lobbying, building networks to central and Euro-government is important. Second within local authorities 'greening the city' or reaping the benefits of decentralisation requires the development of networks which enable different parts of the organisation to communicate effectively with one another. Finally in reaching out to the private sector, through entrepreneurial planning or building bridges with third force organisations, networking skills are essential.

How networks work

We have made the case for designating a third way of working which relies not on hierarchy or markets but on networks. In this section we explore how networks work by examining their core components. This is a difficult task because networks are built on relationships that are often informal and behind-the-scenes. In the discussion below we identify six factors which help to explain the making of networks (see Table 8.1).

Table 8.1:   What makes networks work

• Recognition of dependency
• Pooling of resources
• Exchange of information
• Development of trust
• A mutual orientation
• A commitment over the long haul

Networks exist because individuals and organisations come to recognise that they depend on one another. Diverse interests may be present but each recognises that it can achieve something of benefit to itself by working co-operatively with others. In the light of this factor it becomes clear why networking has come to the fore for local authorities. There is an element of push created by spending restrictions and legislative changes that challenge the ability of local authorities to engage in self-sufficient service delivery. The pull elements include a recognition by local authorities that certain issues — such as economic development, environmental protection, crime prevention — simply cannot be tackled by local government on its own. Meeting the challenges facing cities, as we have already argued, means bringing together a diverse range of interests in a co-ordinated effort.

Networks involve the pooling of resources. Dependency on others often means that you are dependent on their resources (financial, organisational, personnel, legitimacy). In these circumstances sharing resources makes sense. Yet although resources are shared it should not be assumed that in all networks all partners make an equal contribution or receive an equivalence of benefits. Some networks are partnerships between equals but others develop structures of indebtedness and obligation. The involvement of a local authority in a network can often be placed in a patron-client continuum. At one extreme the local authority is the patron of the network: relatively well-resourced, organised and guiding the vision and purpose of others involved. An example, here, might be when a local authority is encouraging community-based third force organisations in a deprived neighbourhood. At the other extreme the local authority may be relatively poorly resourced and unorganised, a client with substantial debts and obligations to a more powerful partner. This situation may occur when dealing with a powerful multi-national corporation undertaking an economic development project in the locality.

Networks are underwritten by the effective exchange of information between partners. Information is a valued commodity within networks and the quality of information exchanged within networks is often very high. Market-provided information tends to be shallow. Hierarchical models, as already noted, can block the flow of information. Networks can be particularly adept at providing efficient, reliable information. As Powell (1991, p. 272) comments:

> The most useful information is rarely that which flows down the formal chain of command in an organisation, or that which can be inferred from shifting price signals. Rather, it is that which is obtained from someone whom you have dealt with in the past and found to be reliable...information passed through networks is 'thicker' than information obtained in the market, and 'freer' than that communicated in a hierarchy.

The quality of information obtained through the long-term lobbying discussed in Chapter 7 would not be doubted by most local authorities. Equally the building of bridges to neighbourhoods through decentralisation or to community-based third force organisations yields to the local authority a previously untapped store of local knowledge and understanding. Looking at the network from the viewpoint of their partners it is plain that many see local authorities as information-rich organisations and therefore attractive participants.

Networks rely on the development of trust between partners. Yet establishing trust presents each of the partners with a considerable challenge. To trust another means a willingness to be vulnerable and recognise that if the trust is abused a severe loss may be experienced. Trust involves choosing to ignore the risk that trusting behaviour involves (*cf.* Lorenz 1991). The great gain from trust is the way it simplifies communication, co-operation and co-ordination. As Arrow (1974, p. 23) comments: 'It saves a lot of trouble to have a degree of reliance in other people's word'. Trust saves time and effort in verification, switching partners and arriving at acceptable terms on which to engage in joint action.

Closely related to trust in networks is a mutual orientation. Organisations and individuals come to define themselves in relation to other units in the network. They share knowledge with one another. They define their status and reputation by reference to the network. They accommodate and compromise to keep members of the network on board as circumstances change. This mutual orientation provided a glue that binds together the various participants.

Both trust and a mutual orientation make most sense in the context of a long-term relationship. As qualities of networks they come to the fore when partners are committed to working with one another over the long haul. In the most developed networks all the participants lose 'some of their ability to dictate their own future and are increasingly dependent on the activities of others' (Powell 1991, p. 274). In new networks participants must present themselves as long-term actors. Here local authorities can often have a considerable advantage, as we argued in Chapter 1, because they are seen as a relatively permanent feature in the locality. A network cannot be created overnight. It is built up through a series of exchanges and transactions within a general pattern of interaction between partners.

The dilemmas of networking

In this section of the chapter some of the dilemmas associated with networking are explored. From the viewpoint of the local authority two related issued need to be addressed. How can the *ad hoc*, informal networks into which officers and councillors are tied be moulded into a purposeful framework for strategic action by the authority? Can the time and effort involved in creating new networks be justified? From the viewpoint of the citizen other issues come to the fore. Can issues of accountability and propriety in public affairs be reconciled with the demands and relationships of networking. Does the promotion of networks undermine or enhance local democracy? We explore each of these issues in turn below.

Strategic framework?

The networks in which officers and councillors are involved are not generally the product of some masterplan or blueprint. Networks can develop on an *ad hoc* basis as officers work with officials from other agencies to make things happen. Councillors are nominated to sit on various outside organisations. Party and ward activities can bring councillors into contact with interest groups and community-based organisations. Other networks evolve, perhaps at the behest of the local authority, to organise a campaign or to achieve some collaborative goal. These networks, again, flow from particular initiatives rather than some grand design.

Should a local authority look to impose some order on what can seem like chaos? The answer we would give is that what is required is a 'light-footed' strategic framework. Anything stronger would run the risk of undermining the informality and autonomy of networks. What would be the main element of such a framework?

The first element is the establishment of a vision, a sense of corporate direction. Such a strategic vision would outline the local authority's priorities and concerns and thus provide its networkers with a framework for their activities.

A second element is the need for enhanced briefing and feedback mechanisms. When councillors sit on the boards and committees of outside bodies how well briefed are they? Do they have some conception of the local authority's policy preferences in the area in which they are involved? Can mechanisms be established to ensure they report back on the lessons they have learnt? There is a danger that the hierarchical mode of organisation within the local authority means that the new thinking and insights generated by networking stay on the periphery of the organisation. Local authorities are data-rich organisations but their capacity to turn data into information which can be used to change policies and performance needs to be expanded.

A third element of a strategic framework, which flows from the discussion above, is ensuring access to the decision-making process for networkers. In the discussion on decentralisation in Chapter 5 we noted how officers in area bases can become isolated from the main structure of the authority. They gain new insights from their close contact with the community but are unable to make a major impact on the decision-making process within the main programmes of the authority. A similar sense of isolation and marginalisation can undermine the work of networking officers involved in economic development, Euro-lobbying, environmental protection or promoting third force organisations. Mechanisms to enable networkers to raise issues and stimulate new decisions at the heart of the local authority are essential.

A final element in any strategic framework would be a system of review. The review process would ask questions of networkers and the networks with which they are involved. Are there some major gaps in coverage of networks? Are some relationships too close and too intensively developed? Should counter-blancing networks be encouraged? We shall return to a discussion of such issues at the end of this section on the dilemmas of networking.

Too much effort?

Networks take time to develop. Networks work at their best when relationships have been built up and a history of shared experience and understanding has developed. Yet the time and effort put into assembling economic development, and urban renewal partnerships during the 1980s and 1990s can appear great against often relatively modest gains or achievements. Working with and through third force organisations to provide services or promote environmental protection can be a very complex and staff-intensive exercise. Especially in the early stages of its development networking can be a rather time-consuming and unrewarding task.

Sometimes just as a good rapport is established the key officers or councillors may move on because of new career opportunities or changes in political direction. Community-based organisations often complain about how, having got used to working with a particular group of officers or councillors, they find relationships disrupted as people change jobs or are assigned different tasks. The stronger, more established networks can withstand changes in key personnel because a group culture has developed which can be passed on. But for networks in the early stages of their evolution rapid changes in personnel can be difficult to manage.

Whether networks are too much effort depends on the local authority's view of the alternatives. We noted earlier in the chapter push and pull factors that have encouraged the development of networking. Given the intractability and complexity of some of the challenges facing city policy-makers we would argue that networking — developing effective responses in partnership with other interests and organisations — is the only viable way forward. We recognise however that commitment to the long haul and the complications of networking sits uneasily alongside the short-term electoral and administrative pressures on local authorities.

Accountability

Can the dynamics of networking be reconciled with the traditional concerns about accountability and propriety in public affairs? As the textbooks suggest the Mafia is in some respects a classic network. Such a model for local government is hardly likely to inspire confidence in citizens. The corruption that has on occasion been associated with the getting of local authority contracts has often been traced to the operation of informal networks of influence. Because the nature of networks tends to be exclusive and semi-private and because networks are driven by loyalty and trust among participants, there are grounds for doubting whether networks can meet the exacting standards of traditional public administration.

One answer might be to suggest that the ends justify the means. Networking ensures the achievement of valued goals that would not otherwise be obtained and, in particular, that traditional hierarchical systems of public administration have failed to deliver. Another slightly less pragmatic response is to suggest that networking requires the development of a new set of public service ethics to guide networkers as to what is appropriate and what is in appropriate action. Such a code of ethics could be an element in the strategic framework for managing networks developed by local authorities.

Equality of access?

Networks, by developing repeated transactions between different interests, inevitably restrict access. Opportunities for newcomers can be restricted. Distinctive patterns of favoured 'insider' networks may develop, leaving other interests unrepresented and excluded. For the local authority networks are both an opportunity to influence and be influenced. It follows that if local authorities only involve themselves in a restricted number of networks, focused around a limited range of interests, then the processes of local democracy and representation may be skewed and biased.

Such concerns, however, are far from new. Indeed the standard political science literature sugests that it is possible in localities to identify clear patterns of 'insider' and 'outsider' interests (Stoker and Wilson 1991). Well-known case studies such as that undertaken in Croydon in the 1970s by Saunders (1980) describe in detail how local business and middle-class groups found access to the local council easy, while working-class tenant organisations were largely excluded. There is a sense in which any local authority is likely to have strong ties to the dominent social groups and organisations within its locality.

The commitment to a more conscious and broad networking system that emerges from the activities described in this book will in many respects challenge the informal and particularist ties that have developed in the past. Networking in economic development or environmental protection has often led local authorities to develop new contacts and new partners. Equally decentralisation and working with third force organisations can open out the local authority to new interests. Networking developed in this way can be seen as improving the quality of the connections between governors and governed, and so an enhancement of local democracy.

Conclusions

In this chapter we have described the activities outlined earlier in the book using the concept of networking. It has proved useful to analyse in a more abstract manner the new style of governance that is at the heart of this book. Networking, at its best, provides a flexible, responsive tool. It enables local authorities to reach out and work with and alongside other interests in a way that traditional hierarchical methods or the newly promoted market mechanisms do not allow. In many respects the networking method follows already established patterns of working elsewhere in European local and urban government (see Batley and Stoker 1991). It also matches developments in some parts of the private sector as firms seek to grapple with a rapidly changing environment and new challenges. The strength of the network model is that it offers local authorities a role in comprehending and defining local needs and then, through joint action, seeking appropriate policy responses and solutions.

Networks, however, are not the only tool that should be in the local authority took-kit. Hierarchy and markets have their place in ensuring efficient and effective service delivery. Further the tensions and difficulties that have to be overcome in building the level of co-operation necessary for networks may be too great. Networks can, especially in their early stages, be fragile and tend to disintegrate. Even established networks may break given a major shock (such as a dramatic loss of funding capacity by one of the partners) or if conflicts of interest are given priority over areas where co-operation has been developed. Networks, in short, are not immune from the strains of operating in the context of a political system distributing scarce resources and driven by competing ideologies and interests.

References and bibliography

Arrow, K. (1974) *The Limits of Organisation* New York: Norton.

Batley and Stoker, (1991) *Local Government in Europe* London: Macmillan.

Brooke, R. (1989) *Managing the Enabling Authority* Harlow: Longman.

Johnston, R. and Lawrence, P. (1991) 'Beyond vertical integration — the rise of the value-adding partnership in Thompson, G. *et al.* (eds) *Markets, Hierarchies and Networks.* pp. 193–202.

Le Grand, J. (1990) *Quasi-markets and Social Policy* Bristol: SAUS, University of Bristol.

Lorenz, E. (1991) 'Neither friends nor strangers: informal networks of subcontracting in French industry' in Thompson, G. *et al.* (eds) (1991) *Markets, Hierarcies and Networks.* pp. 183–193

Powell, (1991) 'Neither markets nor hierarchy: network forms of organisation' in Thompson, G. *et al.* (eds) *Markets, Hierarchies and Networks..*

Saunders, P. (1980) *Urban Politics: A Sociological Interpretation* Harmondsworth: Penguin.

Stoker, G. and Wilson, D. (1991) 'The lost world of British local pressure groups' *Public Policy and Administration* 6, 2, Summer, pp. 20–34.

Thompson, G., Frances, J., Levacic, R. and Mitchell, J. (eds) (1991) *Markets, Hierarchies and Networks* London: Sage.

9 Conclusions

This chapter starts by restating one of the underlying arguments of this book — the need to avoid 'one club' solutions to urban problems. The experience of the 1980s confirmed what was for some at least a lesson that should never have been forgotten. There are no simple solutions to the problems of our cities. The application of private sector-led and property-driven regeneration has not achieved the scale and depth of transformation in our cities that some of its more out-spoken advocates claimed it would. We are not suggesting there is no role for property-based renewal or the private sector. We have argued that what is required is a balanced approach in which private sector regeneration is complemented by other approaches. In the first section of this concluding chapter we develop this argument by suggesting that local authorities shold seek to develop a vision of what is the appropriate mix of strategies for the different parts of their area.

The second section of the chapter steps beyond the form of argument thus far developed — which has been built out of the experience of localities — to make a general case for an elected executive mayor to be placed at the heart of city government. As part of the broader process of restructuring that is underway in the 1990s we argue for a shift to a system commonplace in North America and Europe: an executive elected mayor accompanied by a revamped representative chamber. Such a system offers scope for increased capacity in leadership and accountability within city government.

Finally, although the main thrust of our book has been on the

need for local responses to meet urban problems, we recognise the
continuing role to be played by central government and
supranational agencies. In the concluding section we outline a
framework for national urban policy which is conditioned by the
need to stimulate local activity and innovation.

Getting beyond one club solutions: alternative strategies

All cities present a mixed set of problems and opportunities. There
are areas in all cities where the impact of industrial decline is felt
with abandoned factories, derelict land and other signs of urban
decay. There are also areas where the demand from private
investors remains strong; areas in which land and building prices or
rents are buoyant as new users move in and established users
expand their operations. Some residential areas similarly appear to
maintain a great attractiveness while others become sink areas
where many residents vainly wish for some way of getting out.
Problems with skills shortages and lack of key managerial and
professional personnel can co-exist alongside the tragedy of long-
term unemployment. Parts of many cities have great buildings or
areas brought to life by the arrival of ethnic minorities with
different traditions and new skills. Other parts of cities are blighted
by traffic congestion, pollution and failings in the system of public
transport. In short, the complexity of experience within cities
should be at the forefront of the minds of policy-makers.

The complexity of the challenge facing cities makes the
argument for avoiding 'one club solutions' a powerful one. Many
golfers enjoy the power and the panache provided by their driver.
Watching the ball soar into the distance roughly in the direction
you intended it to go is a great experience (although a rare one for
at least one of the authors). Yet a good round of golf also requires a
range of more subtle shots, not to mention a successful assault on
the mysteries of putting. Whilst not suggesting that the parallel is
exact we would argue that an effective attempt to grapple with the
problems of cities requires a mix of strategies and approaches.

In broad terms there are four strategic options facing planners
and policy-makers thinking about the future of their areas. First
there is economic regeneration. This seeks to find new functions
for run-down areas. This is the strategy of leverage, and entrepreneurial planning that was examined in Chapter 3. It is based on
attracting whatever private sector investment is available, and
planning around it. During the 1980s this became the conventional

approach adopted by urban policy-makers. High-tech offices, waterside developments, and arts and leisure-based investment were amongst the activities promoted in the hope of finding new uses for city land and premises. The competitive dynamic of this approach provides the opportunity for dramatic rethinking and redefinition essential for the future of cities.

Secondly, there is the local needs strategy. This is aimed at problems of poor housing, unemployment, and multiple deprivation. It is based on surveys of the needs of local people, and on developing policies that tackle them. This strategy does not seek a fundamental change in the role of areas based on the bringing in of new users and uses. Rather it seeks to build on the strengths and concerns of established residents. The third force organisations (TFOs) discussed in Chapter 6 provide a mechanism of working from local needs. The way in which small housing associations, trading centres, city firms, community centres, providing for pre-school groups and OAP drop-in centres, and similar TFOs, can bring new heart and life to established residential communities is clear. The experience of decentralisation within local authorities examined in Chapter 5 shows how a focus on the needs of particular areas can be developed. A focused effort, building on the strengths of local residents and meeting the needs they define is an essential city strategy.

A third strategy is politically much more controversial. This is the difficult one of actually closing parts of the inner city down. In areas of loss of population, it would involve decanting particular estates, demolition and greening over. In areas where there are too many people for that, but little prospect of new jobs to reduce high unemployment levels, it would involve accepting that some areas became 'Girotowns'. A strategy of managing decline in this kind of way might be acceptable in some cicumstances. In effect it means making explicit what is already an implicit strategy within many cities. In some circumstances investment-seeking entrepreneurial planning or bottom-up local needs approaches are not viable. To pursue such strategies against impossible odds is a pointless and wasteful activity. Making explicit such dilemmas and recognising that in some circumstances what is required is 'moth-balling' will clarify the choices available to policy-makers. Public spending in such areas then becomes focused on ensuring that life is not too uncomfortable for the residents that remain and that where people have moved out blighted land is landscaped and made as attractive as possible. The hope is that eventually the land will become attractive to investors and new users again, and new potential will be seen.

The fourth strategy — pressure management — arises in those areas of cities where demand for competing uses is strong and investors are bubbling with enthusiasm and new ideas for development. In such areas policy-makers can engage in strict containment, phased land release, traffic management, pollution controls and other regulatory mechanisms. Most cities have such pressure points and policy-makers need to ensure that effective mechanisms for containing demand are in place. Some appropriate mechanisms were discussed in Chapter 4.

Each of the strategies we have outlined make a different demand in terms of the style and approach in decision-making. Entrepreneurial planning requires flexiblity and strategy vision from policy-makers. The bottom-up approach demands responsiveness and an ability to empower others, building on their needs and strengths rather than imposing solutions. The closing-down strategy rests on the authority and longer-term perspective of those in government. If opposition emerges policy-makers may well need all the skills of persuasion and the resources of legitimacy in their possession. The pressure management strategy relies heavily on regulation: having clear rules and regulations and the capacity to enforce them. Again the authority and legitimacy of policy makers is likely to be a key resource.

The successful running of a city requires a balanced approach. In the light of local knowledge and understanding it requires the mixing and matching of a variety of strategies. These strategies in turn call for a range of political capacities and skills. In the next section we consider whether the existing governing arrangements of cities are adequate to the complex range of tasks that we have identified.

Elected mayors: leadership and accountability

This book has outlined the need for local government to develop a new style of governance. There is evidence that local authorities have already done much to promote this new style of working. There is considerable evidence that the new style of governance we have described — which involves working with and through other organisations and interests — is being actively developed in the 1990s. Yet, if the potential of this new style of governance is to be fully developed we believe that certain weaknesses inherent in the established institutions of decision-making within British local government need to be radically reformed. In particular we propose the introduction of an elected executive mayor.

First it is necessary to deal with the reorganisation of city government. The current reorganisation process in England leaves out the metropolitan areas and London. The abolition of the six metropolitan counties and the Greater London Council in 1986 left a system of single tier authorities surrounded by a complex range of joint boards, joint committees and quasi-governmental agencies. The absence of any attempt to establish a London-wide authority is to be particularly regretted. Outside metropolitan areas, a rolling Local Government Commission may well give unitary status to the main city authorities, although they too may be surrounded by a complex orbit of joint boards and local quangos. In Wales and Scotland the reorganisation process would appear to be heading towards giving the main cities unitary status. Again these new multi-purpose city authorities may find themselves operating within a complex set of joint arrangements and special purpose agencies.

The reform process creates a number of dangers as well as some new oportunities. Assuming that the short-term disruption and chaos associated with any reorganisation is overcome, then a more effective system of government for cities may emerge. Unitary status as such will be relatively irrelevant since the new authorities will most likely be hedged in by tight boundaries, facing strategic demands beyond the scope of their immediate powers and unavoidably involved in working with and through other agencies. Unitary authorities will certainly not prove to be the panacea that some of their advocates claim. To achieve good government it is essential that the new unitary authorities continue to develop the new style of governance we have discussed in this book. the achievement of unitary status should not be the end of a process but rather the catalyst for further reform of the way the local authority works and relates to its environment.

This book has commented on the need for civic leadership. Local leadership is needed to make strategic choices and balance the diverse interests of the communities that live in urban areas. In Chapter 1 we outlined the general case for local authorities to take on the mantle of civic leadership and in subsequent chapters we have illustrated ways in which such leadership can be provided. In our concluding discussion we take the analysis a stage further and make the case for a shift in the internal management of local authorities to provide a focal point for civic leadership.

The established system of internal management has three big disadvantages in terms of developing the new style of governance that we advocate. First, most committee systems are designed to monitor the delivery of services. Opportunities to develop strategic vision or to look beyond the boundaries of the organisation tend to get squeezed out. The cycle of committee meetings is driven by operational concerns and issues with little time or opportunity to reflect on the objectives of service delivery or wider concerns. Second, the key actors are often relatively invisible and unknown to the public. The majority of citizens know which party is in control of their authority but only a minority are able to name the councillors for their ward (see Table 9.1). The name of the council leader or the chief executive (with a few exceptions) is unlikely to roll off the tongue of many residents. Finally, despite the huge amount of responsibility laid at the door of senior councillors, they are asked to do their job on a supposedly part-time basis and with the minimum of reward. A point graphically illustrated by Jean McFadden, Leader of Glasgow District Council:

> When I was Convener of the Finance Committee in 1972, in charge of a budget of c. £800m, I was paid one half of what my secretary earned, one-tenth of the salary of the Director of Finance and 2p per hour more than the cleaners.   (McFadden 1993, p. 27)

Table 9.1:   Knowledge of local councillors and controlling parties by region

	% of responsents able to name correctly				
	London	Metropolitan England	Rest of England and Wales	Scotland	All
Party in control of local council	68	80	53	62	61
Party in control of county/regional	77	72	45	62	56
Name of any councillors in ward	15	22	33	42	30

Source: Adapted from Gyford, Leach and Game (1989) Table 25, p. 230.

A common response to the critical points we have raised is to argue that local authorities have adapted to pressures they face by developing informal coping mechanisms. It is true that many authorities now have informal panels of councillors and officers, away-days and other mechanisms for breaking from the treadmill of committee routine. Informally in many authorities there is a *de facto* division between leading councillors who take almost full-time responsibility for particular services and act as the executive board of the council, and other councillors who are less involved and more engaged in casework and representative functions. The internal management of local government has kept the structural skeleton of full council and committees but built a range of mechanisms for ensuring effective decision-making.

Informal coping mechanisms, however, are not in our opinion really adequate. First, there is too great a gap between the formal structure of how decisions should be made and the informal realities. As we argued in Chapter 1, if a system of decision-making is to be legitimate it needs to be understood and comprehended by the public. The current position rests on the public being sold a myth about how decisions are made. Second, the informal rearrangements that have occurred do not provide the institutional capacity for delivering the style of city governance we have been advocating.

We support the efforts of those who have been trying to raise alternative models of internal management to the attention of local government policy-makers. In particular we see a strong case for the move to a system based around an elected executive mayor. This is not the place to discuss the full details of such an argument (see Stoker and Wolman 1992) but its broad thrust can be presented here.

The executive mayor would have responsibility for preparing and submitting the budget to council; the power to place policy resolutions and recommendations before the council; the responsibiity for the excecutive operations of local government and the power to appoint and remove departmental heads. He or she would be in a full-time, salaried post.

The mayor woulc be elected. There would also be a separately elected council thr.t would have the right to vote on the budget, policy resolutions and appointments of the mayor. The council would also be able to make its own policy recommendations and budget proposals. The mayor would be able to veto the council's recommendations subject to a council override by an extraordinary majority. The mayor's proposals would require only a simple majority of votes cast in the council in order to be approved.

The operation of the system would depend on the state of party politics in different localities. The mayor is most likely to be elected on a party ticket and, where the majority in the council is of the same political hue, the basis for co-operation is clear. Given the powers of the elected mayor such a figure is unlikely to be subject to the full force of party control and discipline. The mayor may well provide a mechanism for broadening the base of support and leadership provided by the party; speaking beyond the faithful few to a broader range of elements in the community. In those circumstances where the council lacks an overall majority or is of an opposite political hue to the mayor the basis for co-operation can still be present. However, a high premium will be placed on the ability to bargain across both party and institutional boundaries. In many ways such bargaining is the essence of the new style of urban government we advocate.

Finally the elected mayor's ability to hire and fire staff implies a different relationship with the chief executive and chief officers. The relationship will become more like that of senior civil servants to government ministers. Senior officers will have a much sharper identification with and responsibility to the mayor. They will provide him or her with policy advice, managerial expertise and administrative skills. They will act in partnership with the mayor. The role of chief executive will be transmuted to that of chief administrative officer overseeing the mayor's policies and budget within the administration. The council may require a separate corps of officers to enable it to draw up its own policy recommendations and budget proposals.

What are the main advantages of an elected mayor?

1. One of the main attractions of having an elected mayor is the way it creates a highly visible figure whom the public can hold to account. A valued feature in any local government system is the degree to which locally elected officials are held accountable for their actions by the public, with election or re-election reflecting their local performance and their views on local issues. A prominent and locally well-known elected mayor might well add to local accountability, given the tendency in the current system for national issues to heavily influence local elections. Moreover, it may be easier for the public to identify and attach responsibility for local decision-making to the personality of an elected mayor rather than the more abstract notion of a party group.

2. The mayor can provide a focal point for local lobbying. The elected mayor offers a potentially attractive option in that as a highly visible and prominent local figure the mayor is likely to

be keen to be seen to respond to the demands and preferences of his/her constitents. It would be inappropriate if the elected mayor became the prime receiver of minor complaints in relation to service delivery but it would be desirable if a local political figure became the target for the public's attempts to challenge the major decisions of the council. The elected mayor could provide a stimulus to local political activity.

3. The potential contribution of an elected mayor to service effectiveness rests on his/her greater accountability and separation from the daily grind of service delivery. The role of mayor may also be valuable in those service areas where innovation or co-ordination is a key theme — land-use planning, transport and economic development. It is generally agreed that the internal steering function of local government — its ability to plan, prioritise, direct itself towards coherent goals and organise and co-ordinate itself in order to achieve them — is an important aspect of its overall success. An elected executive mayor would establish a much more centralised internal government structure than the present system; the mayor, at the top, would be in a hierarchical relationship to the rest of city government. Such a structure would provide a potential for stronger internal leadership and management than is presently the case.

4. The visible position and elected status of mayors gives them the opportunity and the authority to speak, negotiate and make demands on behalf of their community. Given the increasing fragmentation that characterises local government — the reorganisation of elected local authorities and the rise of a whole array of non-elected local agencies — the elected mayor offers a means of bringing together the fragments and a focus for community government. As elected, visible, figures mayors offer the potential of providing a counterweight to powerful national political leaders. Mayors of big cities, in particular, might be expected to attract considerable media attention and have the opportunity to present the concerns and needs of local government and their local communities. A network of elected mayors could provide a powerful *political* voice for local government in contrast — or in addition — to the current pattern of representation through local authority associations. A mayoral system may present advantages in negotiating with the European community

because it provides an identifiable executive which is the dominant pattern in Europe (see Blair 1991).

The main arguments against an elected mayor revolve around the concentration of power in a single individual rather than its dispersal among many. Some argue that the potential for corruption will increase. This viewpoint is difficult to sustain. If greater corruption exists in those countries with elected mayors this probably reflects wider differences in political culture rather than the establishment of an elected executive figure. Further fears about corruption can be countered by appropriate procedures and checks to ensure that decisions are made with due respect for their legality and probity.

In formal terms, at present executive authority rests in the council. However in most local authorities power resides at an informal level with a small group of leading councillors working alongside a number of senior officers. Full council meetings, or perhaps more realistically in majority-controlled councils, the majority party group, provide some check on their activity. Yet evidence abounds of the ability of leading councillors to manipulate their party groups. Generally power is seen as concentrated in a joint elite of senior officers and leading councillors who jostle for policy influence. The picture is complicated by the dynamics of party groups and the broader organisational politics of the authority yet few would dispute that considerable power resides in small cabals of senior councillors and officers (Stoker 1991, Chapter 4).

An elected executive mayor in some respects, therefore, constitutes a concentration of power at both the formal and the informal level compared to the current system. Yet looked at from another perspective it can be seen as a clarification of the system of responsibilities and accountability, that in the current situation is confused. The combined executive and respresentative role of the full council is split, with executive power residing mainly in the mayor and representative functions being concentrated in the council chamber. The principle of checks and balances underlies the whole approach. Executive power resides mainly with the mayor but it is checked by the power of the chamber to block his/her measures and propose alternative policy measures. The representative function rests mainly within the council chamber. Assuming that these representatives continue to be elected on a ward or area basis then the elected mayor as a representative for the whole city provides an alternative, broader expression of the area's interests. In short the system of government created by establishing an elected mayor provides scope for not only increased leadership capacity but also increased accountability.

A national urban policy?

This book has made the case for solving urban problems through the development of local leadership. Each locality has its own uniqueness and effective action can most easily be assembled at the local level. Local initiative is required to match the variety of local circumstances. Local authorities working through and alongside other interests can develop a new style of governance which through its flexibility and its empowering style can meet the challenge facing cities in the 1990s and beyond. Far from being sidelined, our approach puts local authorities alongside other local interests in the driving seat.

What are the implications of this perspective for national urban policy? In developing a response to this question it is useful to think in terms of the various urban policy frames identified by Solesbury (1990, 1993). We have rejected simple-minded market-oriented solutions that imply that a *laissez-faire* approach and reliance on private sector imagination and initiative alone is the answer. We also reject the tendency of central government to impose its own demonstration projects in a stream of *ad hoc* responses to urban problems. Enterprise Zones, Urban Development Corporations, City Technology Colleges and other initiatives have created a patchwork of centrally-sponsored agencies each claiming to set new standards and promote new thinking. The time for such demonstrative projects has now passed.

We are not advocating a return to the welfarist model in which measures are aimed at simply ameliorating the demographic and economic misfortunes of our older and larger cities. Our argument has been for a positive, forward-thinking policy. It has recognised that cities are in competition with one another: to retain and attract investment, to find new functions, to renew their environment and to empower their citizens. We have also suggested that the continuing social, economic and environmental transformation of urban areas is necessary. We recognise that change causes pain and means there will be relative winners and losers (*cf* Solesbury 1993, p. 35). Yet cities must change to survive. Strategies for managing change can best be developed and legitimated at the local level.

From our perspective the scope for a national urban policy is conditioned by a view that the driving force should rest in each locality. National policy should not seek to impose solutions or stifle the creativity of localities, rather its task is to foster, underwrite and regulate the process of local problem-solving.

To foster

Central government should foster a spirit of experimentation within localities. Such a process involves encouraging the search for alternative solutions and seeking to draw lessons from those alternatives. A 'free local government' experiment could be developed, following initiatives in Nordic countries, in which local authorities are encouraged to apply for exemption from existing controls or for the granting of new powers (Stewart 1991). In a more dramatic move local authorities could be given a power of general competence similar to that held by many city councils in Europe and North America: a power to undertake any activity within certain limits that is of benefit to the citizens of their area (see Stewart and Stoker 1988 for a fuller discussion).

To underwrite

Central government resources will be needed to underwrite local programmes of renewal. Problems may be in cities but they are not of cities. The challenge posed by, for example, unemployment, family breakdown and poor education requires a mobilisation of resources on a national or even supranational scale. What is important is that there is public funding to support market and non-market orientated local initiatives. The criteria for allocating funds to physical redevelopment can reflect hard-nosed leverage ratio goals but for other projects softer, less hard-edged criteria should be developed. The benefits of a third force organisation running a community centre cannot be as easily measured as those from the underwriting of a business park development. Yet if a balanced approach is to be encouraged central government funding should not be skewed to those projects where hard-nosed benefits can be demonstrated. Further the public funding that is available should not have to come through the complex and diverse range of channels that underwrite many projects at the moment (see for example the case of Wigan Pier described on p. 154). A one-stop approach to available central government funding grants and support should be developed.

To regulate

Finally the role of national urban policy is to regulate. The competition between places should be kept in bounds and regulation also has a role to ensure that the outcomes of competition are tolerable within broad national norms and standards (*cf.* Solesbury 1990, 1993). Unfettered competition driven by unlimited subsidies for businesses to relocate would run the risk of creating a pointless round of musical chairs in investment and job creation. In areas of high demand where problems of congestion and over-heated economies arise national intervention may be required. Equally in other locations where levels of homelessness or racial discrimination may be thought so intolerable that national intervention may well be judged necessary.

The bare bones of our national urban policy that we have outlined compliments the wider discussion of the need for local choice and initiative which occupied most of this book. We hope we have provided some stimulus for thought and avoided any suggestion that meeting the challenges facing cities is an easy task. As the American political satarist H.L. Mencken put it, 'For every complex, difficult problem there is a simply, easy solution...and it is wrong'.

References and bibliography

Blair, P. (1992) 'Trends in local autonomy and democracy in Batler, R. and Stoker, G. (eds.) (1991) *Local Government in Europe* London: Macmillan.

Gyford, J., Leach, S. and Game, C. (1989) *The Changing Politics of Local Government* London: Unwin Hyman.

McFadden, J. (1993) 'The reorganisation of Scottish local government: a councillor's perspective' *Local Government Policy Making* **19**, 4, March.

Solesbury, W. (1990) *Reconstructuring National Urban Policy for the 1990s*, unpublished paper.

Solesbury, W. (1993) 'Reframing urban policy' *Policy and Politics* **21**, 1, 31–38.

Stewart, J. (1991) *An Experiment in Freedom. The Case for Free Local Authorities in Britain* London: Institute for Public Policy Research.

Stewart, J. and Stoker, G. (1988) *From Local Administration to Community Government* Research Series 351, London: Fabian Society.

Stoker, G. (1991) *The Politics of Local Government* (2nd ed.) London: Macmillan.

Stoker, G. and Wolman, H. (1992) 'Drawing lessons from US experience: an elected mayor for British Local Government' *Public Administration* **70**, 2, 241–267.

Index

Aberdeen 34, 54, 148, 157
Accessibility 104, 106
Accountability 4, 6, 15, 103–4,
    116, 134, 188, 194, 198
Administrative Will 85
Agenda 21, 65, 71, 74, 91–3
Air Quality [Pollution] 30, 66–7,
    69, 71–2, 74, 78–9, 83
Area Approaches 97–99, 101–
    104, 113, 116
Area Management 99
Association of Metropolitan
    Authorities (AMA) 5, 19,
    60, 170
Audit Commission 9, 128, 154,
    173–4

Balanced City 1–2, 19–20,
    31–5, 194, 201–3
Basildon 100
Birmingham 21–2, 24–6, 28, 33,
    100, 107, 154, 162, 171
Blackburn 22, 25–6, 78, 125,
    171
Bradford 22, 26, 28, 38, 141, 172
Bristol 21, 38, 47, 82, 157
British Coal 159, 166
Brundtland Report 69, 73–77
Brussels *see* European Community

Bury 162
Business in the Community
    (BIC) 50, 56, 169, 171
Business Leadership 14, 16, 156,
    171, 174, 176
Business Parks 21, 202

Cardiff 51–2
Chief Executive (local authority)
    54, 151, 196, 198
Citizens 32–4
City Challenge 5, 33, 59–63,
    158, 160, 163, 167–8, 171, 176,
    178
City Grant 41, 49, 127, 153, 161,
    163
Civic Leadership 11–14, 195
Civic Trust 125, 169
Cleveland 28, 31, 81
Clydebank 22–3, 25–6, 41
Coalfields Communities Campaign
    158–9, 166–7
Community Government 7
Compulsory Competitive
    Tendering 181–2
Confederation of British Industry
    (CBI) 16, 18
Conservatives 6, 151, 166–7,
    181

Co-ordination (*see also*
    networking)   9–11, 54–5,
    179–181, 199
Countryside Commission   50, 86,
    132, 142, 154
Covent Garden   45
Crime   30–1

Decentralisation
    case for and against   102–3,
        114
    development of   98–102
    in the 1990s   114–117
    scope and limitations   103–114
Democracy   15
Department of Environment   8,
    29, 38, 46, 51–2, 60, 65, 69,
    95, 99, 157, 161–4, 167–168,
    170–1, 173, 175–6, 178
Department of Trade and Industry
    8
Deprived Urban Areas   19–20,
    20–28
Derby   164
Derelict Land Grant   49, 50, 86,
    153–4, 157–8, 162–164, 167
Dialogue   152, 155–159, 178
Dudley   155
Dundee   39

Earth Summit (Rio Summit)   65,
    70–2, 76, 91–2
Economy   20–1
Edinburgh   100
Education   27, 65
    City Technology Colleges   5,
        27, 156, 175, 201
Elected Mayor *see* Mayor
Embedding Strategies   117
Employment   20–1, 32
Empowerment   34–5, 145–6
Enterprise Zone   41, 175, 177,
    201
Entrepreneurial Planning   37–62
    challenge of   57–9
    complexity   42–5
    making things happen   45–57
    stages   39–42

future   59–62
Environmental
    capacities   76–77
    concerns/issues   64–8, 77–83
        (*see also* sustainable
        development)
Environmental Impact Assessment
    68
Equity   73–4
European Commission   21, 151,
    154, 162, 172–4
European Community   4, 47, 51,
    70, 96, 158–9, 173
Exeter   39, 125

Flagships   39
Friends of the Earth   66, 95–6
Futurity   73

Girotowns   193
Glasgow   22, 25–6, 39, 107
Groundwork Trusts   121–2, 125,
    156

Halifax   125, 161
Harlow   100
Health   23, 25
Hierarchy   9–10, 180–1
Homelessness   23, 26, 164
Housing   29
Housing Action Trusts   155, 175
Housing Corporation   61, 142
Hull   38, 163, 175

Implementation   9, 42, 45–58,
    83–8, 120–1
Inter-Generational Equity   73–4
Intra-Generational Equity   74
Islington   100

Kensington and Chelsea   22–6, 121
Kirklees   66, 72

Labour   101, 110–113, 149, 166
Lancashire County Council   64,
    67, 84, 96, 159, 169
Leadership (local)   1, 6, 12–13,
    68

business   14, 16, 171, 174
civic   11–14, 34, 195
third force organisations   130,
    138
Leeds   39, 47–8
Legitimacy   14–17, 194
Leicester   72
Liberals   101, 109–12, 116, 149,
    166
Light Rapid Transit   87, 162–3
Liverpool   8, 10, 22–6, 28, 98,
    175
Lobbying   151–78
tactical considerations   163–7
timing   174
use of statistics   160–2
and Europe   158–9, 172–4
and Whitehall   155–7, 162–3,
    175–6
Local Authorities
financial position   6, 85–6, 153
reorganisation of   114, 195
roles of   6–17
Local Enterprise Companies   5
London   21, 23, 164
London Docklands Development
    Corporation   32, 41, 52, 158,
    165, 167

Manchester   8, 21, 23, 100, 108,
    155, 161–3, 174, 177
Market Models   181–2
Mayors   194–201
Members (Councillors) 8–9, 14–
    16, 84–5, 109–11, 146, 165,
    186, 196–7, 200 (see also
    mayors)
Members of European Parliament
    (MEPs)   172, 174
Members of Parliament (MPs)
    164–5, 169
Merseyside   31, 165
Middlesborough   22, 172

National Council for Voluntary
    Organisations   49–50, 142,
    150
National Rivers Authority   68,

87, 159
National Urban Policy   201–3
Networking   4, 10–11, 86–88
Networks   10, 179–190
dilemmas   185–9
how they work   183–5
New Magistracy   14
Newcastle-upon-Tyne   52, 60,
    162
Not-for-Profits (see Third Force
    Organisations)
Nottingham   22, 26, 40

Officers (of Local Authority)   5,
    198, 200 (see also chief
    executive)
Oldham   155

Participation   42–3, 48, 107–9,
    125–6
Physical Decay   27–30
Planning (new approach)   57–8
Policy Studies Institute   19–20,
    22, 24–29, 31, 36
Poverty   23–24

Quasi-Government Agency   5–6,
    37, 47, 49, 54–55, 68, 87,
    120–22, 135, 152–3, 155, 159-
    -160, 176, 195 (see also new
    magistracy)

Recycling   78, 81–2
Regeneration
economic   59–60, 171
social   59–62, 171
Rio (see Earth Summit)

Salford   22, 24–6, 28, 49, 163,
    168
Scottish Development Agency
    (SDA)   41, 49, 57
Sewerage   159
Sheffield   21, 34, 54
Sites of Special Scientific
    Interest   170
Social Polarisation   21–6
Social Unrest   30

Sports Council   142
Standardised Mortality
    Ratios   23, 25
Strathclyde   172
Subsidies   49–52
Sutton   72, 170
Sustainable Development   64–94
    administrative will   85
    and Agenda   21, 91–3
    and Networking   86–88
    concept of   72–3
    dimensions of   73–77
    importance of   71–2
    mobilising resources   85–6
    operationalising of   77–83
    political will   84–5
    strengthening focus on   68–70
Sustainable Development Ladder
    88–91

Task Forces   5, 153
Third Force Organisations   119–
    150
    advantages   122–7
    disadvantages   127–8
    growth of   119–22
    stages of development   136–9
    strategies to promote   139–49
Tourism   46, 123, 154
Tower Hamlets   22, 24–6, 97,
    100–1, 104–107, 109–16
Traffic Congestion   72, 78–80
Trafford   19, 177–8
Training   27
Training and Enterprise Councils
    5
Trickle Down Theories   32–3,
    59–60

Unitary Development Plans
    (UDPs)   69, 168
Urban Development Corporations
    (see also LDDC)   48, 167,
    169, 177–8, 201
Urban Policy
    for cities   31–35, 191–4
    national   201–3
Urban Programme   33

Urban Regeneration Agency   6,
    49, 153
Urban Villages   56–7, 81, 94
Users   104–8

Voluntary Sector (see Third Force
    Organisations)

Wakefield   64
Walsall   100
Water   68, 79, 81–3
Wigan   42, 154, 156, 163
Wildlife   64, 66–7, 82–3

Urban Groups   88, 123